Under a Croatian Sun

Under a Croatian Sun

ANTHONY STANCOMB

LUME BOOKS

LUME BOOKS

First published in 2020 by Lume Books
30 Great Guildford Street,
Borough, SE1 0HS

ISBN 978-1-83901-250-1

Typeset using Atomik ePublisher from Easypress Technologies

www.lumebooks.co.uk

Table of Contents

CHAPTER 1

APRIL
ARRIVAL

The car ferry whooped its hooter as we rounded the point. The ship heeled and we lurched against the others squashed into the hold as a wave of diesel-scented air blew over us from the engine room. A child at a porthole cried out that he could see the harbour, but jammed between an ancient Deutz lorry loaded with vegetables and a dented Skoda hatchback with a family of seven inside and a pile of cardboard boxes on top, we couldn't see too much. It must have felt like this in a refugee transit camp.

'I feel like a refugee,' said Ivana, showing remarkable thought-reading talent and trying to smooth down her crumpled jacket. 'Do you think I look like one?'

Not a good subject to dwell on. Ivana's family had done their fair share of fleeing in this part of the world and I didn't want all that stirred up again. I smiled back brightly, not wanting to admit that the last time I felt like this was standing at the school gates on the first day of term as my parents drove off in our Morris Traveller. I started to say something suitably upbeat about British explorers, but my words were drowned out by a crashing of chains and a grinding of metal as the front of the ferry began to heave open, and we were left to our individual brands of culturally fed angst.

The angst level was already running high. This was the first day of our new life on Vis, an island thirty miles off the coast. For better or for worse we had upped sticks from London and come to live on this Croatian island. Had we done the right thing? Would it be yet another disaster like the timeshare in Andorra or the ill-fated part-ownership of the barge on the Norfolk Broads? And would we be accepted by the local community – or would we be returning to England at the end of the year with our tails between our legs?

Sunlight streamed into the hold as the bow ground open, and in front of us appeared a frenzied melée of shouting men, waving women, honking horns, weaving scooters and demented whistle-blowing. Pulling our luggage behind us, we struggled past the revving bikes and roaring lorry engines and edged towards the throng, but were halted at the gangplank. A clasping, kissing and pummelling was going on as if the ship had just arrived back from a war zone, and as those concerned seemed quite unaware that their heartfelt embracing was completely blocking the exit, it wasn't until the whistling and shouting of two harassed policemen had broken up the family reunions that we were able to get off.

The air on the quay smelled of fish, tar, coffee, wine barrels and burned diesel. You could savour each one separately, but they mingled together quite pleasantly. Surrounded by a sea of people, all of whom seemed to know each other, we felt very conspicuous and the feeling was compounded by having to jump smartly out of the way of small black-clad women scurrying past with cloth-covered baskets and grizzled old men pushing rickety wheelbarrows through the crowd with sharp axles sticking out like the scythes of Boadicea's chariot. I looked around, feeling like Piglet eyeing a Heffalump trap and wishing Pooh were there to tell him what to do.

A smiling priest appeared in the crowd and, thinking he was smiling at me, I smiled back, but his beam was directed at a dog-collared passenger behind us. They bobbed up and down at each other as we were all swept forward in the melée, and from their noddings it looked as if the visitor was pulling rank on the local man, but they were swallowed up in the throng before I could get a closer look at their markings.

In front of us was a bus that seemed to have attached itself to a large metal litter bin, surrounded by a vociferous squadron of grandmothers who were shaking their sticks and umbrellas at a man in a driver's hat. The stringy-looking fellow with a walnut of a face was standing on the steps of the bus protesting his innocence. The grandmothers, in hats of a more sensible design – though definitely not the latest fashion – had ringed the steps like Indians round a wagon train. One of them, who looked like a cross between an aged Princess Anne and a snapping turtle, was flailing at him with her walking stick while the others accompanied her sabre work with crow-like screeches.

'It wasn't my fault!' the driver called out, gesticulating to the crowd with one arm while parrying the slashing granny with the other, but the granny was getting more accurate and he retreated up the steps protesting. 'Someone moved the litter bin! How was I to know it was there?' he cried from the safety of the bus.

The crowd was having none of it. Another matriarch, somewhat resembling an authoritative-looking sofa, came to the front of the crowd and shouted, 'You fool, Nano! Anyone could have seen it was there!'

Others joined in. 'You're as blind as a bat, Nano!'

'Get the Town Hall to buy you some glasses!'

'Get yourself another job!'

'I can see a damn sight better than you can, Jako!' the driver shouted back. 'You're such a short-arse, you couldn't even see over the steering-wheel!'

The man called Jako was carrying a spade and stepped forward as if he had impromptu surgery involving Nano's head in mind, but others restrained him.

'You put the whole town into darkness last week when you ran over the cables, you stupid idiot!' called a wizened octogenarian with a large white moustache, accompanying his words with appropriate gestures.

I had been learning Croatian for a few months, so had already come to know that, whereas we Anglo-Saxons tend to keep our arms by our sides and use a wide range of vocab to lend emphasis, Croatians go for the good old second language of the gesture – not that this appears to lessen the volume. Croatian is not a mellifluous tongue; not a language of love and romance. It sounds more like an angry farmer telling you to get off his mangelwurzels with lots of Zs and Xs in the words.

Looking at the front of the bus, it appeared that the driver had caught the bumper on the litter bin by taking the turn too wide. The bin, unfortunately, was made of metal and embedded in concrete. The focus of the hubbub now switched to the litter bin where a muscly young man with a sweat-soaked vest and bulging forearms was doing some virtuoso work with a metal-cutter. The crowd was urging him on and comparing him to the driver.

The adverse comparison was clearly too humiliating for poor Nano, and now that the stick-wielding granny had left off the attack, he got down from the bus and slunk off behind a donkey cart that was standing on the quay. The donkey turned and blinked at him with the soulful eyes of a saint on an icon as Nano fished in his pocket and pulled out a pre-rolled cigarette. He lit up and took a long drag, his stringy figure outlined against the bay as he gazed philosophically out to sea. But he was not to be left to his philosophising. The stick-wielding granny spotted him and started up again. 'He's the most useless of all my nephews, and his father, my blessed brother, God rest his soul, was just as useless. In all his years, he could never get that sheep dip of ours to work properly, and now that stupid boy of his is making me miss my only granddaughter being given her first communion by the bishop!'

Nano's face clearly wasn't one that lent itself to displays of emotion, but, by the look on it now, he knew that the incident was going to be part of the fabric of village conversation for some time.

Trundling our luggage behind us, we made our way through the line of umbrella-wielding grannies and the clamouring crowd, wondering if this was a portent of things to come.

The house we had bought was at the far end of the village so we walked down the waterfront. The village was going about its business in its usual way and no one seemed in any particular hurry. Groups of women were chatting outside the shops and walking home with their shopping baskets, and, along the front, weather-beaten old gaffers sat talking on the waterside benches. In front of the houses, men were mixing cement, chipping away at blocks of stone, and chatting as they worked. Beside the sea, fishermen were mending their nets and repairing their tackle beside their gaily painted boats, and little girls in school smocks danced in between stacks of lobster pots, seemingly unsupervised and with no barriers to keep them from falling in. We could hear the sound of banging pots and sizzling oil, and the smell of fish, garlic, coffee and herbs wafted out from the waterfront windows and hung in the air before dissipating into the breeze.

But there was something else there as well; something that wasn't part of the world I was accustomed to, something in the way that the people went about their lives with such slow deliberation, something in the way that the old black-clad women sat by their doorsteps observing what went on. It was something timeless, human, undefinable; but it was there nonetheless.

Ten minutes later, we arrived at our courtyard and pushed the battered, green door creakingly open. Oh, Christ! The work wasn't finished! The courtyard was a complete mess of wood, stones and rubble. Damn! We hadn't been able to afford to do it all up in one go and had only told the builder to do stage one – the *piano nobile* – but even that wasn't finished.

The shambles was a bit of a dampener, but as soon as we were inside it felt like home. The air buzzed with the kind of electricity generated by children in toyshops as we went from one corner of the house to the other, taking it all in – the echoing corridors, the tall Venetian windows, the smell of polished wood, the light streaming through the skylights, the sounds of the harbour percolating up over the courtyard wall. We opened the shutters and flooded the rooms with sunshine. The front windows and balcony looked out over the shimmering bay, and the French windows at the back opened onto an unkempt garden. At least the three main rooms were back to their original sixteenth-century size, and now, with the restricting walls and the hideous lino gone, the wide, dully gleaming floorboards gave a feeling of grandeur, even to the kitchen.

The unfinished work made our piles of furniture and packing cases seem even more daunting, but the excitement gave us the strength of two Pickford's removal men, and by midnight we had got most of the furniture into the right rooms. Then, having chosen the only bedroom with no gaping floorboards or dangling electric wires, we made up a bed, and collapsed on to it.

The next morning, I threw open the shutters. In front of me was a silvery expanse of water glittering in the sunshine ringed by green hills with fluffy white clouds in the vast blue basilica of sky above. In the courtyard below, the soft breeze ruffled the leaves of the pink mimosa and a flock of yellow butterflies fluttered around the purple bougainvillea. The only sound was a solitary fishing boat puttering across the bay and sending gentle ripples skating over the glass-like surface.

I stood at the window feeling the peace that passeth all understanding.

CHAPTER 2

FIRST
STEPS

The morning mist was evaporating off the slopes of the hills by the time we set out for the village market. Silhouetted against the sky, the cypresses on the green slopes trembled in the rising heat and the village basked in the sun. So compact, so vibrant, so enchanting. I don't know why, but the sight of clustered terracotta roof-tops never fails to gladden the heart. What is it about Mediterranean villages that makes them so appealing? Maybe that's just what happens when you've got stone to build with instead of bricks and there aren't any gardens to separate the houses.

It was ten o'clock and the bay was still as calm as a pond. The sunshine glinted off the water and a handful of fishing boats were coming in from the open sea, their engines chuntering and with flock of gulls swirling like a cloud behind them. The gulls wheeled in perpetual motion, swooping down and soaring up, their wings angled against the wind and hovering before they dived again. The flight of a gull is something of extraordinary beauty. If gulls were rare, people would travel across the world just to watch them.

The morning ferry was rounding the headland, blowing out a lot of black smoke (someone ought to see to those piston rings). It glided across the bay towards us and the captain put it into a sort of aquatic ballet, weaving the bulky shape with surprising elegance between the fishing boats. Arriving at the dock, it towered above the village like a colossus, its

7

engines growling and churning up the water. While seamen ran up and down its decks, shouting frantically and heaving heavy ropes over the side to men on the dock. Then with a hideous grinding of metal the bow began to yawn open, and the quiet waterfront was suddenly transformed into the same frantic turmoil of yesterday, with people, bikes, cars and lorries jostling for position. We tried to make our way through, but had to jump smartly sideways to avoid being run over by a Lada pickup driven backwards at speed by a wild-haired man with the inane grin on his face of Keith Moon driving a Rolls-Royce towards a swimming pool. Until, with a sickening crunch, his trajectory was halted by an iron gangplank. This brought shouts of abuse from the deckhands, but the driver clearly had a talent for living in the moment, and continued to grin around seemingly unconcerned about the damage he'd caused to his van. Was this kind of thing normal? I wanted to ask.

The village was in full swing when we got to the market. Cafés were full, vans were delivering and fishermen were offloading their catches. The market itself was a scene straight out of a child's painting book; stone slabs piled high with brightly coloured fruit and vegetables, jars of honey and cheeses. To the side were wooden trestles sagging under the weight of the hundred and one alcoholic concoctions they make from grape leftovers in this part of world, and, behind the stalls, wrinkled-faced women in black cackled to each other in shrill voices as leathery-skinned men wearing shirts with no collars heaved boxes about, muttering oaths to no one in particular. In between the stalls, village housewives were bargaining and gossiping and clouting their chickens or their children, whichever were nearest at hand. There was no queuing; people just elbowed their way in, squeezing tomatoes, prodding lettuces, sniffing melons, snapping carrots and complaining loudly when they came across anything substandard. The stallholders gave back as good as they got with raucous references to the miserly habits of the customer and the last two generations of their family.

The women all seemed to be shopping for a regiment and baskets were being put against a wall where a group of men, whom I presumed to be husbands, were waiting to carry them home. They sat on the wall puffing at cigarettes held between first finger and thumb (the lighted end in the palm, mean hombre style), while they made their mid-morning snack. Goat's cheese and tomatoes were sliced with penknives and spread on to long crusty pieces of bread, and in between the bites and the puffs they swigged from a bottle of red wine that seemed to be held in common.

We filled our baskets and made our way out though the stallholders' vans parked behind in a somewhat haphazard manner (that is from the standpoint of someone accustomed to parking in the supermarket car parks of South West London). Most of them looked as if they had assembled from a do-it-yourself car kit bought at a street market in Bled. Many had novel open-space designs in the front instead of passenger seats, and their wings seemed rather over-reliant on gaffer tape to keep them in place.

Across the square, there was a steady trickle of fishermen heading from the quay to the bars to brace themselves for the day, and at the far end of it I spotted the unmistakable figure of Nano the bus driver's aunt – still in the same Miss Marple hat but now using her umbrella to calm down some scrapping dogs.

Over the next few days, we noted that most of the boxes on the stalls were empty, and, wondering why, Ivana, who speaks Croatian quite well, asked the bearded, bear-like stallholder who was a cousin of our builder.

'The early bird wipes its beak and the late one wipes its bum, like they say,' he replied, grinning and revealing some frightening gold dental work. 'It's the nuns; that's who. They're here the earliest so they get the pick, don't they? Not that they eat much themselves by the look of 'em, but they feed all the old 'uns in the old folk's home, and come early to get all the best while the likes of you are still in bed.'

'Any chance of putting something on the side for us?' I asked tentatively, not wanting to start a vegetable turf war with the local gang of nuns in our first week.

He gave a throaty laugh. 'You'll get no special treatment here. The way things are going with my ex and my kids, I'll be needing a whole coach-load of nuns to put in a good word for me at St Peter's gate, if I'm ever going to get in!' (Our builder had told us that his cousin was in disgrace ever since he'd run off with a neighbour's daughter half his age.) 'But if *you* got out of bed at five in the morning to say your Matins and Lauds, *you'd* be here in time to buy the best, too!'

We made do with the remainders.

Actually, I'm an early riser, but Ivana will happily sleep on until kindly hands bring her a cup of tea. (In fact, without her morning tea and a fair time to brood on life for a bit, she's not up for much.) So, leaving her sleeping, I'd slip out of bed at the first glimmer of dawn – and that was something worth getting up for. Opening the kitchen shutters I could watch the sun creep up over the hills behind us and unleash itself with awe-inspiring splendour over the bay. The fort on the headland, like a loyal sentry at the gates of the sun, was the first to be touched by the burning shaft and the radiance would flood down the slope, illuminating the translucent layer of mist over the water and making the fishing boats look suspended above the surface. The light then spread along the hillside, suffusing the village roofs with its glow and making it stand out like a theatre façade against the backdrop of the hills. The air that blew gently in from across the bay was tinged with burning wood from kitchen stoves, and in the distance I could hear crowing cockerels and barking dogs.

I don't know why, but the dawn in South West London never seemed to have the same effect on me. Somehow, looking out of my bedroom window in London I'd never managed to get that enthused about the mystical properties of daybreak over Fulham Broadway – but here, it took my breath away every time.

Nothing ever happens the way you plan it, I mused as I lay in bed watching the moonlight filtering through shutters and listening to the sea soughing gently to itself on the other side of the courtyard. We had lived in London for thirty years without a thought of ever leaving, and here we now were in the middle of the Adriatic. But then, does any amount of planning ever prepare you for the next bend in the road?

Twenty years ago, I set up a company to sell the work of contemporary British artists to galleries overseas – which is hardly a disagreeable way of earning a living I know – but, after I turned fifty, the strain of running what had become a multinational organisation had begun to tell. When I started the company, I'd been under the impression that, once you had built up a successful business, it would just tick over nicely; but what in fact happens is that you have to work even harder to maintain its success than you did when you built it up in the first place. So, by the time I hit fifty, I was travelling constantly and my problems were getting bigger and bigger – more difficult clients, more irascible artists, more stubborn bank managers and more 3 a.m. wake-up calls brought on by letters from the Inland Revenue. Before long, I found myself sitting at my desk planning my escape like Harry Potter in the cupboard under the stairs; dreaming of places where the sun shone brightly, where food and wine were plentiful, and where we could enjoy a good life without needing a Goldman Sachs-like salary to fund it.

As usual with my grand plans, the idea stayed stubbornly in the land of fantasy, but, when the war broke out between Croatia and Serbia and Ivana started running relief convoys down to the refugee camps, a location was played into our hands.

Ivana was actually Croatian by blood – hence her ability to speak the language. Although born and brought up in Argentina, her parents were Croatian and taught her to speak it. They also sent her off to Croatia when she was twenty to discover her roots, but that was a journey never completed. She had stopped off in England, been taken by a friend to a May Ball, and it was there I spied her dancing on a college lawn in the light of the moon; her sylph-like figure sheathed in a sequinned gown and her dark eyes and sparkling smile flashing in the moonbeams. Luckily, in the obscurity, she couldn't see that my dinner jacket had spent the previous night stuffed under my flat-mate's bed and that the trousers didn't quite match the jacket, and, by the time she'd discovered my congenital scruffiness, we were already an item.

So that was it, and for the next thirty years she was imprisoned like a dark-haired Rapunzel in a tower of long winters, cold houses, woolly clothes, frosty in-laws and fish fingers for supper. Who could have predicted that, instead of reaching the sun-kissed shores of her homeland, she'd end up in an Edwardian terrace off the Fulham Road with a dog-eared Englishman and a couple of tousle-headed children?

At least that was the case until the war between Serbia and Croatia broke out and the hitherto little-known corner on the wrong side of the Iron Curtain was suddenly beamed into everyone's sitting rooms with unsettling proximity. But what she saw on the screen was nothing like the sunlit homeland she had imagined. What she saw were anxious women, angry men and scared-looking children; children who looked much like our own – and, instead of a dream waiting for her on an idyllic coastline, Croatia suddenly turned into a cause. Within a month, she and some friends had assembled their first convoy, and for the next two years she rattled up and down Europe in a collection of battered Ford Transit vans with supplies for the refugee camps (with me tagging along whenever work allowed).

And finally, the link with the land of her forefathers was made.

12

CHAPTER 3

KARMELA

At the end of our first week, a terrifying-looking woman, dressed as if she was going to a Queen Victoria impersonation competition, appeared on our doorstep. In her sixties and with a face like a weathered block of granite, it looked as if someone had given her some bad news in 1958 and she was still chewing on it. She announced that she had come to be our house keeper.

Taken aback, we started to say that we were managing OK on our own, but she cut us short with a disdainful snort. According to Lenko, the builder, our belongings were still piled up in unidentified heaps and we were clearly incapable of looking after ourselves. Slightly shaken by the summary judgement, we thought we had better ask her in. Once upstairs, she perched on the edge of the sofa as if she knew something unclean was lurking beneath the cushions, and, instead of waiting for us to ask the first question, she fixed us with a glittering eye, like the Ancient Mariner, and began her interrogation.

'Why have you come to live here? Why haven't you cleaned the house yourselves? Why have you done all this building work? Why did you put in so many bathrooms? When are you going to finish it?' And all this in a voice that could have boned a herring at twenty fathoms. Even Ivana looked somewhat cowed – and that's saying something, given that Ivana is the fiercest person I've ever known (except for her mother that is).

Not having the courage to say we'd think it over, we lamely agreed that she could start the next day.

That night, Ivana hardly slept that night but once they started working the next day, they found they had a lot in common – in particular, an ultra-Thatcherite attitude to other people's working habits and a deep distrust of anything suggested by men.

With black eagle-like eyes and a hawk-like nose, Karmela's face resembled one of those fierce-looking Medusa masks you see on wall-mounted fountains in garden centres of the Home Counties, and I, like Perseus, soon began to feel somewhat cautious around her. Nor was it only Perseus and me. Any man who came into the house was pinioned by the glare of a crocodile that had just spotted its lunch, and the look followed them around like a wartime searchlight until they had left.

Cantankerous and stubborn, and with extremely intolerant views about the world in general, Karmela would have been very much at home at the Basingstoke Women's Institute circa 1950, and, if I had a bent for cross-stitch, I could have created a sampler a day of her best aphorisms. But, to us, her observations were pearls of a new kind of wisdom, and we listened in awe to her lectures about the dangers to our health that lurked round every corner. The most common directives were:

Never stand in the sun between ten and four – it addles your brain.

Never sit in a draught – it damages your liver (particularly men's).

Never sit on cold stone – it affects your 'parts' (particularly women's).

Although, in fairness, we were given the same dire warnings by other village women – particularly concerning draughts and men.

Now, I had been raised by a mother with a bad case of wartime penny-pinch and thought I was about as frugal as it comes, but my childhood training was eclipsed by Karmela, who had been recycling long before the Greenies turned it into a new religion. By the end of each day, anything surplus to requirements was stripped from the house with Germanic fervour – vegetables to the neighbour's pigs; bread to her cousin's chickens; tea slops to someone's compost; sheets of paper used on one side only whisked out of my wastepaper basket and taken to the school. Likewise, every scrap of clothing was reused; frayed cuffs snipped off and turned into dolly dresses or dusters.

Another task that Karmela quickly took upon herself was to warn us about our neighbours. We were taken down to the square outside and shown the houses that harboured criminals or were cursed with bad luck and so were similarly to be avoided.

'Beware of those ones there!' she said, indicating a building. 'She's a witch and he's no better. And, as for those in that one beside it; a well-coloured lie counts for the truth in that household, I can tell you. And you be very careful of anyone who comes out of that broken door there.' She pointed a bony finger. 'If you're not careful, they'll be in your garden stealing your potatoes the moment your back is turned. Their youngest son got arrested for trying to rob the garden centre in Split last year and their eldest waters down the milk he sells us in the market. He thinks we don't know, but we do. Terrible people! Don't even talk to them.'

We were also told who not to do business with.

'Now, a farmer you can trust. Give him your left arm and he'll return it with interest, but don't you ever lend money to a fisherman. He'll drink it or forget where it came from. My husband, God rest his kindly soul, gave some money to that Grubic family when their boat sank in a storm – and did we see any of it back? Did we ever! "We thought you gave it to us in return for the wine we gave you at Christmas," they had the cheek to say a year later! As if we didn't have perfectly good wine of our own to drink. Pah! You save a dog from drowning and that's the one that bites you! May their fish rot in their van before they get it to market!'

Like most of my countrymen, I'm more likely to enter myself for *Strictly Come Dancing* than let my fellow beings know what I think of them, so I had a sneaking admiration for the way Karmela came straight out with what she thought about people. I would have thought that in such a small community this ultra-direct approach would have got her into trouble, but Karmela was clearly above such concerns.

We had barely finished unpacking when Karmela told us it was time for spring-cleaning. She then set about flinging open windows, scrubbing floors, sluicing steps, polishing flagstones and hanging bedclothes out of the windows. On the second day, she began to lug our furniture outside, and I was about to tell her that she shouldn't when I saw that our neighbours

15

were turning the square outside into what the inventor of the car-boot sale must have visualised when he first dreamed up the idea.

'But we really don't need to put everything outside, Karmela,' I said, gesturing to our prized collection of tastefully distressed French Provencal. 'We've only just unpacked it.'

But, like Balaam's ass (with whose edifying tale the reader is doubtless acquainted), Karmela wasn't to be dissuaded. 'Ha! What that all needs is a good painting. Look at the state of it. The paint's come off everywhere! But a good dose of sunshine should do it a power of good all the same.'

Once almost everything was out in the courtyard, the news of its lack-lustre quickly spread and the village came to see if what they had heard was true. We stood at the back of the balcony watching the shaking heads and listening to the tutting – 'Nice linen, but all that awful old furniture …'

Communism had brought a novel approach to interior design. Wood had given way to Formica, carved Venetian windows to plastic ones and big old doors that creaked replaced by snappy-looking MDF pairs with frosted glass. As for colours, ever since a team of Soviet psychologists in Omsk during the 1950s had discovered that the colours purple, orange and a particularly frightening shade of green induced a mood of gaiety in gerbils, the landscape of the Eastern Bloc was never the same again. Assuming that humans would react in the same way as gerbils, the politburos had scaled the theory up, like doubling up a cake recipe, and the unfortunate combination of purple, orange and bilious green has been blotting the landscape from Plovdiv to Vladivostok. In the New Dawn of socialism, bright colours and new materials were milestones on the highway of progress.

One of our neighbours, a middle-aged lady of a decent size, had a sofa of livid orange, which she hauled out into the square and, after whacking it for a bit, left it for everyone to admire – which they did. Our collection of furniture, on the other hand, failed to attract a single appreciative comment.

On the third day of spring-cleaning, I noticed an ominous group of female seniors gathering around Karmela, and, pretending to be absorbed by a problem with my Black & Decker, I moved in to eavesdrop.

'What can Mrs Ivana have been thinking of, spending her money on

16

such rough-looking things?' said one with a face even more hatchet-like than Karmela's.

'No good housewife should ever have spent her money on such peasant-looking furniture!' said another, accompanying her words with an impressive display of face pulling.

'And as for those rugs!' exclaimed one with the figure of a Russian shot-putter. 'It looks as if they were made by a tractor driver!'

'It all looks suspiciously second hand to me,' said the fourth, who looked like a well-upholstered armchair.

'And they look like they could well afford to buy themselves something new,' said the Russian shot-putter.

I couldn't hear Karmela's reply, but, when I brought up the subject later, she glared at me. 'And they're quite right too! Hard wooden benches were all our parents and grandparents ever had to sit on, and, now that we can get all those nice, easy-clean Draylon sofas in our shops like in the rest of the world, we should buy them.'

Unable to spot a flaw in the argument, I stood in mute assent, as if I was back in the study of my primary school headmistress.

'And why you've brought out all this old furniture with you, I just don't know,' she continued. 'It's so difficult to clean, and look at all the extra work I have to do because you've taken up that perfectly good linoleum and left me with all these terrible floorboards. They're old and ugly and they let the dust get everywhere! You should put the linoleum back; that's what!' She pointed her bony finger at me for emphasis.

Karmela pointed her finger at me a lot and I did find it rather disconcerting. I'd had it instilled in me by my mother that pointing at people was rude, and I had assumed that other mothers had done the same, but, once again, Karmela was above such conventions – as was another great user of the pointed digit: Margaret Thatcher. And, as Mrs T's ex-colleagues can testify, being the subject of a pointed female finger can be somewhat intimidating.

I did see Karmela's point, though. Our old furniture *was* more difficult to keep clean and the old floorboards *did* let the dust in – and I dare say that, if we had lived here all our lives, we too would have chosen practicality over perceived notions of elegance and left the floorboards covered over. But please… not with lino!

Trying to display the suave indifference of an Englishman in total control of his manor, I made as if I had something important to do and retreated to the study feeling like a pageboy ticked off by Queen Elizabeth I.

It's a sad day when a man is no longer the master in his own house.

Karmela said that during the winter the entire village had come to see the havoc we were creating and had criticised every stage of it. It had been a black mark against us, she said. What had appalled them most was that we had restored the rooms to their original sizes. This would mean fewer rooms than before! What kind of people could we be? And as for leaving all those old rough beams and stone exposed… Why, the whole thing was as perverse as that place in Paris where they put the pipes on the outside! Some things were just meant to be covered up!

Karmela also said that no one could understand why we had bought such an old building and then had to spend as much money on it again, when for that amount we could have bought ourselves several really nice new apartments. But, when one considered that most of our neighbours struggled to make ends meet (even now few of them owned a car), all this was understandable. Island life revolved round sheep, goats, fish, wine and olives, and the kind of money we were spending was more than many of them would earn in a lifetime. That the same amount of money would only have bought you a garage in Fulham was not the point. They didn't know that.

This was going to need some careful handling.

CHAPTER 4

THE ROAD TO
THE ISLAND

We hadn't delivered any supplies to Vis on Ivana's convoys, but it was on one of them that we first saw it.

'Vis has a magical charm,' said one of our fellow aid workers as we looked at the island hovering mistily on the horizon. 'When you are there, you feel as if you've stepped inside a fairytale. There people still live according to the wisdom of the earth.'

'Yes,' said another, wanting to air his knowledge of English literature, 'Vis is like the island of Caliban in your Shakespeare. "Full of noises, sounds and sweet airs that give delight."'

Vis had been a secret hidden from the world ever since 1945 when Tito took a liking to its isolated location and made it into an excluded military zone. So, having heard about its beauty and its 'sweet airs', as soon as the war ended and the convoys weren't needed any more, we hired a boat that summer to explore the Croatian coast and stopped at Vis. Entering the narrow straits flanked by a cannon tower and a fortress that shimmered in the sunlight like armoured sentinels as we found ourselves in a wide horseshoe of calm water with a fishing village at the far end nestling below steeply rising green hills, its stone walls and terracotta roofs picked out by the afternoon sun. It reminded me somewhat of Dawlish in Devon, in that the hills seemed to be tipping it into the sea; only, unlike Dawlish, the hills were lined with vine terraces and the sun was shining. As we motored across the bay towards it, a cracked bell from a monastery on the water tolled five o'clock.

Drenched in the late-afternoon sun, the village looked drowsily delightful in that sleepy way so characteristic of Croatian coastal villages. Except for a solitary figure lobbing a fishing line into the sea from the sea wall, the only moving object was a desultory fishing craft chuntering across the harbour, the smoke from its engine hanging lazily in the air behind it. The siesta was clearly in full swing.

We looked for a space among the fishing boats and, after finding a gap, tied up to the sea wall and climbed ashore. The heat hit us like a hammer. It ricocheted off the flagstones, bounced off the walls, and made the façade of the village flicker like a mirage as we walked along the front. It felt as if we were walking past an abandoned stage set.

The planners seemed to have had little influence on the hotchpotch of housing. It appeared to have grown out of the hillside and meandered down to the water on its own. The houses were mainly Venetian and some were in perfect condition with their original façades and balconies, but some were covered with concrete or had cafés and shops on the ground floor. A large tabby cat strolled languidly out from one of them and stretched itself on a flagstone, balefully eyeing a fat seagull that was sitting on the quay. Too hot to move, the cat just narrowed its eyes and blinked at it, and the seagull, knowing it was siesta time, stared defiantly back.

Entering the village, we made our way along stone-paved streets worn smooth over the centuries. Most of them were so narrow that the green shuttered houses gave shade to each other and created a welcome eddy of cool air, which wafted over us. The village seemed laid out like a maze to baffle anyone who might stray away from the waterfront, so, taking the slope as our guide, we headed upwards. Households were waking from their siesta as we wound our way along; shutters were being swung open and people were appearing in doorways, rubbing their eyes and blinking owlishly before setting off on their business.

Emerging at the top, we turned to look over the rooftops. A shimmering sliver of moon was already up in the sky and the sinking red sun had turned the surface into a pool of liquid gold, making the monastery and the fort stood out against the purpling sky like two black silhouettes. The green hills cascaded gracefully down to the bay where white sails glided across the glass-like water, and speckled lights were appearing in windows along the shore. Out at sea the lamps of approaching yachts flickered in the blue dusk. We stood there listening to the soft murmur of the village and breathing in the scent of lavender, rosemary and fennel that wafted up to us on the warm evening air.

I think it was then that we first fell in love with the island.

After a supper of grilled fish at one of the waterfront restaurants, we went back to the boat and sat on the deck watching the evening promenade taking place. It was August but it wasn't crowded and there was a pleasant murmur of voices in the warm night air as the locals and the few holiday-makers milled around the square or strolled along the waterfront. Groups of teenagers mooched moodily around the church steps, and one or two food shops were still open where some were doing their last-minute shopping, picking up loaves of bread for the morning's breakfast or stopping to talk and laugh with those they knew. With the Venetian church behind it, the square resembled a scene from an Italian opera, and, as I watched this timeless evening pageant taking place in front of us, I was overwhelmed by a sense of wellbeing – like James Stewart at the end of *It's a Wonderful Life* when he looks out of the window at life going on in the street and sees that all is well.

Why was it that we always felt so comfortable in places like this? I said to Ivana. Was it simply the lack of neon lights and signs of consumerism, was it the comforting sense of life's continuity, or was it simply that we always felt at home in places like this?

'It's what happens when you stop rushing around the world like a madman and stay still for a moment,' Ivana replied.

We sat in silence as if we were in a world with its own sense of contentment.

The strollers thinned out, waiters folded up chairs and turned off lights, and soon only the soft glow of the moon lit the sleeping harbour. Sitting on the deck in the balmy night air, listening to the soft lapping of the water and the muffled creaking of mooring ropes, I felt in complete harmony with everything around me. We looked at each other. We really had fallen in love with it and this was where we were going to find the life I'd been dreaming about. In the morning, we would look for a house we decided, and with a certain sense of finality we went down to our bunks.

Knowing that estate agents hadn't really existed under communism, we went into the nearest café for breakfast and asked the owner where we could find out about houses for sale.

'Houses?' he responded. 'But no one wants to buy a house here!'

When we assured him that we really did, he scratched his head. 'Well, I suppose there might be some Serbian houses for sale. *They* won't be coming back here in a hurry. Maybe you should ask Tonko. He insures most houses, so maybe he might know.'

It didn't sound too promising, but off we went. As direction-giving is an imprecise art in a small village where no one needs directions, it took us some time to find the place, but, eventually, above the old fire station, we found the office and opened the door. A prematurely grey-haired man sitting at a heavy forties desk jumped as if startled. He can't have had many visitors. After we told him what we were looking for, he fished around in a drawer for some keys and told us that there were three houses belonging to Serbians who had left when the war started. They were referred to as 'absentee owners' as the word 'Serbian' now stuck in people's throats, he said.

He was surprised by our visit. 'You're the first people wanting to live here since World War II. After Tito made the island a military zone in 1945, no one, not even our own people, could come to the island without permission. 'But at least it saved us from all the development that happened along our coast. That's why we're the most beautiful island in the Adriatic.' He smiled. 'I knew that one day the world would find us again.'

The first house he took us to was tiny, but, at a price of £15,000, it had an immediate attraction.

'Look!' I enthused to Ivana. 'Three bedrooms and a kitchen big enough to be a living room.'

'All you'd get into these bedrooms is a bed. No room for any cupboards or chests of drawers. No space for clothes at all!'

'But we won't be needing much in the way of clothes out here, will we?'

I got a look which said: 'If you think you're going to keep me holed up on a distant island with nowhere for clothes, you've got another think coming.'

I'd pictured our life here in terms of sandals and shorts, but I should have known my wife better.

Tonko didn't speak English, but Ivana's look crossed language barriers and he clearly got the drift of it.

Once back on the street, Tonko enthused about the second house. He was sure Ivana would like it. Spacious, modernised and well maintained, he assured her. But it was dismal. The communist vogue for concrete had turned what might once have been a charming house into something that had all the appeal of a dental clinic. We shook our heads and, feeling like Goldilocks running out of options, we followed Tonko in silence. Emerging into the square at the end of the village, he stopped and gestured to a derelict building on the water, almost falling into the sea. We stopped in our tracks. There in front of us stood the most magnificent tumbledown affair I had ever seen. Ramshackle and unkempt, it stretched from the water to the next street; an entire block of magnificently dilapidated sixteenth-century Venetian architecture. The shutters hung lopsided on their hinges, the roof sagged and parts of the balconies had fallen off, but, as I looked up at the crumbling façade with the afternoon sunlight bouncing off the weathered stone, I wanted it to be mine.

We went through the derelict courtyard and found a complete mess inside. The plumbing hadn't been touched since the thirties, there was one bathroom for the six bedrooms and in the kitchen was a single dribbling tap, a cracked lino floor and some terrifying electric cables with wire sticking out of the crumbling cord casing. The place needed complete renovation – roof, floors, plumbing, electrics – and it certainly needed a few more bathrooms – but there was an air of magic about it that made all other considerations immaterial.

It was much bigger than we needed, but, according to Tonko, all this could be ours for the cost of a garage in Fulham. I totted up the rough cost of the works and it came to as much again, but I'd already made my decision. This was the one for us.

Tonko went off to get the papers and left us on the terrace. It was that magical hour somewhere between teatime and drink time when nature slips into torpor. The late-afternoon sun was streaming down, the bees were humming in the mimosa and the sweet, heavy scent of jasmine floated up from the courtyard. Ivana put her arm around me.

'Well, here you are at last with your own tumbledown house on a distant island. Isn't this what you always dreamed of?'

'But there's a hell of a lot of work to do, and we can't possibly afford to do it all in one go. We'll have to do it up in stages, and you know what that means. Living with the builders; like after we got married. Remember?'

There was a slight hesitation as she recalled the first months of newly wedded bliss that we'd shared with half a dozen Irish builders and a lot of rubble.

I willed her to say yes.

'Well, I suppose we'll have to do it again.'

'Are you sure? We can still tell Tonko we've changed our minds…'

I was flashed a heart-stopping smile. 'I've got a feeling that we're going to be very happy here. Particularly you.'

I hugged her.

Standing there, drenched in the late sunshine and listening to Ivana enthusing about what we'd do to the house, my whole being drooped with happiness like one of the mimosa branches in the courtyard weighed down by the weight of its soft pink flowers.

24

CHAPTER 5

TRYING TO
FIT IN

Once we were back in London, I wondered if this urge of mine to go and live on a distant island was something deep-seated in me or only just part of the new-found travel preoccupation that now affects the middle classes. It used to be the young and intrepid who went off to far-distant places, but it seemed to have become the prerogative of the middle-aged. Our local Waterstones was full of those 'A Hundred and One Things to Do Before You Die' kind of books, and on my way home I'd sometimes have a browse, but after a hard day at the office they only served as a rather depressing reminder that yet another day had gone by and I still hadn't climbed Mont Blanc, gambled in Las Vegas, swum with a shark, hang-glided over the Himalayas or dated Liz Hurley.

Ivana had begun to tell me I sounded like Victor Meldrew.

After a few false starts, I sold the company to an old competitor in the business – a Mr Scaglione from Detroit, a man of great flair, vision and energy – and within two months every-thing had gone off to America. That done, I started to learn Croatian and threw myself into the move.

It was around that time that I started to have my first nagging doubts. Was island life really going to work for me? Would I find enough to do? I had some projects in mind – a restaurant, a delicatessen, a boat charter business, house renovation – but, if they didn't succeed, would I feel frustrated?

If all there was to do was lie in the sun sipping chilled wine, would I turn to drink in the time-honoured manner of white men in far-off stations or take to whisky and leering at local talent, like that failed Colonial Police Chief in the Graham Greene novel?

There were a lot of things I was going to miss, particularly our two children, and also my friends and my cricket. I told myself that these were the kinds of worries to be expected by anyone remoulding their entire existence, but it still didn't stop the worries having the same 3 a.m. wake-up effect on me as letters from the Inland Revenue. Sometimes in the middle of the night, plagued by thoughts of being the only outsider in a close-knit island community, I'd slip out of bed to sit at my desk looking at pictures and maps of the island and tell myself for the umpteenth time that we really *had* made the right decision.

For Ivana, I wasn't so worried. Whereas I've never been able to shake off an innate hesitance to befriend complete strangers, she's the kind who collects new best friends wherever she goes. Anyway, she'd be living in the land of her forefathers, and I'd seen how similar her features were to those we met on the convoys. With her straight dark hair, almond eyes, olive-shaped face and gymnast's figure, she could have been anyone's sister. So much so that, despite the ethnic diversity of London, no one had ever taken her for English in our thirty years together. (Although that might have had something to do with her exotic way of dressing, her expansive way of gesturing and her habit of approaching everything with enthusiasm, fury or implacable feminine logic.) But life had been rich with colour and our marriage had prospered.

Nonetheless, I could see that even she was beginning to worry about giving up all that our metropolitan life had to offer – Planet Organic, Harvey Nichols, Zara, her girlfriends, bridge clubs, fitness clubs, yoga clubs, book clubs, dental hygienists, theatres, exhibitions; not to mention dry-cleaning, 24-hour shopping, fashion magazines, sliced bread, full cream milk, oven ready food and all those other terrific little inventions that make the world such a jolly place to live in.

Most of our friends and family had the bizarrest notions of how we were

26

going to live. Some asked if malaria pills were needed, and just before Christmas my brother rang to ask if I'd like the new survival book that had just come out.

'Come off it,' I said. 'I'm not going out there for adventure. I'm after a quiet life these days.'

'You don't fool me, A. If you were asked what you wanted to do most of all in the world, I bet it'd be something like winning a DSO leading a squadron of Marines into Tobruk or something equally daftly Biggles-like.'

'You've just never got over me getting the Frensham Pond Boy Scout of the Year badge instead of you.'

The next week, someone gave me a book entitled *Living on an Untamed Island*, and other books authored by writers with a thing about khaki were to follow. Most were pretty drear, but there was one that was un-put-downable – *The Life of Ragnar Hairybreeks*, a Viking who discovered the Orkneys and Iceland. What a man! If there was any derring-do to be done, he was the man to do it. What a role model! Perhaps rape and pillage were a trifle high on his agenda for my taste, but I'd take him with me to Tobruk any day. Once I had my boat, he was the man to model myself on.

I took all the books out with us, but except for the Hairybreeks one, the others we never read again. Although two weeks after our arrival, I remembered that in one of them I had read the old adage that, when you move home, the first thing to do is to join a club. That sounded like a good idea. I'd make some friends and ask advice on the projects I'd been thinking about.

It didn't take long to find one. There was only one – the Old Men's Club.

Like all good clubs, it was well tucked away down a side street, and, arriving at a battered green door, I stopped to peer inside. A shaft of light cut through the wreath of blue-grey smoke revealing a bare high-ceilinged room with men in hats sitting around heavy-looking tables. Some with impassive faces were picking up and discarding cards, some were talking in low voices and slapping down dominoes, and at the back a discussion was going on that seemed to involve a lot of table thumping. This was a man's world. No wife or daughter would dare venture in here and order them home for lunch in a bossy tone as I'd seen them do when the men were on the benches.

The moment I stepped inside, the talking stopped and all heads turned towards me. I was as if I'd stepped into a superannuated spaghetti western scene. Near the door were three wizened honchos with the sort of faces you see on those Red Indian totem poles in the British Museum, so I turned to the nearest and said hesitantly, 'I'd very much like to join your club if that's possible. What do I have to do to join?'

There was a rather chilly silence and the oldest of the totem poles cleared his throat. Managing to capitalise his words phonically, he said, 'This is… THE OLD MAN'S CLUB.'

'Yes I know. But how do I join it?'

'You must wait.'

How silly of me. Of course, any club worth joining had a waiting list.

'Well, I belong to two clubs in London,' I said cheerily to show I was a clubbable sort of fellow. 'How do I get my name on to the waiting list?'

'The what?'

I tried to think of a better translation while the totem poles looked at each other as if to say 'Where did this dope come from?'

Then in a slow voice, as if addressing a child, one of them said: 'YOU MUST WAIT UNTIL YOU ARE OLD.'

With the eyes of half the Vis demographic aged seventy to ninety fixed on me, I backed towards the door and hurried off. If this was a spaghetti western, the telegraph operator with the visor and shirt-sleeve bands would be tapping out: *English middle-aged moron at large stop trying to join old man's club stop*.

I had made a fool of myself and the word would soon be around the village. I needed Karmela to do some emergency PR, and quickly.

Actually Karmela had already taken on the role of Greek Chorus. The village was kept regularly informed about everything to do with us, and we, in turn, were filled in on all village goings-on. Of course, true to universal village custom, the news was never a simple nugget of information. Karmela had a belt and braces attitude to news. We were fully briefed; there's no other word for it. So for an engagement, we were first given three generations' worth of history of the families concerned and then by daily updates on how each side was coaching the one in their corner to respond to the latest move from the opposing corner. And this included the all-important commercial side of the match that involved plots of land, vineyards, sheep, goats, olive trees, fishing boats, second-hand trucks and part shares of pizzerias.

The only drawback was that Karmela's reports could reschedule a day and sometimes we found ourselves pinned down for half the morning. With her prodigious talent for non-sequential thought process, we could have entered her for a James Joyce stream of consciousness competition. Although, come to think about it, Joyce can't have invented stream of consciousness. All self-respecting mothers in Ireland and the Mediterranean must have been practising the art of it for centuries before Joyce ever came up with the idea.

Having failed to join a club, I thought that lending a hand might be a good way of making friends, so, when I saw a neighbour's wife unloading some crates of wine, I went out to help. It was an infuriating job, but, after ten minutes of scraping my knuckles in an infernally cramped cellar, I had got them all stacked up nicely. Then thinking she might appreciate a neighbourly chat about how we were getting on in our new home, I hovered with a 'Yes, I'd love a coffee' expression. But she just said thank you and waited by the door for me to leave.

'Maybe it wouldn't have looked right to invite you upstairs if her husband wasn't there,' said Ivana when I returned. 'They're still a bit old-fashioned about things like that.'

The next day, I saw two men unloading some wood and tried again. This time, the job took a lot longer, but once again, despite my boyishly expectant expression, all I got was a curt 'thank you' and they drove off. Rather Anglo-Saxon of me, I suppose, to have expected a chummy invitation for a beer, but I felt slighted.

'I know what,' said Ivana seeing my long face. 'Why don't you go and help the fishermen to tie up when it's rough? I'm sure they'd appreciate that.'

So the next time a stiffish early-morning breeze was blowing in, I paced the quay pretending to be admiring the scenery, and waved cheerily at the first boat that came bobbing in. And yes, my friendly indication was accepted and they threw a line. The wet rope slapped me in the face and got tar all over my trousers before I managed to get hold of it, but I did a fairly seaman-like job of a half-hitch round a bollard and they came alongside. But not a flicker of human interchange crossed their craggy faces. All I got was a perfunctory grunt of thanks and they went about their business as if I wasn't there. No mention of a beer one evening – or even a free pilchard.

'Try and look on the bright side,' said Ivana when I got home. 'They must have always treated all outsiders in the same way – Romans, Greeks, Turks, Italians. They're not just picking on us.'

It never ceases to amaze me how Ivana manages to find a sunny side to most things. I've tried to do the same, but I just don't have the knack, it seems. Mind you, if there were any courses on it and this rejection therapy dished out by our neighbours was going to continue, maybe I should sign up.

I cheered myself with the thought of Roman centurions desperately trying to ingratiate themselves. 'Please feel free to borrow my pilum any time you want, my good fellow – no, really!'

The first rude awakening to the actual local hostility was not long in coming. One morning, Karmela press-ganged a solemn-faced fisherman into helping me carry a table upstairs, and once we'd done the job, thinking that he might like to see what we'd done to the house, I offered him a coffee and to show him around. The fellow looked at me as if he'd bitten into a bad apple and, with an expression on his face that reminded me of Norman Tebbit, he said he was busy and left.

I sat down on the sofa with Ivana and we looked at each other in despair. This was what we had feared the most – rejection. Were our doubting friends and family going to be proven right? Would we be returning to the white cliffs of Dover with our tails between our legs before the year was over? It was the scenario of our nightmares. I looked out of the windows at the sparkling bay feeling like Piglet up the oak tree with the water rising and throwing down a bottle with a message in it saying: 'HELP! PIGLET (ME)'.

Karmela had heard my exchange with the fisherman and came in from the garden. 'You mustn't take it badly,' she said. 'This is how we are – suspicious of everyone. It's small wonder, though. The only visitors we've had for as long as I can remember have been the military, and as we say: "You can't prevent the birds of ill-fortune flying over you, but you can stop them nesting in your hair.'"

We looked at each other in dumb despair, and seeing our faces growing even longer, Karmela added, 'Well it's no good you sitting there goggling at each other like two dead halibuts. You're both so friendly I'm sure they'll get to like you in good time.'

Cold comfort.

CHAPTER 6

COFFEE
HOUSING

At least the fisherman's reaction made Karmela determined to see us accepted by the community and the first thing to do, we were told, was to be seen regularly in the cafés. So we chose Marko's as our 'regular'. Marko's was in the main square and, set against a background of the Venetian façades, his wicker tables and chairs made a charming tableau. It was also a prime position, as sitting there you could watch the activity on the waterfront and look out over the bay at the same time. Marko could have charged extra just for the view.

At first, we thought it was the setting that had made it the focal point of the village, but it was Marko himself who made it the 'Café de Ville'. An ex-naval officer with a square chin and a steely eye whose speech and bearing spoke of quiet command, Marko presided over the square as if it were his quarterdeck. His battleship-grey hair was never out of place and his shirt and trousers were as well pressed at three o'clock on a hot afternoon as they were in the morning. Even the way he moved was precise and economical, and, although the coterie that hung around him were a pretty garrulous lot, Marko spoke quietly and chose his words carefully.

When I first introduced myself, he told me in his slightly stilted English that he was the Hon. Sec. of the Vis Anglo-Croatian Military Society, which he had formed five years ago with the British officers who used to come up from Bosnia and Kosovo during lulls in hostilities.

'Why did they come to Vis? I asked.

'To visit all the British military sites and cemetery, of course.'

'*British* military sites?' I said in surprise.

Marko looked at me in equal surprise. 'But you occupied our island on two occasions. We were the base for your Navy when you were fighting Napoleon, and again in World War II.'

'I thought we just passed through on our way north.'

'You were here for nearly two years and our harbour was full of your ships. You even built an airfield up in the valley. In the Napoleonic war, you were here for ten years. That big fort over there is called Fort George, after your King, and that little island there is called Hoste Island after your Sir William Hoste, the captain of the fleet. Do you know the family?'

'Er… I don't think I do.'

He looked disappointed.

'I'm afraid I had no idea about all this,' I said. 'It certainly wasn't in any of our school history books.'

'Please, I did not mean to give offence,' he said quickly, clearly embarrassed at showing up my ignorance. 'Please do not feel that you should know such things. We were also not taught about it in our schools. We were only told about the brave deeds of our fearless Comrade partisans who fought with their bare hands for our freedom! He gave a wry smile. 'The brave deeds of the British were never mentioned. It did not suit our Glorious People's Revolutionary history. And I am sure that in England there were more important campaigns for school children to learn about.'

A practised diplomat.

When I got to know Marko better, I discovered he was also a practised master of the inconspicuous question – but, by the time I found that out, he'd already got all there was to know out of me.

After a week, I discovered that he acted as the village Citizen's Advice Bureau. He had an ability to put people's problems into perspective and explain how the outside world worked. Every day villagers came to ask for his guidance – how to write a letter to the Ministry, how to get legal advice, how to find out if they can get a grant, how to get their son a place at college… and, whoever they were, Marko would invariably sit them down, offer them a drink and chat about this and that before asking why they had come to see him. Most of the questions, he told me, were about how to deal with the authorities, and added that, because the same people that ran the country under communism were still in charge, dealings with the authorities were as Byzantine as they had always been.

Marko's counsel was invariably down to earth. 'No, I really wouldn't ask them about it yet,' I heard him say to one of our neighbours. 'If you do that, they'll have to inform the Fisheries Department, and that'll put a stop to everything. You'd do much better to talk to Kristo in the Port Office and let him have a word with his brother in the Tourist Development Office. Once *they* give their approval, no other department will dare to object.'

Another time I heard: 'Don't even mention it to your mother-in-law or she'll be at your poor pa-in-law with the frying pan again. Just go ahead and do it, and, when she's here having coffee with her cousins after church, get your cousin Nada to tell her about it. She won't want her smart cousins to see her getting angry, and she'll think it was Nada's side of the family who engineered it rather than you and your pa-in-law.'

It sounded as if there were many in the village who had been saved from the frying-pan treatment thanks to Marko – although there were those who were not fans of his, and Karmela was one of them. But, for her, Marko was something of a rival, both of them being in the information-distribution business. 'That Marko expects everyone to ask his advice about everything,' she told us. 'About jobs, houses, cars, donkeys, children and mothers-in-law. And, if you don't ask his advice, he tells the whole island that whatever you're doing is wrong.'

I raised my eyebrows.

'Oh yes he does! And that's not a good thing in a village as small as this. We have a saying: "Teeth are hard, but they soon fall out. The tongue is soft, but it lasts forever!"'

I felt like mentioning the pot, the kettle and the colour black, but my Croatian wasn't quite up to it. Anyway, perhaps there was something in what she said. Marko was somewhat proprietorial. Whenever we hadn't been in for a few days, the next time he saw us he'd say in a slightly disapproving voice: 'Oh! I was wondering where you've been,' as if we had been straying away from his protective network. But I appreciated his concern and I was grateful that he was always quick to notice if any of his customers didn't respond when I tried to talk to them. Whenever he saw this happening, he'd come over to start a conversation and include me in it to show I was a friend of his.

I had found a Godfather.

The best place for meeting people was, in fact, the ferry. Everyone had to go over to the mainland at some point, and being at sea seemed to create a kind of camaraderie that made it easier to talk.

The ferry journey to the mainland was a trip back in time. At daybreak, we'd climb the iron companionway past the evil-smelling engine room and rancid latrines and up to the smoke-filled cafeteria where everyone gathered. The scene there resembled an old French movie. Crew members stood at the bar with the truck drivers knocking back shots of *rakija* (the local vodka-like gut rot), gnarled fishermen in berets sat with their drinks, playing cards and smoking Walter Wolf cigarettes (an oddly named but favoured brand in this part of the world), Town Hall officials huddled over their papers, and at the back an old granny or two skulked in the gloom with a live chicken in a basket.

On our first journey, I went into one of the minuscule toilets and was in the process of unzipping when the door banged into my back. Damn, I hadn't shut it properly. I quickly tried to push it shut with a foot, but I was flattened against the urinal. Craning my neck round, I saw an agitated bearded face, and given that the square footage of the toilet was that of a phone box, we eyeballed each other at six inches. At school, I'd always practised the paralysing karate chop that I'd give to anyone trying something on in a public convenience, but, squashed against the porcelain, I couldn't even secure a first line of defence by doing up my zip, let alone delivering a paralysing chop.

'*Oprostite, Gospodin!*' stammered the intruder, and, seeming to recognise me, he continued in English. 'Please, Sir, I must hide myself from some person!'

Scenes from spy movies flashed through my mind. He must be an agent

35

on the run. What if the Stasi or a KGB hit man were after him? Innocent bystanders like Michael Caine and Harrison Ford were always getting caught up in situations like this, and then spent the rest of the movie escaping from the hit men themselves. (But, as somewhere along the line they'd get to persuade someone like Nicole Kidman to take off all her clothes, it usually turned out OK.) I began to panic. This was what was happening to me right now *sans* the Nicole Kidman bit.

'What's going on?' I said, trying to put a gritty Michael Caine-like edge into my voice.

'I must hide myself! Someone they look for me!'

Oh my God! A man toting one of those guns with big silencers!

'Who is it?' I trembled.

'Grandma Dragulic!'

The Richter adrenalin scale level dropped by fifty points as the pictures of men with big silencers were replaced by black-clad grannies wielding umbrellas.

'Oh, really!' I said, as if that was the most natural thing in the world.

'Yes. For many days, she is waiting for my answer, but in this case I do not have answer for her!' the man said, the words tumbling out in staccato. 'She is on ferry and, if she find me, she shout at me and all will hear!'

My fear turned into self-consciousness. I was conducting a conversation squashed between a stranger's stomach and a urinal and I now remembered where I had seen him – at the Town Hall signing some of our endless paperwork. (The Croatian civil service system still hadn't changed since the fall of communism, and the amount of paper we had so far acquired must have been equal to the amount of paper needed to tie Great Britain into the European monetary system.)

'Maybe she's already passed by and it's safe now?' I suggested.

'You go look? Yes?'

'But I don't know what she looks like.'

'She small and wide and she wear black!'

Like any Vis granny then. There were at least a dozen of them on the ferry. But my worry was that the granny might have rumbled us and was waiting outside with leg of ham and ready to clout me over the head with it. I put my head out gingerly. The threat had passed. A small but ominous black shape was disappearing down the corridor. I relayed the information to my companion who squeezed himself out, thanked me profusely, and hurried off in the opposite direction.

As the village was so small, we thought that patronising one café was enough, but Karmela considered that slacking. How were we to get a true perspective of anything with only Marko's gossip to go on? Why, with only his view, we'd never get to the bottom of any story.

I was quite happy about this as I've always found the concept of a café society rather appealing. Drifting in from the street to order a tonsil-numbing liquor or a coffee so strong it almost dissolves the spoon and then striking up a conversation with anyone around is something I've wanted to do all my life. You couldn't do that kind of thing in Fulham – or, at least, you'd get some very strange looks if you did – but out here the cafés were full of people willing to reciprocate.

Marko's was more of a coffee place than a drinking place, but it seemed that Western coffee culture hadn't yet filtered down this far, so on the Vis waterfront there were no cinnamon lattes, decaf macchiatos or skinny mocha Americanos. Here, coffee was either small and black or large and white, but at least it meant one didn't have to waste time making up one's mind.

Acting on Karmela's advice, as our second 'regular', we chose more of a watering hole – Zoran's, a small rundown place near the front. It was more of a bar than a café, in that it attracted more of a bar-type clientele (that is, men), and its décor certainly wasn't chosen by someone in touch with their feminine side. The interior was largely taken up by a bar and the remaining space was filled with a shabby collection of mismatched café furniture. There were also some chairs outside, but they looked as if they had started a fight and been sent out into the street to finish it, and were rarely used. Zoran's regulars were largely impervious to the beautiful surroundings and preferred to stay in the dark interior where they could drink unobserved and weather down Zoran's paintwork with the nicotine from their Walter Wolf cigarettes.

Zoran had been born on Vis, but he had left for Texas in his twenties where he had picked up a Texan swagger and an addiction to wearing boots, and had added an American drawl to his gravelly voice. With his hawk-like features, meaty lips and wavy, long black hair, he looked like a bad-tempered Red Indian, but there was always a glimmer in his hooded eyes that hinted that a quip or a sardonic comment was never far away. He had sharp-tongued opinions about everything and everyone, but he rarely talked about himself, and, if he did, he would shroud it in humour. Usually, it takes me a while to get people into focus, but I soon had Zoran in sharp definition and I warmed to him – in particular, his way of treating the whole world as a joke that had somehow gone a bit wrong.

On weekends, Zoran's was full of people from the mainland, most of whom Ivana suspected of being skippers of smuggling boats or mercenaries on leave – at least she was sure they looked as if they had just come in from killing someone or something. Zoran loved the weekends. There was a lot of shouting and *rakija* drinking, and he could hold forth like a compere on a TV show. Standing at the bar, he'd thump the top with one arm and wave the other, which sported an eye-catchingly large Rolex. Cushioned in a thick bed of arm hair, Zoran's watch looked particularly unattractive. I must say, I do think those big chunky watches must be the most unbecoming male fashion accessory since the codpiece.

We tended to avoid the weekends and saved our visits for the weekdays when his minion, Dragimir, did most of the work and Zoran could spend his time holding forth to the cabal of large-bellied men of the village, who, having nothing better to do, hung around his bar for most of the day conducting their conversations in a somewhat curious way. Like in a Greek classical play, Zoran and his bar-proppers didn't so much discuss things, as make speeches to each other, and this did make exchanges of opinion a rather more protracted experience than usual. It certainly filled the hours, though.

It wasn't long before the subject of Croatia joining the EU came up.

'I'm told you guys in the EU have towns you "twin" with. Right?'

'Yes, but I'm not sure my hometown has a twin. I don't think too many European towns were queuing up to twin with Fulham.'

38

'Mebbe now that Croatia's gonna join the EU, I could set up a nice little suicide pact between your Fulham and our Solin?"

We had been to Solin and it was a place so crushed by its heavy industry that it made Dagenham look like an area of outstanding natural beauty.

'I could get you a nice little trade goin' with Solin,' Zoran continued. 'You send 'em your pork pies an' they can send you their goat-hoof fritters in return. They've also got an industrial landscape down there that could be a great inspiration for your poets, an' there's enough pollution goin' on to keep your conservation lovers busy for years.'

Zoran drank steadily throughout the day. It was a mystery how a man could absorb so much alcohol and still be able to function. I sometimes thought he might have developed some sort of resistance to the substance. A side benefit of his drinking, however, was that sometimes it made him drop his guard enough to talk about himself. 'When those goddamn Serbs invaded us,' he said to me at the end of a long evening, 'I gave up my job in Texas, sold my house an' came back to fight them. But once we'd got the bastards off our back and I came here to Vis full of ideas of what I'd get goin', it only took me a week to see that nothin' new was gonna happen on this little island of ours.' He pulled a long face and stubbed out a half-finished Walter Wolf. (At Zoran's, no one, including the proprietor, paid much attention to the new smoking regulations.)

'It's the old communist thick-necks we've still got runnin' this country; that's the problem. It's still the same goddamn clods that ran the show under communism. The only difference now is that they can line their pockets from it. These days, politics sure pays a lot better than crime!' He pulled another award-winning scowl.

I made condoling noises.

'And with that flabby-arsed lot we've got in our Town Hall,' he continued, 'nothin's ever gonna happen. As the gypsies say: "They keep such a tight hold of the reins, the horse can't move."' (Much of Zoran's conversation was peppered with these kinds of aphorisms, the meaning of which sometimes took me a moment to work out.)

'But it must be a lot easier now you're free,' I ventured.

'Not here it isn't. Those Town Hall bastards love their goddamn horse so much, they sit on its goddamn head!' He paused. 'I'm just tellin' you this so you know what kinda place you're livin' in. It's tough for a free-thinkin' man who's got his own ideas. A place like this can bend iron.'

More upbeat news.

CHAPTER 7

LOCAL CUSTOMS AND LOCAL TRANSPORT

One morning we were sitting at Zoran's when we heard the clump of his boots and he barged in brandishing a local broadsheet. 'Look what the stupid bastards have come up with now!' he shouted, thwacking the paper on the bar. 'They're so far up their arse with this heritage stuff, we can't change a single bollard. How the hell do they think we can get a tourist industry goin' if we can't get any more moorings put in? Jesus! What a load of dumb-asses! God knows when I'll get the goddamn permit for my pontoons now.' He sat down beside us, scrunched up the paper with a large fist and threw it on the floor. Then he heaved himself up and paced round the room, his bulky frame contorted in anger. 'Crap, crap, crap! That's all I ever get from that flabby-assed bunch of idiots! And you know what else? At the same time as they won't allow me to get my business goin', they say they need more employment. Assholes!'

He circled the room and sat down heavily. 'Sometimes those damn bastards really get me down. I've wasted months on this!' He glared at the crumpled newspaper for a moment and got to his feet again. 'I think I'll go and walk around for a bit. Maybe I'll feel better.' He shouldered his way out of the door and clumped off down the waterfront, his curses and the scrunch of his boots dwindling away in the breeze.

When I got to know Zoran better, I found that, although he was always dreaming up new projects, he seemed to have lost some of his fight. Had he been a bit younger I think he might have thrown more of himself into his schemes, but most of his time seemed to be spent presiding over the big-bellied coterie that hung around the bar. I once asked him why he thought his clientele spent so much of their time there and he replied that this was how the islanders kept their fingers on the pulse – not only about whether the grape harvest was going to be early, the prices of olives and the movements of the anchovy shoals, but also about whose wife had been seen in the car of somebody who wasn't her husband. He said he liked his bar being used as an agricultural forecast office, a Stock Exchange and a neighbourhood watch rolled into one.

After a few weeks, I was getting on quite well with some of the regulars, but there were several who were still uncomfortable in my presence. Shaking hands and saying hello to everything that moves usually does the trick, I've found, but it didn't work at Zoran's. Even Zoran, who could have majored in insensitivity, noticed their hostile attitude – not that I got much sympathy from him.

'This is Croatia, not Italy or Spain. You won't find any friendly grinnin' locals aroun' here. Not in my bar you won't. A few centuries of bein' invaded by all you foreign bastards hasn't made us the world's most friendly nation.'

More encouraging news. When was the fun going to stop?

Some days later, seeing another of my attempts to converse falling on stony ground, Zoran put a hand on my shoulder. 'Don't you worry, my friend. You jus' kiss the hand you can't bite. Like I said, they're not used to outsiders here, so you jus' keep on tryin'. They'll get used to you sometime.'

'Sometime? And when do you think that'll be?'

He gave me one of his infuriating grins and disappeared behind the bar.

Hardly reassuring, but I felt that I had found myself another Godfather – albeit one who looked more like Big Chief Sitting Bull on a bad hair day than Marlon Brando.

One afternoon, Zoran clamped an arm round my shoulder and said, 'It's about time you got yourself a car.'

'I've been thinking about that.'

An' we'll have none of them English Jaguars or Range Rovers. A car of the people is what you gotta get.'

'I don't care what you say. I'm not having a Skoda or a Wartburg. Our children will laugh at me.'

Zoran raised a hooded eyebrow and gave a dismissive shrug.

'You don't have kids. You just don't know how mean kids can be to their ageing fathers when it comes to matters of taste. It's bad enough when it's just a matter of my ties.'

'Don't you worry; I'll find you somethin' decent. An' if you don't like the image, you can always beef it up with tiger-skin seat covers an' matchin' suitcases.' He looked at me with the twinkling eyes of George Clooney and the heart of Al Capone.

What kind of car was he thinking of?

The favoured form of island transport was a sort of motorised wheelbarrow with handlebars on the front – you see a lot of them in Spain and Italy. (I had rather fancied myself on one of those, but I went for a ride on the back of our builder's one and found it the most painful way of travelling known to man. They must be popular with men who don't want their wives to go into town with them.) The next vehicle in the island pecking order was the Renault 4; the oblong box on wheels with the pull-push gear lever on the dashboard – and that's what Zoran had in mind. 'Tito did some deal with the French back in the sixties,' he said. 'We made Renault 4s under licence and sent the French container loads of pickled gherkins and tractor tyres in return.' He gave a snorting chuckle. 'I think we came off best outta that deal.'

By the end of the week, Zoran had found a suitable model and we were sent to Split to buy it – a twenty-year-old Renault 4 belonging to an elderly man who (surprise, surprise) turned out to be a cousin of Zoran's. However, the old man had plainly cherished it for twenty years and spent nearly an hour telling us about all its eccentricities. I couldn't see in the rear-view mirror, but I'm sure there were tears in his eyes as he watched us driving it off into the sunset.

Ivana was consumed with guilt as we waited for the car ferry. 'He was so sweet. Do you think he noticed I was bored when he showed us everything? He must have thought me so rude.

'It doesn't feel right; just rolling up like that and buying his most precious possession with obviously no hardship. His life's savings probably aren't much more than what we've just given him.' She was silent for a minute. 'I hope he thought I liked his car and I'd look after it. Do you think he did?'

'Yes, my sweet,' I replied, as I usually do when I'm not quite sure what she means. Ivana has never so much as raised a car bonnet in all our years together, but perhaps she meant that she'd do it if she had to – which she probably would. She'd drive to Bulgaria and back in an old banger if she had to, as she did to the camps with the convoys, yet, if asked to perform the simplest of mechanical tasks, she gets the vapours. I've never quite got my head round it. Our children say their mother is a curious mixture of Xena Warrior Princess and Margot Fonteyn in *Swan Lake*, and she does, in fact, look something like a combination of the two. (As you can imagine, this combination does make for a slightly unpredictable home life – but at least she's never learned kickboxing.)

Three hours later, we clattered off the ferry in our four-door wheelie-bin on wheels and, after dropping Ivana home, I took it over to Zoran's. After pulling up in front, I dusted off my trousers like Clint Eastwood hitching his burro to the saloon rail, and swaggered into the barroom as happy as the day I brought my first car home to show my brother and sisters.

The bar trooped out to inspect my purchase, tyres were kicked, teeth were sucked, and a lot of knowledgeable nodding went on. My confidence had a slight wobble when someone lifted the bonnet, but he looked up to say, 'Engine's clean. Someone's looked after it all right.'

'No sign of rust on the sills, either,' said Filip the tax collector.

Zoran opened the driver's door and looked inside. 'Seats a bit worn. Better order up some of those tiger-skin seat covers.'

The others looked puzzled.

We went back inside and regrouped around the bar. 'And now,' said Zoran, clamping a hairy arm around my shoulders again, 'we're gonna find you a boat.'

The farmer who lived in the street behind us had a Renault 4 of a similar vintage, and I was looking at it for rust spots (being by the sea brings them on like a rash of measles), when I noticed small black pellet-like objects on the roof. I was curious to know what they were, but the owner was a terrifying-looking fellow with a crushed purple strawberry of a nose and a mat of hair that stuck out in every direction, and I didn't want to show I was ignorant of something that was obvious to a local.

A week later, I was looking down from the window when I thought I saw something move on his car roof. I couldn't work out what it was at first, as one doesn't quite associate animals with car roofs, and it wasn't until it moved again that I realised that two sheep were tied on to the roof rack. Our first visitors, a cousin of mine and her two boys, were staying with us for the half-term, so I called the boys over to look and they quickly scampered downstairs. Sheep that didn't run away when you tried to pet them were a rare commodity, and by the time I got down they were in deep conversation with them. Just as I arrived, I saw the Renault's owner lumbering out of his door; a terrifying hulk of a man, he looked as if someone had dug him up by the roots. As he came barrelling towards us shouting something unintelligible, I felt what an English piker must have felt like at the battle of Bannockburn.

He came to a halt. 'Hah! You English people!' he said in loud, guttural English and grinned at us, revealing a startling row of brown multi-directional teeth. 'Always English like animal! Why Englishman so like animal? Croatian man, he like girl!' He roared with laughter at his joke.

Being of an age at which animals are preferable to girls, the boys looked perplexed.

'Why are they on your roof rack?' the older one asked. 'Are you going to sell them at the market?'

'No, no! These are my bad sheep. These two they make much trouble. If I leave them when I go in town, they go jump wall and run in road – and all other sheep they follow – like sheep!' He laughed loudly at his joke again.

'Don't they miss their friends when they're on your roof?' asked the younger one.

45

'I give them sweet food when they go on roof, so they like.' He cuffed one of them over the head and ruffled its ear. 'This one my best friend. I call him "Hrabo" (Brave). He go fight dog and sometime he go fight man if he no like.'

One of the sheep was casually chewing at the ear of boy No. 1 and the man noticed. 'But look! He like you. You come see my farm. You see all of sheep and you help give food and water. Yes? You bring Uncle too. He come drink my new wine.' He winked at me.

Watching his Renault bounce away down the cobbled street with the two sheep, I realised I had just received our first island invitation. Had there been a sea change in local attitude? Maybe the predictions of Karmela and Zoran were wrong?

'Maybe the locals aren't so standoffish after all,' I said to Ivana as she made us knock the sheep pellets off our shoes before we were allowed back inside.

But my optimism was short-lived. Hearing reports of a storm brewing up at the end of the week, and seeing that the floating jetty attached to our wall looked ready to jump ship at the first strong wind, I thought I'd ask the fishermen what to do about it. So the next time I went by Marko's and saw four weathered salts sitting there in a range of assorted nautical head-gear that you'd never find at Harvey Nichols, I squared my shoulders, straightened my back and approached them. (It's astonishing how much a ramrod posture can do to your confidence.) Seven eyes and an eye patch turned towards me as I hastily explained my problem, and one who had a face that looked as if it had been carved by a second-year sculpture student looked up to say, 'There's no difference how you tie it. Whatever you do, if the wind's strong enough it'll break it loose.'

The one beside him, a sunken block of a fellow, grunted in agreement. 'You'll learn soon enough.'

There are many times in my life that I've wanted to pull out a gun, point it at someone's head and say, *Go on, punk, make my day!* Or, like the Scarlet Pimpernel, make some witheringly witty remark while flicking a speck of dust off my lapel. But, unable to think of anything suitable to say, I pretended I didn't feel at all slighted and walked away trying to look as nonchalant as I could. But I don't think it fooled them one bit, and I could feel their watery, mocking eyes on my retreating back as I went down the front.

I got home to find Ivana on the phone to the children (as usual checking they were OK for underwear), but, seeing my expression, she told them their father wasn't looking quite himself and rang off. She then joined me on the sofa for a bit of fond arm stroking and head shaking while I held forth about our neighbours' blatant unhelpfulness, plain rudeness and lack of common courtesy, and the unfairness of life in general.

'But just think of all the other things we have now we're here,' Ivana said soothingly when I eventually ran out of steam. 'Why don't you go and get yourself a drink and we'll sit on the terrace and watch the sun go down while we think of other ways of thawing the neighbours out.'

I poured myself a large gin. Such a comfort in times of trouble, gin. No wonder it was the Queen Mum's favourite. Must have been such a help to their Royal Majesties during our national emergencies and their own family ructions.

We sat on the terrace with our drinks looking over the bay as the light began to soften, turning the hills hazy blue and the water into a limpid pool of gold. Sometimes the combination of sunlight, sea and warm air can do something quite narcotic and sometimes it can lift you on to another level entirely – but, by the time the sun had disappeared, we still hadn't thought of another way of thawing out the neighbours.

We did feel a lot better, though.

CHAPTER 8

MEDICINE
MATTERS

In the end, it was Karmela who set us off on the right path. As there was no hospital on the island, Ivana had brought out enough medical supplies to kit out a frontline field station, and, when we eventually unpacked it, Karmela picked up a carton and glared at it. 'Ha! Made in a German factory I see! And what do they know about our illnesses and accidents? I ask you. Now, if you ever have an accident – and here we see so many terrible accidents – Grandma Gokan will give you something much better than all these chemicals.'

'Are the roads really that dangerous?' said Ivana, her eyes widening as she no doubt imagined me upside down in a Renault 4.

'No, it's the fishing, not the roads!' replied Karmela.

Ivana exhaled. The life-expectancy rate on the roads of Vis was not somewhere in between Mogadishu and Helmand Province.

'What with all their knives and their hooks, our fishermen have the most terrible accidents! Such dreadful wounds I've seen, and, as nothing ever heals in the salt water, they can turn into gangrene and we lose another of our sons.' She crossed herself. 'Oh yes. God might give us the sunrise every morning and the flowers in springtime, but that doesn't seem to stop him taking our sons from us whenever he feels like it!'

Seeing the fishermen on the quay every day, I had noticed that a surprising number of them had missing body parts. Ears, eyes, fingers, toes and sometimes whole feet were often absent; not that your average fisherman looked the picture of health even when whole. Years of being sandblasted by the elements had clearly played havoc with complexions and no one on the island seemed to be pushing skincare products too hard.

'Well, as I don't want to join the fishing fleet and end up like them,' I said, 'I don't think we'll be troubling Grandma Gokan just yet.'

'Ah, but the roads can be dangerous!' responded Karmela, as always a glass half-empty person. 'Look at the state of our vans and our drivers! That Bozo Sanda is the worst of them. He drinks too much and drives that dreadful van of his so dangerously. They shouldn't allow either him or his van on our roads. He'll wipe out half our congregation one day, you mark my words! If you're not careful, you'll be rounding a corner one day and you'll find that Bozo coming straight at you on the wrong side of the road.'

I hadn't met this Bozo yet, but several times I'd had an unnerving awareness of my mortality brought on by the antics of other island drivers. Back home, that kind of driving was largely restricted to shaven-headed people between the ages of seventeen and twenty-five in cars with spoilers and alloy hub caps, but here it was the preserve of middle-aged men looking like Mr Toad behind the wheel of their Skoda vans with dangerous glints in their eyes.

'Several others make cures as well as Grandma Gokan,' continued Karmela, 'but you be very careful who you buy from. Some are getting too old and they forget which herbs are which.'

By the time Karmela left, Ivana was humming with ideas and pacing up and down the kitchen.

'I'm going to visit all medicine-making grannies. Most of them live with their families, and it's a wonderful excuse to get to know more people.'

'You can't just knock on someone's door and say: "Hello, do you have a granny at home and does she make medicines?"'

'Oh, I'll tell them you're suffering from something. They'll never think that I'm making it up. Karmela says that everyone thinks you're so thin and straggly that you must be ill. I'll tell them about your back – or, even better, I'll talk about our family illnesses. Everyone over sixty likes talking about illnesses, and it'll make us lots of friends, I know it will. We'll get to the village through the grannies. See if we don't!'

The next evening, Ivana marched me off to Grandma Gokan's and knocked on the blackened door. A pleasant-faced girl opened it.

'My husband has a bad back and I wondered if…'

'Come in, come in! You want my grandmother. She's out the back killing chickens. I'll go and fetch her.'

'Killing chickens!' I whispered to Ivana as the girl went out.

'Now don't you dare spoil it,' she hissed back.

I looked around. In the middle of the low dark kitchen was a large wooden table, and on the floor underneath were baskets of oddly shaped roots. Along the walls were shelves lined with strange-looking jars and the light from the window gave their murky liquids an eerie, alien glow. Were they for drinking or for rubbing on to the affected area? From what we'd heard about grannies getting their potions wrong, you wouldn't want details like that to be lost in translation.

The pendulum clock on the wall ticked unnervingly loudly and a blackened pot on a thickly encrusted stove at the back of the room bubbled ominously. The smell coming from it suggested pig's face boiled in grease. Was it too late to do a runner? Then a clack-clack-clack of footsteps came down the corridor and a tiny old black-scarfed woman with a fearsome expression appeared in the doorway. Her voluminous black skirt made her look almost as wide as she was tall, and I was alarmed to see white feathers clinging to the skirt.

Without introducing herself, she pointed at Ivana. 'Is it you?'

'Oh, no!' said Ivana, momentarily flustered. 'It's my husband. His back is really bad.'

I gave her a 'let's not exaggerate' grimace.

'Well, it's not that bad, I suppose,' she faltered. 'It's more of a dull ache.'

Damn. I shouldn't have put her off the script.

'Lie here!' said the granny, pointing to the kitchen table. With no obvious exit at my disposal, I got up and stretched out on my front. She hauled up the back of my shirt, yanked down the top of my trousers and prodded me

50

fiercely at the top of my bottom. I whimpered. I'm a pretty accomplished actor when it's a matter of just 'appearing ill', but, when it's the real thing, I can be very realistic. She now stopped prodding and I heard the clack-clack-clack as she moved round the table to my head. I tensed. Was she about to yank my neck about? She bent down to peer into my face and for the first time she smiled. She must have recognised a nervous patient.

'Artichoke root, birch bark and egg are what it needs,' she said over her shoulder to Ivana, ignoring me completely. I remained face down and listened to the screech of metal steps as she dragged them over to the shelves, and then I heard the clink of the jars. The footsteps returned to the sink and there was the sound of cracking eggs and whisking as she beat away at what I presumed was the 'root in viscous'. The footsteps then came back to the table and a bowl was clunked down. It gave off a strange, pungent smell and I looked round to see her scooping up a dough-like substance and slapping it on to the small of my back. I stiffened, but it didn't hurt.

'There! That'll pull the inflammation out of you in no time at all,' she said, patting my bottom in what I considered to be an over-familiar manner. 'I'll strap it up later,' she said, clack-clacking over to Ivana. 'You make sure he keeps it on until tomorrow, and don't let him have a bath or he'll get a bad burn. We'll go and sit next door,' she said, and turning to me she raised a finger, Barbara Woodhouse style. 'Now you stay where you are and keep still!'

'Yes. You stay there and be good!' said Ivana, grinning.

It was the knobbliest table I'd ever lain on, but in case they came back I lay there with my chin out like an obedient Golden Retriever. The poultice was cold and clammy, but for some reason it gave a strong sensation of heat and the small of my back began to feel numb. Despite the knobbliness of the table, I must have dozed off and was in the middle of a dream involving chickens when I woke to find a terrifying vision from a science-fiction movie six inches away – a wrinkled face with a toothless mouth. I jumped in fright, but bony fingers grabbed my thigh in a vice-like grip and a sharp command was barked. I didn't know what it was, but I froze.

'She's telling you not to move,' said Ivana, as the granny cackled something else.

I looked up.

'She's asking if you were dreaming about flaxen-haired maidens,' said Ivana, laughing.

The granny fumbled about my middle with a bandage, hoiked up my trousers, and patted my rump again as if I were a child on potty training.

Ivana giggled.

As soon as we were outside, Ivana started to laugh. 'You jumped like a rabbit when she woke you!'

'Well, at close quarters she looked like the Bride of Darth Vader – and you saw what she does to chickens!'

'You were very brave, darling.'

'Was I really?'

'Yes, I was very proud of you.'

'I didn't look silly, then?'

'Well… I have seen you to better advantage.'

'Oh…'

'Anyway, it was all a great success, even though there weren't any other family members to make friends with. But she told me all about her family and I told her all about ours – about the illnesses, I mean. She loved it. We're going to visit all the others that Karmela told me about and we're going to make lots of granny friends, you'll see!'

'But do I really have to be the patient every time? Why don't you go on your own and just tell them what I'm suffering from?'

'Maybe that's not such a bad idea. They might not want to talk with you around. Look how Grandma Gokan only told me what she did when you weren't there.'

'Good plan.'

The following evening, Ivana went off on her own to the next medicine maker, and over the following two weeks she worked her way through the rest of them. And she was right about family illnesses. They were the best possible talking point, and not only did she hear some wonderfully grue-some stories in eye-popping detail, but she also gave good value in return. Apparently, all our old family favourites went down a treat; in particular,

Uncle Sidney drowning in his bath when under the influence and Great-Aunt Lydia being trampled to death while trying to defend her herbaceous border from her herd of prize bullocks. What also went down well was Uncle Arthur dying from a heart attack while on top of Aunt Mavis and Aunt Mavis spending the rest of her days trying to cover it up.

The only downside was that Ivana now came home with strange concoctions to dose me with, and, without exception, they all tasted revolting. Funnily enough, though, most of them seemed to do the trick.

The most successful were:

Coughs – Boil nettle leaves. It certainly dealt with an itchy throat.

Diarrhoea – Mugwort and angelica. Boil in vinegar and drink. It would persuade anyone's bowels to shut up shop.

Colds – Elderflowers with all their leaves. Boil and drink. This one even tasted quite good.

Insomnia – Lemon juice and honey before bed. I added whisky.

Cuts – St John's Wort. Crush until a paste and put on the wound.

There was also a potion for blood pressure – one dessertspoon every morning of lemon, onion and sugar mixed in equal measures. I didn't think it was working, but Ivana was adamant it was. Without a doctor at hand, it was hard to prove either way, but Ivana has never been one to let things like that get in her way, and I was made to keep taking it.

Ivana's infiltration of the aged underbelly of the village continued, but, although I was let off the hook on many occasions, I still found myself spending more evenings than I would have cared to on people's kitchen tables, wondering how fate and one's wife could bring a man to such a state of indignity. Wives and grannies never treated their men like this back home, but I suppose Health and Safety probably clobbered the last healer to the ground sometime in the reign of George V. It was just my bad luck to have ended up in one of the few places left in the Western Hemisphere where potions were not only legal, but also family sized and Triple X strength.

I was then struck by a really terrifying thought. What if Ivana took an interest in potion making herself and started brewing up with my bowels in mind? It didn't bear thinking about.

Matters of health were by far the most common subject of all village conversations, even among the middle-aged, and the most common form of salutation was *Zdravi Bili!* (Be Healthy!). This salutation was not only exchanged when taking your leave, but it was also a greeting. There was, however, a downside. While islanders were naturally reserved, once they started on the subject of health, natural propriety was cast to the wind and it was open season. This meant that no one had the slightest compunction in laying bare the personal intimacies of their family members in public – and, as someone who blushes at the mention of any bodily function, I found it excruciatingly embarrassing.

I was queuing at the corner store one afternoon when an elderly lady came up to me and without any preamble said, 'What happened to you after your meal at Jacov's on Sunday? We were there having my Dina's birthday lunch and we all had terrible wind for the rest of the day. It's those chickpeas Jacov puts with everything he cooks. I know it is. I was making such terrible noises I didn't dare go to evensong. Were you the same?' And she waited for an answer as if she'd asked me the way to the bus station.

Bereft of speech, I stood there like a ventriloquist's dummy propped up against a wall with its mouth open.

The same happened at the market. 'I always buy my Pero these beetroots,' a septuagenarian neighbour said to Ivana as we were choosing our mangold. 'He's got such a problem passing water these days. Does yours have the same problem yet?'

Ivana was chatting with the next stallholder and didn't hear, so the old lady turned to me. 'Does it sting when you do your pi-pi?' And she fixed me with a gimlet-eyed look that required an answer.

I felt my face reddening as I tried to attract Ivana's attention. 'Well, um… yes, beetroot is really good for you…' I stammered. 'Yes, it's such a good vegetable…' But Ivana was still steadfastly refusing to look in my direction and so I burbled on. 'And tomatoes are really full of good things, too, aren't they… Just look at those ones there… Magnificent specimens…' I willed Ivana to look up, but obdurately she still wouldn't pick up on my distress signals. Mercifully, a stall holder then said something to the old lady, and, seeing her momentarily distracted, I made a quick escape.

From then on, I was on red alert every time I went to the market in case another inquisitive granny might be lurking behind a pile of beetroot, but it was a small price to pay. Health talk was definitely the way to the hearts and minds of the grannies – and they were a powerful pressure group. Besides, who knows, given a few more years of island living, even I might learn how to exchange the intimacies of my bodily functions with my fellow beings in the full light of day.

Something to look forward to, then.

CHAPTER 9

CHILDREN
AND GRANNIES

After a month of being on the island, we could still remember the state of euphoria we were in when we returned to London after deciding to sell up and move. Euphoria had put our house on the market, euphoria had found us a tiny flat and euphoria had got my company ready for sale. Though when it came to breaking the news to our two children, it failed us.

Now in their late twenties, our children had serious doubts about our ability to cope with such a change. Like most treasured offspring, they had started life as dear sweet little things, and after a few ghastly years of teenage strop they mercifully reverted to the endearing people they used to be, but they had recently started on a new phase of treating their parents as old duffers who needed a watchful eye kept on them. They considered our decision irresponsible and were clearly worried about what it might lead to next – joining the Moonies, running amok, spending their inheritance? The lectures came from all angles, and, when I was foolish enough to let slip that I was looking for a boat, things got worse. Knowing that their mother's argumentative powers were more than a match for them, they didn't start right away, but, as soon as Ivana left the kitchen, they closed their chairs on me in a pincer movement like two of Rommel's tanks.

'Now,' said Milena in a voice she borrows from her mother, 'this boat. You *are* going to have it properly serviced, aren't you?'

(Both my wife and my children have an unfairly jaundiced opinion of my DIY expertise. I should never have tried to fix the hot water system in 1983; it's given me a reputation that's dogged me ever since.)

Milena continued, 'Because, unless you have it properly serviced, none of us will be able to sleep.'

I held my ground. 'I'm quite capable of doing it all myself, except for the electronic stuff.'

Milena shot a look at her brother.

'Dad,' said Christopher, 'Vis is the last island before the open sea. If you're out there with Mum and the engine packs up, you'll drift over to Italy and no one's going to save you. Did you ever see *Dead Calm*?'

'Yes, I did,' I said testily, 'but conditions in the Adriatic aren't anything like that. And I do know how to look after an engine on my own, thank you very much.'

'You could always just do trips around the island or go to the mainland,' said Milena hopefully. 'You'd be safe enough then.'

'But the whole idea of a boat is to explore. I can drop anchor in hidden coves and Mum and I can sit on deck with a bottle of wine watching the sun go down. And we'll sleep with the hatch open and look up at the stars to marvel at the wonders of the universe.'

Irreverent giggling from both my offspring.

'Has Mum been giving you the magic mushroom pills again?' asked Child One with a smirk.

'And what about poor Mum having to listen to your poetic outbursts?' Child Two chortled.

'Dad, I'm sure you'll look terribly romantic reciting poetry on your poop deck, but imagine Mum with a force eight gale coming up and you beside her going on about the wonders of the universe!'

'You are talking to your father to whom fear is a stranger. I'm a man who can look into the eye of an approaching storm without flinching – or into the eye of a charging elephant, for that matter!'

'Dad, be sensible. This isn't Rudyard Kipling.'

'It's all very well for you playing Captain Pugwash, but Mum will be really frightened.'

'But there are so many islands to explore,' I countered. 'And they're right on our doorstep. We could even go over to Italy. Mum would love that.'

'Mum won't if she knows you've been tinkering with the engines,' said Child One.

'Maybe Mum liked doing dangerous things when we were little,' said Child Two, 'but now she gets frightened. Remember Portugal two years ago when you took her up on that hang glider.'

(How could I not? Her cries could be heard in the next county.)

'Well, a boat is different to flying.'

Christopher sighed. 'You don't have to explore the Kalahari just because it's there, Dad. You really shouldn't be doing dangerous things anymore. We do worry about you, you know – now that you're getting on a bit.'

'I beg your pardon! I'm only in my fifties,' I retorted indignantly. 'And it'll be a very sorry day when a man can't take his boat out to sea when he feels like it!'

'Damned Zulus!' said Milena (in a most inaccurate impression of me). 'The Gatling's jammed and the Colonel's dead, but just wait till I've got my colonial shorts on and I'll sort the natives out!'

They got the giggles again and I called for Ivana.

Ignoring my offspring, I continued with my plans. Once I had my boat, I'd explore the coast like Ragnar Hairybreeks. I'd show the children.

So, from the moment we set foot on the island, thoughts about boats had seldom been out of my mind, even when I woke. Each morning I'd take my cornflakes on to the terrace as the fishing boats were coming in from their night's work and watch as they chuntered in, sturdy and duck-like, a white cloud of seagulls wheeling behind them and the men calling out to their wives and daughters waiting for them on the shore. Once alongside, they heaved off their night's catches in big baskets and poured them into smaller boxes, the fish cascading in a shimmering, silvery torrent as the wet scales caught the sunlight. After the boxes were on the vans and the women had driven off, the men came to sit on the wall below me to smoke and chat for a while, before returning to their boats, fags still on the go. There they would squat beside their nets to repair the night's damage, and, hunched and tense with concentration, they'd stay for another hour working away at the intricate knots with knives and needles as they had done on a thousand other mornings.

By the time they had finished, sailing boats were beginning to leave the harbour and were drifting past, their white sails billowing gently in the morning breeze in what seemed like slow motion. The water was so clean that I could see the stones gleaming on the sea bed thirty feet down, and the air so clear that the mountains on the mainland stood out crisply against the blue sky, their barren, steely peaks glinting like encrusted gold as if touched by a bright knife of sun. Grouped like a family with the higher formations looming majestically over the foothills, they looked like older relatives who had given birth to the lower hills and were now hovering watchfully over them as they retired slowly backwards into the blue distance and greyness of time.

The bay was bathed in sunshine, seagulls wheeled above me crying like risen souls and from over the water came the faint chug of fishing boats. It was all so far away from my usual frantic start to the day – bolting my breakfast and then scrambling to work like a wartime air-squadron pilot. I stood on the terrace marvelling at the world around me. There was such a special feeling to this early-morning life on the bay. The air was warm, the light was sharp and the tang of salt, seaweed and burned cork hung in the air. Standing there with the sun on my shoulders and my bare feet warmed by the flagstones under me, I almost gasped with a sense of wellbeing. This was better than waking up rich.

The oncoming spring brought an atmosphere of expectancy to the village, as if a curtain was about to rise. Pink and white blossom were appearing on the fruit trees, thread-like green shoots were peeking up from the earth and geraniums kept inside for the winter were emerging on to balconies and windowsills. In front of the houses, women were sweeping the streets and the squares to turn them into living spaces for the summer months, and along the shore men were peeling off tarpaulins from their upturned boats and beginning the laborious job of scraping and painting. The smell of blowtorched paint permeated the air.

The island was in fact full of 'sweet airs' as the Bard put it. The strongest were up on the hills when we went for walks along the headland. It was covered by yellow broom, which gave off an overpowering honey-like fragrance and coloured the slope like a brightly dyed carpet. Walking along our usual track, a new scent would waft over every few yards – lavender, thyme, rosemary, fennel and myriad others we didn't recognise. Beside the track, red poppies, blue periwinkle, yellow buttercups, white daisies dotted the rough grass with colour, and walking over them released even more perfumes to the air.

The track led along the top of the headland and down into the valley, and, although we rarely saw a soul, the passing presence of man was everywhere in the form of derelict houses, stone walls and goat sheds. Over the hill, green slopes coloured by lavender fields, young vines and cherry blossom dropped into the valley where vineyards, olive groves and fallow fields stretched along the valley. Flocks of sheep meandered slowly across them and in between the olives and vines, their bells clanging faintly in the distance. It resembled one of those illustrations in a Bible storybook.

Oh my newly adopted homeland, how do I love thee? Let me count the ways…

Now that the warm winds of spring had begun to fan the island, windows were left open and we could hear the women calling out across the streets to each other in that strident sound of women over the age of sixty around the Mediterranean. It's like a caw of a crow or the squawk of a parrot, and at full decibel it can knife through your eardrum and judder your spine. For some reason, Anglo-Saxon women don't seem to produce this ear-jolting screech, but any grandmother from Vis could drown out a Guards drill sergeant any day.

Our nearest granny was the possessor of a particularly terrifying screech. Her appearance was pretty terrifying too. Large, stately and dressed in regulation black, Grandma Klakic had the hatchet face of a Borgia Pope and a temperament to match. She was universally feared, as all domestic matters in the village came under her scrutiny – although Karmela told us that many thought she was just an interfering old busybody, even though they didn't dare to say it out loud.

Grandma Klakic began her summer reign of terror by sitting by her doorstep in her carpet slippers with her stockings rolled halfway down her legs. A solid block of black-clad belligerence, she sat like Jabba the Hutt emanating a dark energy, and, like her Star Wars doppelgänger, she'd shoot out a malevolent croak at anyone who was foolish enough to pass by without giving her appropriate salutation.

In contrast, her timid sister sat hunched and silent three doors down as if she was waiting for her dinner or her death, whichever came first. So obviously overshadowed by her dominant sibling, I felt sorry for her (I had a sister like that), and one morning I went over to make neighbourly conversation. But, just as I started, we were interrupted by a long-haired youth in an official hat knocking loudly on Grandma Klakic's door. The door opened and the bulky figure appeared, arms crossed defensively. Not a good sign, both of us knew, but the youth didn't, and, instead of running for his life, he took a paper from his leather satchel, stood to attention and read it out. The Town Hall wanted her to pay the rates for a member of her family who had failed to de-register when he left the island two years ago.

The sister and I waited tensely for the explosion to come. It came. The blast of her armour-piercing shriek delivered at close range literally rocked the boy back on his heels. The sister and I flinched too, and we were twenty paces away. The youth took off in terror. He ran down the street, one hand on his hat and the other clutching his little satchel, as Grandma K's screeches ricocheted off the walls behind him like high-octave tracer fire.

'Is this all you can do at the Town Hall these days, you useless lot of good-for-nothings? Is this what your grandmother and I fought the Germans for – to end up being persecuted in our homes by our own grandchildren? Oh! If your sainted grandmother Vera were alive today, she'd give you such a clout, you stupid boy! You dare come round to my house again and you'll get a saucepan in your face!'

A few passers-by had gathered in the street and were smirking.

'Poor boy,' I said to Zoran who was with them.

'Don't worry about him. His boss will understand. He'll have heard it. His office is only a hundred metres away. You can hear Grandma Klakic at three times that distance.'

The others laughed. 'They're so terrified of her in the Town Hall,' said a man, 'that they'll just forget about the tax rather than have to face up to her.'

'I suppose I should have warned you about her when I heard you were buying the house at the end of her street,' said Zoran.

'Oh, I'm sure there won't be a problem.'

'You'll see,' he said with an evil leer.

When business was slow, Zoran would sit outside the bar, waiting for someone to come along with whom he could argue. Poised like a terrier for someone to throw a ball, he sat on a chair outside the door, and, if he spotted me, he'd get up and come to clap an arm around my shoulders and propel me in. Once inside, he'd take up position against the bar and hold forth on a bewildering range of topics – American foreign policy, Greek mythology, EU fishing rights or the effect of the Chernobyl fallout on Balkan cattle herds. He liked to flaunt his knowledge in front of his coterie, but, although he occasionally threw a rhetorical question at them, he didn't like to be interrupted and was visibly irritated if anyone did. The most frequent culprit was Domigoy, his goofy, bearded younger cousin who looked as if nature had meant him to be a gorilla but had changed its mind at the last minute. Not being the sharpest knife in the drawer, Domigoy had never twigged that his interruptions annoyed his cousin.

The two topics never discussed by the bar-proppers were the recent war and their past communist affiliations. Oddly, after several weeks, Marko admitted that he'd been a member of the Communist Party, but he said he wanted me to know so I would understand how life had been. If you wanted to get on, you had to belong to the Party, he explained. He had never liked the system himself, he told me, but it was the only way of getting a good job, a car, a decent apartment and the best education for your children – and so what did you do if you wanted the best for your family?

Would I have done the same? I always wondered. I'd like to think that an obdurate Anglo-Saxon instinct to dig one's heels in at the first sign of any coercion would have made me refuse to go along with it – but who knows how they'll react until the situation occurs?

The war was even less talked about. It had lasted for several years, thousands had been killed and three million had been displaced, but bad memories were swept under the carpet and no one wanted to dwell on it. If not caught up directly in the violence, they had all lived in fear, looking nervously at the skies every day, watching the news on TV, and waiting while the West made up its mind whether to help them or not.

For me, the war had come as a particular shock. Like many others, I had thought that in Europe this kind of behaviour was now behind us, but it's extraordinary how easily savagery can be whipped up anywhere in the world.

To find out more, I often tried to bring the war into the conversation, but I'd get blank looks and non-committal murmurs, and, whenever they did discuss it between themselves, they talked in grunts, and there was something fiercely stoic about the short exchanges.

It was as rare for Zoran to talk about it as anyone else, but, after a boozy lunch and when the bar was empty, I brought the subject up again. 'Those were shitty times,' he replied with a scowl. 'An' all the time those goddamn Serbs were poundin' away at us, you guys were sittin' aroun' not makin' your goddamn minds up. That John Major of yours spent two years sayin' "something must be done" and did nothin'. Your Margaret Thatcher wouldn't have stood aroun' like that. "We must give them arms to defend themselves," she said. But you booted her out an' all we had was John Major and his bunch of wussies!'

Zoran's view on the reason for the war was equally unequivocal. 'Even when we had Tito and were Yugoslavia, those Serb bastards ran the show. Despite all that crap he used to give out about "Brotherhood and Unity", Tito ran the show from Serbia, an' all his guys were Serbs – military officers in particular. So, when the war started, the bastards just got into our tanks, ships and airplanes and drove them off to Serbia. All we were left with were policemen with pistols and truncheons.'

CHAPTER 10

HOME AND GARDEN

At the beginning of our second month, our days started to fall into a sort of pattern. I began the day on the terrace with my cornflakes, and every day I'd feel the same kind of sensation – that sort of thing Wordsworth was always going on about – an empathy with nature; a mystical union with our surroundings; a sense of life's continuum, or something along those lines. At first, I tried to brush the feeling away. I shouldn't be indulging in this kind of whimsy at my age; that was for younger men. But then why not? How often in life do you come across a scene so awe-inspiring that it gives you goose bumps? Why not relax and enjoy a good old mystical experience when you get the chance?

After this brief dalliance with the transcendent, I'd do jobs around the house or go to my desk and work on a book I'd started to write about local history until I heard Ivana's alarm go off. Then, after taking her a cup of tea, I'd go downstairs, open the courtyard door, dive straight in and swim out as fast as I could to the middle of the bay. Once there, I'd float exhausted and wallowing in the warm water with the bay spread out at eye level around me. I could see the swallows circling the church tower and the figures moving on the waterfront and over by our house the women who were hanging out their laundry and mopping down their terraces. The familiar sounds of clanking buckets, squeals of playing children and scolding cries of grandmothers drifted across the water to where I floated in my watery rapture.

Once I'd got my breath back, I'd swim back, doing a slow crawl, and then dry off on the flagstones in front of our wall before going in to have a quick shower and join Ivana, who by that time had got a spot of breakfast inside her and was more or less in the land of the living. Then, collecting some baskets, we'd set out for the market.

What a pleasure to be able to walk everywhere you needed to go to. We'd take the same route to the market every day, but it always looked as if someone had rearranged it overnight – the sunlight broke through the gaps in the houses to splash the street with its random shafts of gold, the geraniums on the balconies speckled the stone with their startling colours, and the jasmine, honeysuckle and bright-purple bougainvillea arching up over the alleys seemed higher than when we'd last seen them.

After having coffee at Marko's, we'd move on to the Hotel café where town officials, mechanics, builders, architects, digger-drivers, fruit-fly exterminators and almost everyone else we had business with took their coffee break – and, as the break was taken as part of the working day, no one was bothered if people sat down and talked business with them.

By now, we had got to know most of the officials at the Town Hall. Because the old regime's systems were still in place, there were endless papers and permits that we needed to be able to exist. We already had two filing boxes of licences, resident's permits, alien documents, citizen identification credentials, tax authorisations, tsetse fly certificates and beriberi inoculation papers – plus all the ten-page documents we'd needed to be allowed electricity, telephone, water, drains, dentists, doctors, car passes, rate cards, post boxes, dustbins and so on. Tito, being a shrewd old fox, hadn't taken long to realise that the more forms his comrade citizens had to fill in, the easier it would be to keep tabs on them. Even something as simple as having your electricity connected required the same amount of consultations and documents as a Hollywood divorce case. It was so overwhelming that I thought of not complying, but Marko advised me strongly against it. The authorities had made processes of opting out or objecting so onerous, he said, that it discouraged anyone except the suicidal.

But what was going to happen when I tried to start any of my projects? Was Zoran right – did the Town Hall really sit on the horse's head? Would they be bogged down from the beginning? And, if that was the case, what was I going to do with myself with nothing to work at?

After we'd done our downtown chores, we'd walk back along the waterfront – the 'Riva' as they call it. We passed the fishing boats stirring gently on their moorings and fishermen squatting beside them mending nets, repairing tackle and scrubbing out octopuses, the thick ink-black dye staining the amber stone around them. In front of the church, men were pushing wheelbarrows of bricks, mixing cement and chipping away at blocks of stone, and little girls in gaily coloured pinafores and boys in oversized shorts ran about between them.

Once home, Ivana, who is a novelist, went to her desk in the drawing room and I went off to the Town Hall or the library to do more research for the book I was writing. There was a wealth of information at both places, but the library was my preferred place of study. The librarian, a delightfully enthusiastic man, was so happy to have an outsider interested in local history that he let me take papers to the comfort of the bar next door and read them there. It seemed to suit him, too, as he would often come and sit beside me to work on his own papers away from the hard seats and the gloom. It was a wonderful arrangement. Every library should have a bar attached to it. Not only can you sit and read in comfort, but it also makes getting a drink so much easier.

The only drawback was the Croatian biros. They leaked, and after an hour's session I'd end up with splodges on my shirt or my nose and Ivana would get cross. It was all very well for her, though. She only had a laptop to contend with, but those of us up at the sharp end of the business armed with biros can't avoid getting splodges on our noses. Ask Samuel Pepys, Edward Gibbon or Jeffrey Archer.

Usually, we worked until lunchtime and then had a short siesta. The bliss of an afternoon siesta! Happy hour, once you're over fifty, is an afternoon nap. Having spent the past thirty years trying to cram as much as I could into a working day, I now revelled in a siesta. Sometimes I wouldn't even sleep; I'd just lie there, my mind occupied with a dozen little trifles that didn't need a solution, or simply gaze up at the ceiling following the path of a buzzing fly, my mind a complete blank.

After our snooze, we'd tumble downstairs still half asleep, open the courtyard door and dive in. Plunging into sparkling, clear water in the heat of the day must be one of the most heavenly sensations known to man. The heat and drowsiness is whisked away in an instant, and you rise weightlessly to the surface, sleekly enveloped by water and feeling a blissful harmony with nature. Having swum over to the monastery, we'd come back to lie in the sun and then, feeling refreshed and ready to go back to our books, we'd be at our desks until it was time for the social highlight of the day.

The evening promenade was definitely the highlight of the day. When the light began to fade and the heat subsided, the waterfront was transformed into a spectacle of festivity and action. The whole village was there, perambulating up and down, chatting, laughing, exchanging courtesies and catching up with the gossip. Every age group was represented; the old, the middle-aged, the young marrieds, snotty-looking youths and gaggles of heavily made-up teenaged girls – and in between the legs of everyone ran little children, squealing and playing games.

By the time the promenade finished, it was time for supper and after that Ivana went back to her desk and I went out to sample the downtown highlife at Zoran's or Marko's.

Now that I was spending more time at the bars, I was getting to know some of the regulars. Some had very entrenched views and were difficult to talk to, but others, like Filip the town tax collector, were open-minded and liked to argue the toss. Aged forty-five with an overly high forehead, a lantern jaw and a nose you could hang a hat on, Filip might have had the most lugubrious face on the island, but he was extremely knowledgeable, a prolific reader and played the French horn in the town brass band. He was also a P.G. Wodehouse fan – quite surprising for someone who looked like Boris Karloff without the Frankenstein bolts.

I usually stayed at the bars until ten, and, if Ivana hadn't finished, I could put in an hour or so's writing before bed. It was good to be writing again. I'd actually started off in the brave new world of writing when I finished my studies, but, like the seed that fell upon stony ground in the parable of the seeds, my ambitions had sprung up and withered. As soon as school fees, dentist bills and all the rest of it began to appear, there was a rapid erosion of my ideals and a swift descent into the world of commerce. And it wasn't until twenty years later when the reminders from the school bursar stopped landing on my breakfast table that I started to think about rising like a phoenix out of the ashes of my bourgeois existence and being reborn as a woolly English liberal scribbler once again.

Sometimes, sitting at my desk and looking out of the window at the panorama of the bay, I almost had to pinch myself. What a joy to be able to sit in such beautiful surroundings and write with no deadline. I'd quite forgotten what a pleasure it was to wade through pages of fascinating material and then try to make sense of it all – in my case to find some pattern to the frightful strife and grinding hardship of the people who have lived in this part of the world for over two millennia. I'd also forgotten what a privilege it was to work with the English language. It gives you such exquisite tools of beauty and precision to play with. I could quite happily fiddle around all day trying to weave my words into a beautiful, delicate and steely web of telling commentary or captivate the reader with my wry appreciation of the world we live in (I wish!).

For the past few weeks, I had been looking at the back garden with despair. It had traces of being well tended sometime in the distant past, but it looked as if no one had taken a fork to it since the death of Franz Joseph. Even Alan Titchmarsh would have scratched his curly locks at the sight of it – a thick arboreal dreadlock stretching from the house to the fortress tower at the end. The top floor and most of the battlements were missing, but a fringe of honeysuckle and capers hung attractively from the ramparts and its dilapidation lent a decorative touch of rakishness to the scene. Most of the garden was covered by the *mattogrosso*, but outside the kitchen was a flagstoned area shaded by mandarin, orange and lemon trees and in the middle sat a large stone table where we ate most of our meals. With the trees now in blossom, coming into the area was like walking into the Harrods perfume department.

After watching football, gardening is apparently an Englishman's most popular pastime, but, not having had a garden since leaving home, I'd rather stuck with the football and wasn't quite sure where to start. There ought to be some gardeners in the village I could ask, and what could be a better way of breaking the local ice than garden talk. I could see myself leaning over gates on balmy summer evenings, chatting about greenfly, black spot and bindweed, and, anyway, the role of gardener would be a definite improvement on that of guinea pig for the ongoing medical experimentation of the grannies.

A large part of the jungle looked as if it must have been a lawn in the nineteenth century, so why not get it going again? They would probably have had a scullion in britches cutting it for sixpence with a pair of scissors back then, but, although I knew it would take up a lot of time, what the heck. Time was something I had a lot of.

The lawn area was liberally endowed with a national collection of thorn bushes, so I pulled them up, removed a few hundredweight of stones and started to level the ground. That was the hardest part. The baked dry earth had the density of concrete and getting a fork into it gave me a reminder that there was no osteopath on the island. But then recalling a scene in *Manon des Sources* (that jolly French film about a grumpy old man with a large moustache who gets killed by the combined onslaught of his neighbours and his own garden), I remembered Yves Montand's technique of spitting on his hands and whacking the fork down with a vigorous thump. I tried it out and it worked. I felt a tingle of primitive satisfaction as I began to turn over the sod. Digging is a deeply primal action, I thought. We've been tillers of the soil since time began, and this was probably the sort of man I'd be if I hadn't started reading too much Russian literature, paying school fees and pretending to be a Captain of Industry. So here I was at last taking my place in a long line of tillers – a pleasingly virile concept. I progressed across the garden in a systematic manner as passers-by looked over the wall and acknowledged my manly labour with their smiles. No doubt neighbourly gardening conversations about topsoils, mulches and leaf-droop would soon follow. For a man who had forsworn the sin and shame of the commercial world and turned his back on ambition, stress and credit card debt to return to his roots as a doughty digger, how could my newly adopted community of fellow tillers fail to embrace me?

Two days later, I was seeding the lawn when a couple leaned over the wall and asked what vegetables I was planting.

Here we go. My first horticultural exchange. I put down my rake and called up: 'It's grass.'

From their stunned expressions, I might have said chewing gum plants or marijuana. They shook their heads and walked on.

To tell the truth, I didn't get a lot of positive feedback on the home front, either. Ivana has never been able to understand the affection we English have for our gardens. I'd thought she might come round to it, now that we had our own (and I must say, a little enthusiasm would not have gone amiss), but, when I came into the kitchen with mud-covered hands and my face covered in mannish sweat to tell her about what I'd done, I was told that it was only the English who took such an interest in green and leafy things. 'Who else would spend their weekends kneeling in borders ruining their hands like your mother or doing their backs in mowing, raking and throwing sand all over the place like your father?'

'But ploughmen and woodcutters have always been held up as a sort of masculine archetype in children's books all over the world, I'll have you know,' I retorted, but the iron had entered her soul.

Preserving the demeanour of a resolute gardener, I strode stoically back to my solitary travail.

Another assumption I'd made was that I'd be able to borrow someone's mower when it was time to mow, but, since mine was the only lawn on the island, no one had a mower, and I had to go over to the mainland and buy one of those electric plug-in jobs.

When the day came for mowing, attracted by the noise and the pleasing smell of freshly mown grass, a posse of neighbouring aunties put their heads over the wall. At last, a gardening conversation, I thought, and turned the mower off. I looked up eagerly as the first of them said, 'I've seen them on the television.'

'What, a lawn?' I replied.

'No!' She stabbed a bony finger. 'A lawn mower!'

'I never knew grass smelled so good!' said the second.

'It's English grass,' said the third. 'That's why it smells so nice.'

'The Queen's lawn must smell like that?'

'With a smell as sweet as that,' said the first, 'there must be something you can make with it. Grass soup? Grass juice? Egg and grass sandwiches?'

I glowed with reflected pride at the appreciation of one of my nation's unsung products – though, after a boyhood of lying on the boundaries of cricket fields chewing on grass and daisies, I didn't hold out much hope for any of their recipes making it into Jamie Oliver's next Mediterranean cookbook.

The discussion about grass foods continued, but not a word was said about the lawn itself or any of the many other fine features of my burgeoning garden. Eventually, they walked on, locked in earnest debate about the culinary possibilities of *herba vulgaris*, and I was left wondering if my idea of a village garden fraternity had been a delusion. Now that I thought about it, all the flowers in the village were in pots or tin cans and everyone's backyards were full of bicycles, car parts and broken washing machines rather than flowerbeds. Clearly, fishing villages had not been designed with herbaceous borders in mind.

Not wanting to waste all the information I had downloaded and all the theoretical knowledge I now had about lawns, I wondered if I might drum up some local interest in the noble art of lawn growing. An entree into the community, perhaps? Evening classes in the Town Hall? And, if I wore my battered straw hat and posed as a horny-handed son of the soil, I might make a rather good impression on some of the better-looking middle-aged ladies of the village. Monty Don has a huge middle-aged fan club. They don't get him on TV down here, so there'd be no competition.

As might be expected, I found scant support on the home front. 'You never understand what people want. No one wants to hear about rolling, scarifying and edge cutting. Honestly, what will you think of next – croquet?'

(Not having the advantage of an Anglo-Saxon education, Ivana had no notion of one's duty to disseminate the benefits of one's cultural heritage to less fortunate people in distant lands. No sense of missionary spirit at the Eva Peron High School for Girls.)

In the end, I was forced to admit that gardening was perhaps a peculiarly English preoccupation, and it certainly wasn't going to make me any friends. I was even laughed at when I made the mistake of talking about it at Zoran's. And what capped it all was when Zoran popped his head over the wall and saw me clipping my edges.

'What are you up to down there?'

'I'm clipping the edges. What does it look like?' I called up testily.

'You wouldn't catch John Wayne doin' things like that,' he called out and his head disappeared.

I felt as if I'd been caught practising ballet steps in a tutu.

CHAPTER 11

AN ENGLISH
LEGACY

Somehow, my gardening activities came to the attention of the Franciscan monks and I received an invitation to their monastery garden. Arriving at the gate, I knocked on the big wooden door and after a lengthy wait I heard the flap of leather sandals, a rattling of keys and a muttering that sounded very much like muted swearing. (Are monks allowed to swear?) The door creaked open and a friar in a brown habit stood blinking nervously in the sunlight (definitely more of a Father Dougal than a Father Ted). The minute I announced myself as the English gardener, though, the nervousness disappeared and I was beckoned inside and led down a long dark hall as cool as a sepulchre. What had made him so nervous? Had he thought I was a Bible salesman – or, worse, the episcopal VAT man on his rounds? But then, perhaps the Brothers just didn't have many visitors these days.

We emerged into a riot of green and leafy things. Neat rows of well-hoed vegetables – beans with bulging pods, lettuces tied up with raffia, purple eggplants glistening in the sun, tomatoes swelling on vines. By the sea wall, beets and parsnips poked up perkily from well-mulched earth, and a small orchard of apple, peach and plum trees heavy with fruit nestled against the cemetery at the end. You could have fed two dozen Brothers and a legion of poor with a garden like this. Surprised to see everything growing so well right beside the sea, I asked the Brother why, and this was the excuse he had been waiting for. He now listed every single plant that did well by the sea and every single one that didn't, and standing in the sun I was beginning to feel dozy when I was suddenly jolted awake. 'Your Royal Navy used most of this as a field for their cricket pitch when they occupied the island?'

'Cricket! Here? Are you sure?'

'Our records say that your Navy played the game on our field for many years.'

'I can't believe it!'

'I thought British people always played this cricket when you were fighting your wars. Is this not true?'

'Well, I've never thought about it, but maybe we did when we weren't too busy polishing our boots or painting our battleships. But they must have had a club if they were playing here for nearly ten years. They probably had a pavilion, too.'

I thanked the Brother for showing me the garden and left with my ears still tingling. I could hardly believe it. Of all the islands in all the world, I'd landed on one where they'd played cricket! Was that fate or what? I'd given up the idea of playing again, but maybe I could start something up, even if only beach cricket. Yes, this would be my first project. I hurried home to tell Ivana.

'You won't believe it! Our Navy used to play cricket on the monastery field. Isn't that incredible? Maybe I can start it up again. I know I said I'd never play again, but this changes everything. My own team! Now that's something I've only ever dreamed of. They play down in Corfu so we could have an Adriatic cup. The "Adriatic Ashes"! How about that? I'll be back in the world of cricket again.

I got a look that could have soured milk.

'I thought my days of making teas for thirty and spending my weekends sitting at home or waiting in the car for your wretched game to finish were finally over.'

Whoops! I should have angled it more carefully. I backpedalled madly. 'Oh, there'll be lots of locals to make the teas. You wouldn't have to lift a finger.'

'But you'll always be home late again.'

'On an island only six miles long, I couldn't ever be late. I promise.'

'I know you!'

I quickly changed the subject to the repositioning of the tumble dryer.

I thought it might be politic to spend the rest of the day at home to try to assuage the fears – a good bit of assuaging usually pays dividends in our household – but I was feeling like a missionary on his way to the Congo with a trunk full of bibles. What a turn-up.

Considering the matter later that evening, I had second thoughts. It did seem a bit of a long shot. For a start, would anyone want to learn how to play? Besides, the village might think it rather pushy – trying to start up one's own national game so soon after our arrival? It might be a black mark against us. But then, if it caught on, it could be the best way yet of bonding with our new community.

The next morning, I left Ivana at the market and went to ask Marko if he had heard about the Navy playing here.

He had.

'Last year, Luka, one of our young winegrowers, told me he had read in a book about Napoleon's Adriatic campaigns that the British played the game on Vis. He was at a school in Australia during the war and he played your cricket there. He said it was a good game that required much skill.'

My heart rate quickened. There was another cricketer on the island! That might do a lot to ease any adverse local reaction.

'Why didn't you tell me this before, for heaven's sake?'

'But you have never talked about this game.'

'Well, I didn't think anyone would be interested.'

'Do you play this game yourself?'

'I used to play a lot, but these days I mostly follow it – and that takes up quite a lot of time if you know the game. Do you think it might be possible to start it up again? Maybe some of your young men might like to give it a go. I'm just a bit worried that it might antagonise some of the community. Would they think it a bit arrogant, starting up an English sport?'

'You must meet Luka. He has been talking about starting the game, and if he is doing it, the island will not think it wrong. It will be good to have a special game played on our island. A special sport will bring attention to us. We must think of tourism these days. When Luka returns, you will teach some of our young men to play. Yes?'

'Well, I've never actually coached anyone.'

Marko laughed. 'But you are an Englishman, and we all know that Englishmen are always too modest. I am sure you are very good at this game and you will teach it to our young men.'

'Hmm…'

'A special game will bring great honour to our island, I am sure,' he replied, smiling broadly, no doubt picturing an All England XI in caps and blazers striding off the ferry to take us on for the Adriatic Ashes.

Ivana came back from the market and, hearing the word 'cricket', gave me one of the dirtiest looks seen on the waterfront that morning. I changed the conversation, but Marko brought it back again.

'Tell me. Which other peoples play this cricket game?'

'Well, England, Australia, India and Pakistan for a start, and then there's South Africa, the West Indies, New Zealand…'

'But these are all countries of your Empire.' He laughed. 'So you conquered these people to make them play your game because you had no other peoples to play against? Yes?'

'Well, no. It wasn't quite like that…'

'So our island has been invaded by the men of Nelson and then the men of Churchill, and now another English invasion – this time of cricket men!' He winked at Ivana and said to her in Croatian: 'And how are these cricket men as husbands?'

Ivana laughed.

I pretended I hadn't understood.

There was a whiff of drains in the courtyard when we arrived home, but, as it soon disappeared, we thought no more about it.

The next morning, it was back at twice the strength.

'Phaugh! What's that awful stink?' said Ivana as I put her morning tea on the bedside table. She sat up, wrinkling her nose. 'It smells like a pig farm!'

'But there aren't any pig farms on the island.' I stuck my head out of the window and was assailed by that rank mix of sewage and vegetation that the Mediterranean does so well. I quickly shut the window and went down to investigate. After rootling around, I found a tell-tale stone slab in the far konoba and levered it up with a screwdriver. A dark and evil liquid vision confronted me. I quickly dropped the stone back.

'Did you know we had a cesspit?' I asked Karmela when she arrived.

'Of course you have one. All large houses used to have one. But it's not blocked. It's just the south wind.'

'The south wind? You mean it's the wind that's bringing the smell?'

'No, it's the cesspit drain. When the south wind blows, it makes all our drains smell that aren't connected to the main sewer. Nearly all our houses were connected up twenty years ago, but the Town Hall thought connecting this house up would cost too much. Mind you, what our Town Hall spends our money on, I just don't know! If you knew how they throw it away, you wouldn't be able to sleep at night. If only they stopped spending our money on all the stupid things they do, they could double our pensions. And they won't spend a single kuna on getting water to Grandma Velikov's house. She still has to walk all the way to the pump and fetch it. At her age, too! It's a disgrace! And as for poor Mrs Babic by the…'

'But where do our drains run to?' I interrupted.

'Why, into the sea. Where else did you think they'd go?'

'What? Right outside our door? But that's where we swim! And so do the village children!'

I flushed a loo and ran out to check. Sure enough, it came out right where we dived in. Horrors! What might we have been swimming in as we gloried in the clear blue water? I rang Lenko, our builder, and half an hour later he had worked out the cost of connecting to the mains. The figure he arrived at showed why the Town Hall hadn't done it before. It was more than we'd budgeted to spend on the house in the whole year. This was a severe setback.

'Maybe the south wind doesn't blow that often?' I said hopefully when Ivana joined us.

'I've already asked Karmela about that. It's the first time it's blown with any strength since we've been here, but it's the prevailing wind for the summer months. Anyway, even if it only blows once a week, it's bad enough. The smell's so awful that you'll have to stand beside me all day with my smelling salts or I'll be swooning like a Victorian mother-in-law.'

'Ah…'

'And what does that that "Ah" mean this time?'

'Oh, nothing in particular.'

'Oh yes it does! "Ah" usually means you're thinking how to get out of doing something…' Her voice tailed off and she jumped to her feet. 'Eureka! It's just what we've been waiting for! If we make the children's bathing spot pollution-free, the village will be so grateful that it'll more than compensate for the expense. To hell with the cost!'

So to hell with the cost it was.

Karmela, who had relations in most key places, marched us off to see her second cousin, Mr Samka, the Director of the Town Drains Department. Mr Samka was a florid, portly man with a permanently worried expression, and who was perspiring copiously and mopping his face with a large handkerchief behind a large untidy desk when we arrived.

We explained our problem as he puffed at a Walter Wolf.

'This is a major project. It'll be a dirty job but we're the ones to do it,' he said after we had finished explaining. He wiped his brow and got up to consult a chart on the wall. After looking at it fixedly for some time, he turned to announce that, although all his team of sanitation experts (blokes with shovels) were busily engaged on many other important projects, if we paid in advance, they would be put at our disposal at the earliest opportunity. 'Like priests and prostitutes,' he said with suitable gravitas, 'sanitation experts need the money on the table before they give their services.'

I expressed my instant agreement, and for the first time he smiled.

We went to the bank to transfer the money, and, after getting the island's only architect to draw up some plans, we all met at Mr Samka's office to look at them. The architect mentioned in passing that, because our building was under protection, the Ministry of Heritage would have to be involved, and I noticed Mr Samka's florid face blanched visibly at the news. I couldn't think why, but we were soon to find out.

* * *

The following week, the air-conditioning packed up. I hadn't actually wanted air-con and had only agreed to it after severe pressure was brought to bear, but now we had it I was very glad that we did. On the days that the temperature got up to 35 degrees, even the lizards that scurried up and down the garden walls loafed about in a semi-stupor, barely bothering to move when we appeared, and our squadron of manic bluebottles that usually buzzed hysterically about the house only managed to do lazy loops around the ceiling or sit on the wall. On days like that, coming back into an air-conditioned drawing room was as near to heaven as you could get.

When it was that hot, any movement drained you of energy, and the moment you stepped out, the sun hit you like a hammer. To my surprise, the locals seemed just as affected by the heat as we were and moved about as if they were pushing their way through the heavy air and took double the time to do anything. The most intelligent of them seemed to spend most of the day snoozing behind closed shutters.

I had a go at fixing the air-con unit myself, while Karmela buzzed annoyingly around me like a blow fly, but, after an hour of barking my knuckles and cursing, I found that the thermostat had burned itself out. Feeling thoroughly irritable (the damn thing was almost brand new), I rang the supplier in Zagreb. Accustomed as one is in the West these days to twenty-four-hour delivery, when told I wouldn't get the part until the end of the week, I became even more irritable and was about to make a facetious comment about walking to Zagreb to get it, when I managed to stop myself in time. I shouldn't be behaving like a spoilt foreign brat, I told myself. Slow delivery was just one more thing I'd have to get used to now we were here.

Sweltering in the heat, I waited until Friday came and rang the supplier again.

'What about my thermostat?' I said, as my sweat dripped on to the receiver. 'It's thirty-six degrees down here.'

'It was put on the ferry from Split on Wednesday afternoon,' the man replied. 'We tried to ring you, but we couldn't get a telephone signal.'

(Sometimes, the island's signal did tend to wander off for a few hours.)

'Damn! Well, put it on the next ferry.'

'It is still on the ferry.'

'That's fine then. I'll be at the dock when it comes in this evening.'

There was an embarrassed cough at the other end. 'I am very sorry, sir, but the ferry has continued on to Dubrovnik and it is not returning to Vis for another four days.'

'What! But you could have rung the ship's Vis office and asked them to keep it for me. They would have told us they had it.'

'But there was no signal. We could ring no one.'

'Blast!' The sweat was now streaming down my temples.

'I am so sorry, sir,' the man said, sounding genuinely sympathetic, 'but you will have to wait until Wednesday morning when the ferry returns to Vis.'

Grinding my teeth, I nevertheless made myself put the phone back carefully instead of banging it down, and I went to find Ivana. She was in the garden reading in the shade.

When I had finished venting my spleen, Ivana put down her book and said, 'Now you really must stop getting yourself upset like this, darling. That's not what we've come out here to do, is it?'

She was right. It wasn't. I went into the kitchen, opened the fridge and stood in front of it to cool down and console myself with some of Marko's chilled white wine.

CHAPTER 12

NEIGHBOURS

Early the following day, I was woken by a terrible crashing and banging outside. Thinking it might be Mr Samka and his sanitation experts, I got out of bed and looked out. But it wasn't Mr Samka, it was Boyana, our grumpy, jam-making neighbour who lived on the other side of the garden wall and who bore a distinct resemblance to Marjory the Trash Monster in *Fraggle Rock*. She was loading her empty jam jars into the back of her car and making the most appalling din with it. I looked at the clock. It was only six o'clock, for God's sake! Maybe she didn't realise what a racket she was making. I'd better go down to tell her.

The few people in the square looked surprised at the sight of me in my striped pyjamas, but, with the clenched jaw and the no-nonsense step of an Englishman undaunted by circumstance, I strode across the square. Boyana's broad beam was protruding from a back door like a life raft accidentally inflated in a confined space, and, thinking it impolite to address her in that position, I made a discreet cough. She heaved herself out like a hippo extricating itself from an African mud hole and turned to face me. Red-faced from the effort, she now looked more like Les Dawson playing Widow Twanky than Marjory the Trash Monster.

'What then?' she snapped.

Undeterred by this less than cordial greeting, I gave her a winning smile and started on the Croatian version of my well-practised John Le Mesurier *Dad's Army* routine that had served me well on many other occasions. 'I say… sorry to bother… but would you mind awfully not making such a frightful racket? It's only six o'clock in the morning… and, if you could just wait a couple of hours, I'd be glad to give you a hand… we could polish the job off in no time at all if we did it together.'

She looked at me witheringly. 'If I want to rattle my jam jars at six o'clock in the morning, I'll rattle them, and I'll do so on my own, thank you very much. And I'll be doing the same every Tuesday and Friday until the jam-making season ends.' She crossed her arms defiantly.

I searched for inspiration but drew a blank. 'But it's just… the noise… so early… I'm sure there's some way I could help…'

She gave the kind of snort that said there was little chance of us ever exchanging Christmas cards, and got back to work.

My *Dad's Army* routine hadn't done the trick and clearly no amount of arguing was going to bring her round. Passers-by had stopped to watch us and standing there in my pyjamas I was feeling rather vulnerable (the stiff upper lip was beginning to wobble a bit), but, moulding my face into a suitably inscrutable mask, I retreated across the square to the door with as much dignity as one can when wearing striped pyjamas.

During the promenade that evening, our neighbour with the roof-rack sheep came up to us to say that he had heard about the incident. Putting a sympathetic hand on my shoulder, he said, 'No worry, my friend. She do same to all in village. When I say please not put car at my door, she shout at me like she shout at you.'

So at least we weren't being singled out; not that that gave us much comfort. Anyway, there wasn't much we could do about it. At this stage, the last thing we wanted was a row with a next-door neighbour.

That afternoon, Karmela told us that the jam-making season went on until the winter.

Ivana, of course, saw the cheery side. 'No one likes Boyana. Think of all the villagey conversations we can now have with everyone about difficult neighbours. Best of all would be if we could somehow find a way to win her over. Then everyone would see we're the sort of people who try to get on with their neighbours however difficult they are. That would really impress them. We ought to work on Boyana together – like a tag team.'

I wasn't so certain, but over the next week I tried to engage her in conversation – at the corner store, outside the church, at the ferry, on the benches. But she was as stubborn as they come. The first time, she looked at me as if I were trying to sell her holiday timeshare apartments in Bulgaria; the second time, she said she was busy; and the third time she just ignored me.

And Ivana didn't fare much better.

I had already resigned myself to being treated as a pale-faced Englishman for some time, but I had thought that by now they would have been treating Ivana as one of their own. She was Croatian, after all, and she spoke the language – albeit with a funny accent. But it wasn't until the end of May that we made the breakthrough discovery. *They just didn't like anyone who wasn't from their own village.* And another strange thing – the people they disliked the most were those from the island's only other village – Komiza – and they've inhabited the same island for over two thousand years.

Our first inkling of this was when we were walking down a dark alley one night and bumped into someone putting a large, mewing sack into a van. Embarrassed at being caught *in flagrante*, the man told us that several times a year he rounded up the stray cats that gathered in his alley and dumped them in Komiza. 'I don't feel bad about it,' he said, 'as they dump all their stray dogs on *us*. Haven't you noticed all the starving dogs around lately? They're not from here. We feed our dogs properly in Vis.'

(Being the island 'capital', our village is also called Vis – as in New York, New York.)

Gaining confidence, the man put the mewing sack down. 'And rumour has it that they've started to send all their dogs with diseases over to us. Just like Castro did when he sent everyone in prison to America. That's just the kind of dirty trick you might expect from Dog Town!'

Like the Hundred Years' War, the Vis Dog/Cat War was evidently a slow-burning one.

Komiza, a tiny village even smaller than Vis, on the other side of the island is only five miles away, but, surrounded by steep cliffs, it was unreachable until recent times, except by sea. Cut off from the rest of the island, until the government dug a road into the rock face, hardly anyone ever left it, not even to come over to Vis. The only time they left it was to fish, and being so isolated for so long they developed their own language – Komisese, which is still spoken today. There's even a Komisese dictionary.

One morning, we were at the market talking with Karmela and some other village grannies when a family came past speaking Komisese.

'When your children come out,' Karmela hissed to Ivana, 'you make sure they don't hang around with any of those young people from Komiza!'

At the word 'Komiza', the others weighed in.

'Yes, you make sure you keep them well away,' said Grandma Gokan. 'In Komiza, all the young do is lie in bed all day and take drugs all night!'

'And you make sure your children never marry any of them,' said Grandma Gokan with a dire expression. 'They make bad wives and bad husbands. No good in the home or in the fields.'

'They just sit in the cafés all day drinking,' echoed Grandma Draginov. 'Why, half the village can't even swim. They're too lazy to walk the twenty paces to the sea!'

'And they're no good at sports, my nephew says.'

'And they're bad losers, my grandson says.'

'Too much inbreeding,' said Karmela, giving me a significant look.

We assured them that we'd watch our children like hawks from the moment they arrived, and went back to the car. We got in and looked at each other grimly. If that was how they felt towards their fellow island inhabitants, what chance did we have?

A few nights later, we were on the terrace when we heard raised voices coming from the recess outside the courtyard wall, and looking down we saw the struggling shape of a neighbouring teenager being hauled out of it by her mother and grandmother. She was in her vest and knickers and they were pulling her by her hair and shouting at her. It was in dialect I couldn't make out anything except the words 'Komiza *!!x*!', but Ivana got the gist of it. Someone had spotted the girl canoodling in the recess with a boy from Komiza and had alerted the Home Guard.

84

The grandmother was holding a pair of jeans, so it looked like some heavy petting had been going on, but more ominously she was holding a large wooden spoon. Had she rushed straight from the kitchen; was it to beat off the boy, or was it for later? – in the eyes of the village a very suitable punishment, I'm sure, for the kind of girl who goes off snogging with a boy from Komiza. That kind of thing had to be stamped out!

We didn't catch sight of the Lothario. Maybe he had seen the advancing granny-and-spoon combo and had high-tailed it back to his side of the island. But, if I knew anything about the island telegraph, another utensil-wielding granny (his) was lying in wait for him.

By the following morning, the incident was front-page village news and Karmela made her opinion clear when she arrived. 'A terrible going on it was, and only stopped just in time! Pah! When *will* those dreadful Komiza boys stop buzzing around all our girls? It's always the same story. A quick wedding before the baby is born and the boy then runs off leaving another wretched girl to bring up a child on her own. That's what you get from Komiza!' She paused for the requisite disapproving sniff. 'And their girls are no better. Not that I'm saying that most girls these days don't throw themselves around like I don't know. Look at that daughter of the Ragostas. She might have gone to university and can speak four languages, but it seems she doesn't know how to say "no" in any of them! Pah!'

'But Marko says that, despite the centuries of enmity, the young of Vis and Komiza started to fraternise the minute the road was built,' I said.

Karmela's eyes swivelled in my direction like twin gun turrets, and I faltered. 'I don't know if you've heard of Margaret Mead, the American anthropologist,' I continued hesitantly, 'but her findings showed that, despite the views of their elders, the younger members of rival tribes were usually interested in forging links – particularly with the more attractive ones of the opposite sex. Don't you think we ought to encourage the young to get to know each other and relationships might improve?'

'Pah!' (Karmela's anthropological studies had clearly been learned in the field.) 'I've never heard of the woman, but it sounds like she should have found something better to do with her time than writing such nonsense.' She gave me a withering look as if daring me to contradict her.

I didn't dare.

'Anyway,' she went on in a slightly less belligerent tone, 'inbreeding has never been a problem in our village. We've always had enough merchants and seamen passing through our harbour to stop that sort of going-on. Unlike that Sodom and Gomorrah of Komiza, where it's been going on like an epidemic since time began. Those people! Pah!'

She scuttled off like an angry beetle.

When I asked the bar-proppers at Zoran's about the Komiza/Vis two-thousand-year war, Bozo, the fattest member of the coterie, reckoned that, because both villages could now abuse each other on Facebook and Twitter, the conflict would probably run for another thousand years.

'The conflict hasn't gained official recognition by the UN yet,' added Filip the tax collector, 'but it won't be long before a motion is tabled.'

I hadn't got to know Bozo well, but there was an appealing air of wistful resignation about him; the look of a benevolent alien who had been dropped into a world he didn't really understand. Even his appearance was slightly out of kilter with the others. Most of the group had a fairly universally bashed-up look to them, but everything about Bozo was soft and spherical. His chubby face was dominated by an attention-grabbing Viva Zapata hedge-growth, but above it were a button nose and kindly, round brown eyes, and below, a rounded chin. The rest of him was a bulging tummy that stuck out like an advance guard of a royal procession and underneath that were two stumpy legs.

As well as having the largest moustache on the island, Bozo also had the largest konoba, and he was respected because of both attributes. The konoba was a prime spot and Bozo had recognised its potential as soon as the first tourists appeared. Walking along the promenade, they passed in front of it, and its wine barrels and stacks of bottles attracted curiosity, and, now that the weather was warm, Bozo took up position every evening in front of it on a backless chair. Unshaven and with his belly sticking out from under his vest, he looked very much the *patron* – and, should anyone stop to look, he would rise munificently to extol the wonders of his wine.

I was sitting with him one evening when a hefty-looking woman suddenly burst out of the side door and came barrelling towards us. I got up to introduce myself, but, ignoring me completely, she put her hands on her hips and gave Bozo a terrific bollocking. It was in impenetrable dialect, so I couldn't understand, but after a minute she flounced off in a flurry of skirts and slammed the door behind her.

Bozo looked at me and blinked.

'Well, what was all that about?' I asked.

He tugged his moustache (he always did that when nervous) and mumbled, 'Oh, nothing really. Nora was just telling me something about the house.'

The virulence of the bollocking didn't quite bear that out, but I left it at that.

A few minutes later, the door banged open again and this time Nora marched straight past us without even a nod. The alien-on-the-planet look came over Bozo's face as he sank back on his chair, his sad brown eyes drooping like a forlorn spaniel, and looked dejectedly out to sea.

What was going on in that household? I'd better ask Karmela.

CHAPTER 13

COOKING

Every few days, I checked to see if the cricket-playing Luka had returned, and I kept an eye out for young men with the right physique. I had already spotted a few when I was told by Ivana that this blatant eyeing of the well-set-up young men of the village would make people jump to the wrong conclusions about my sexual proclivities and I was to stop.

A week later, Marko heard that Luka would be staying in Germany longer than expected, so I thought I'd start on one of the other projects I had in mind – a restaurant. I've always liked to cook, even though most of what I produce comes from the *Blue Peter* school of cooking (the sort that involves tins of tuna, sandwich spread and a lot of crumbled digestive biscuits), but what could be a better way of becoming part of the local scene than running a local restaurant?

I first thought of Mediterranean cuisine, but, as every restaurant already had that, why not English cuisine? After all, bringing your home cooking to your newly adopted homeland is what people have done for generations – Italians, Indians, Chinese and whoever it was who invented the kebab, to name but a few. I'd never, in fact, come across an English restaurant abroad, but maybe we'd always been too busy planting coffee and moving our battleships around, and we'd never had time to get round to the catering. But what the heck; why shouldn't I start an English restaurant?

Ivana, imagining the interim chaos in our kitchen, wasn't so enamoured of the idea, but I enrolled in an Internet cooking course, ordered some cookbooks and started to think up exotic English menus. I took Hugh Fearnley-Whittingstall as my role model, as my style of cooking was more like his (and I looked more like him than any of the others – well, not quite so chubby, but similarly scrofulous).

In a short time, my skills improved greatly, despite Ivana telling me that my cooking was slapdash and that I made a frightful mess of the kitchen (no sense of what true artistry involves). This, however, did make me think that there was a cookbook waiting for me to write – *The Slapdash Chef*. I could see myself sporting a knowing grin on the cover of a large, glossy cookbook and looking as if I knew a thing or two about life – and what about the TV guest appearances, *Slapdash Chef* demonstrations and swapping witticisms on air with the likes of Nigella, Gordon and Jamie and other great thinkers of our age?

I didn't tell anyone about my plans, but I looked around for a suitable site and investigated the four existing restaurants. Doing this, I got to know Ranko, the best cook on the island – 'The Best in the Balkans', as he so modestly put it. Bald-headed, barrel-chested and fierce-eyed, he had a voice like a bark and dominated his end of the Riva. He had been a sea captain and had retired when the war ended to turn his home into a restaurant. Outside he had erected an awning and put long tables underneath, and it made a pleasant place to eat, but indoors it looked much like a canteen in a Soviet gulag. No one ate there unless it was raining, but the sight of the bar alone could put anyone off drink for life.

Ranko was anarchic, abrasive and always in trouble with the authorities, but for the locals he was a man who had seen the world and they looked on him with a certain amount of awe. He was also highly astute, and, although he drank too much for his own good, even when drunk nothing escaped his notice – and this meant that in the short time he had been operating he had managed to insult half of the population. Actually his favourite pastime when drunk was insulting Germans, but, when there weren't any on hand, he'd happily insult anyone. Despite this, the restaurant had quickly become a village social centre – although, whereas at Marko's you got the benefit of the proprietor's wise advice, all you got at Ranko's was the proprietor's prejudiced opinion.

Being on a strategic corner of the waterfront, Ranko would sit under his awning and glare out at passers-by like a disapproving duchess, either beckoning to them with a wave of a hand, or waving them away as if giving a royal command. As he treated the restaurant like a personal club, many were not welcome – and, being Ranko, he made no bones about who they were. Nonetheless, he was effusively hospitable to those he liked and I started to spend a lot of time with him talking about food and exchanging insults, and, whenever he had cooked up something he was particularly proud of, he'd invite us to join him for supper.

On one of these evenings, we found him in an apron covered with blood and looking as if he'd spent the afternoon butchering piglets in a slaughter-house. The wives of the other guests were trying to take it off him, but he was protesting vociferously that it served as a reminder of the unavoidable relationship between a violent death and their dinner. But the wives were resolute, and in the end he was made to take it off, leaving them free to attend to the life-threatening draughts that their men might be standing in.

Once the matter of the air currents had been attended to, we all sat at the long table and the feast began. A large tureen of fish soup, which was simply delicious, was put in the middle and an equally large tureen of snails cooked in olive oil and garlic followed. Thinking that this was all, I had seconds of both, and was sitting back with my stomach bubbling away like a test tube in one of those Frankenstein films, when I saw Ranko's squat frame emerging from the kitchen with another even bigger cauldron. Hare cooked with plums (*Zec u Slive*), he announced as he placed it on the table and lifted the lid. It smelled heavenly, but I was absolutely full and down the other end of the table I could see the look of panic on Ivana's face. She knew how our polite requests for small portions were always ignored.

Exchanges with Ranko would go something like this:

'Come! Eat more!'

'Thanks, Ranko; that was simply delicious, but I'm really full.'

'A small piece. Please!'

'I really can't. I've eaten too much of your wonderful cooking already.'

'You have eaten nothing!'

'But I've eaten a huge amount. Even I will get fat if I go on like this!'

90

'Hah! So our English friends do not like our cooking. They eat at restaurant in London and Paris and on island we not so good! Eh?'

And, of course, we'd have to capitulate.

Ranko ladled out the food from the cauldron and I mushed the sauce into the baked potato. Delicious! Both tangy and creamy at the same time. The combination, everyone agreed, was a new height of gastronomic delight.

Ranko's friends all wanted to know about English food.

'What is it like? What do you eat at home?' asked a friend from Ranko's Navy days. 'I have heard of roast beef and fish and chips, but what else do English people eat?'

Keen to pave the way for the English restaurant, I gave a glowing account of English cuisine and told them there were more Michelin stars awarded to restaurants in London than in Paris.

No one believed me.

'Who's ever heard of an "English" restaurant?'

'I've never seen one anywhere in the world.'

'There are many English pubs in Europe now, but no restaurants. What is wrong with English food?'

The picture I'd been treasuring of my English restaurant juddered in its frame and Ranko's naval friend continued to heap scorn on English cuisine.

'But why have the English never learned to cook?' asked a professor from Split. 'The French invaded you in 1066, but my French colleagues tell me it never made a difference to your cooking. They say that the only dish the English ever cooked well was Joan of Arc!'

Ranko gave his barking laugh.

'There are even German restaurants in foreign countries,' the professor went on, 'and we all know what we think about German food!'

'Yes, I went to Germany once. My son married a German girl,' said the naval friend, who, by his size, looked like he ate a lot. 'You can't believe how plain the food is there. All they eat is kraut, kartoffel, knobslauchs gristle or some other unmentionable parts of the pig. And they drink beer with everything. Do they do that in England, too?'

I opened my mouth to defend my country, but he continued. 'And my daughter-in-law feeds it all to my grandchildren and my son doesn't complain. Not wanting to offend, I couldn't say anything myself to her, but I told my son he should get her to feed them properly. I think he's afraid of her, though.'

'Our sons aren't the men of the house anymore,' grunted Ranko.

Murmurs of assent from the other men around the table.

Ranko turned to me and said in English, 'And German man he eat the horse. Croatian man he not have money like German man, but no Croatian man eat his horse. And I think no English man eat his horse. Yes?'

'Well, I don't think we would unless we had to,' I said guardedly.

'I am eating snake and crocodile in Africa, and once I am eating a rat,' said the naval man in English, 'but I am eating a German before I am eating my horse!'

At this, Ivana promptly did the nose trick and trying to recover she half fell off her seat. Ranko reached over to steady her and pat her on the back, and, when her spluttering had subsided, he finished wiping the hare juice up with bread. 'Croatian man, he always eating good,' he said. 'Even in Roman time Croatian man eating good. But English man – what he eating in Roman time? Stew of dog and turnip. Yes?'

Once again, I rose for my country. 'But look at all the celebrity chefs we've got!'

'Chefs not celebrity peoples,' said Ranko dismissively.

'Not anymore. Celebrity chefs have star status these days. In our day, pop stars, film stars and sportsmen were the celebrities and chefs wore funny white hats and were kept out of sight chopping liver in the kitchen. But these days chefs are up there in the spotlight along with Madonna, David Beckham and Pippa Middleton's bottom. You could do with some celeb chefs down here.'

Ranko gave a snort. 'In Croatia, chef not on television wearing silk shirt and yellow trouser. He in kitchen working hard!'

The company took their cue and were full of praise for the skills that Ranko had displayed that evening. Ranko waved his hand like a magnanimous king telling his lackeys he was glad they'd enjoyed the feast he'd just given them. 'Best in Balkans!' he called to me across the table and thumped his chest. 'Maybe England BBC make Ranko new "celebrity chef" and he make much money! Yes?'

The argument about English food continued, but, not wanting to give Ranko any more anti-English food ammunition, I discreetly omitted to say that what was eaten in English restaurants wasn't exactly what English people ate at home. Thank heaven I hadn't told him about my restaurant plans.

'Something will have to be done about England's position in the world cooking league if my restaurant's going to take off,' I said to Ivana as we walked home.

'Well, it's going to stay at the bottom of the league as long as your mother's still cooking,' said Ivana.

(Ivana has been unfairly prejudiced against English cuisine ever since her introduction to it by my mother, whose signature menu is boiled mince with mash and carrots followed by gooseberry fool.)

Ignoring Ivana's disrespect, I continued with my cooking course and tried out recipes in the cookbooks. But I didn't dare go near the cooker when Karmela was around. Given her views on men in the kitchen (and men in general), I kept away, and for half the week we ate whatever she cooked for us. There was a *Brodetto* she made out of sprats, eel and squid that was positively inspirational, but most of what she dished up must have come from a Red Army Canteen Cook Book. I spent years at a boarding school where we were fed on pig's crotch, tapioca, margarine and cocoa, and I'd always thought that I could eat anything, but that was before I'd tried some of Karmela's specials. The worst was a meaty mush she called *Pasticada* that had the consistency of wallpaper paste, and the next worst was a hostile-looking sausage thing covered in a gelatinous substance that would have come in handy for plugging holes in World War II aircraft fuselages. (I never found out the name of that one, but avoid it if you ever come across something that looks like that.) We pretended we ate everything, of course, but, as Karmela checked the bins daily in her never-ending quest for recycling opportunities, I had to bury it under cover of darkness. Someone did once remark about a smell of dead dog down that end of the garden, but I managed to put them off the scent with some upbeat talk about the strength of Croatian fertilisers.

With no one except Ivana to talk with about my restaurant plans (I didn't want anyone in the village – and Ranko in particular – to know about it yet), I felt at rather a loss. I'd always had people at work to talk to, or my fellow cricketers on weekends, so I missed having others to talk over my ideas with. The Test Match had just started, too, and I really missed not having my friends around. We used to spend hours watching the Test together (and all the endless replays). Sad, some might say (and my children certainly say so), but perhaps that's what cricket is all about – a bunch of blokes going over what should have happened while getting steadily more plastered. I suppose it must seem very odd to someone not English that so many reasonably intelligent men the length and breadth of our green and pleasant land spend so much of their time doing this, but I do remember Frank Muir once saying that the mark of an Englishman is someone who opens his newspaper at the sports page before turning to the news.

The oddest part of all, come to think about it, was that our chosen team was almost invariably the loser, and most of the time we'd be watching an England sunk for 185 with the Aussies at 462 for six – and, although none of us would say it out loud, at the beginning of a game we'd be expecting that, even after a long struggle, a plucky retaliation and a stubborn last-ditch fight, we'd end up as the losers. What's more, I swear I could detect an expression of wonderment on the England faces whenever we did happen to win; as if they hadn't believed that victory was really on the cards. But, then again, that's all part of being English, I suppose.

CHAPTER 14

THE LEGACIES
OF WAR

It was at Zoran's that I got to know Marin, a Bosnian in his mid-thirties who was the skipper of a power boat belonging to a Zagreb footballer. A handsome young man, he was tall and broad-shouldered like most Southern Slavs and, with his chiselled features, olive skin and grey-blue eyes, he looked like a darker version of David Beckham. He even had the slow grin and that slightly serious Beckhamish air about him.

Marin was another casualty of the war. After graduating, he had worked for his family's business in Bosnia, but when the war started he had to flee to the coast with his mother and two sisters, and had provided for them by doing menial work until it was safe to return. But, on their return to their village, they found that most of their family had been ethnically cleansed and their house and small factory burned down. Their savings now gone, he left his mother and sisters in the care of the surviving relations and went back to the coast to find himself a proper job. With most of Croatia's shipyards now closed down, unfortunately his degree in Marine Engineering didn't count for much, and he had to settle for the job of a skipper on a power boat belonging to a Croatian footballer.

The reaction of the village to a Bosnian was a further insight into the way the islanders viewed anyone coming from the outside. I was sitting with him outside Marko's when Karmela went by and threw me one of her Mrs Danvers-like glares before passing on. When I got home, I asked her what it was all about.

'He might be as good-looking as Montenegrin pirate, but he comes from Bosnia so don't you let him get too near. You can never tell what they're up to, those Bosnians.'

'Well, I'll make sure we count the spoons whenever he leaves,' I said, trying to make light of it, 'but don't you think it's a bit unfair to treat someone who seems a nice young man with such suspicion?'

She pursed her lips and I was fixed with the Mrs Danvers look again. '"The more beautiful the lizard, the more it wants to be a crocodile," as we say.'

'For heaven's sake, Karmela! If God made everyone equal, as you're always telling me, that kind of attitude is very un-Christian, if you don't mind me saying so.'

'Sometimes God doesn't see all that we do. Never trust people who don't belong!'

'Come off it, Karmela! That's just not fair. He's polite, kind and hard-working, and just the sort of man you want around if there's any kind of trouble. Whatever has he done to deserve this kind of tarring? The village will be suspecting *us* of something at this rate!'

'Well, now that you mention it,' she said darkly, 'people do ask why you and Mrs Ivana came to their island. You must have a hidden reason, they say.'

It wasn't the first time we'd heard this. Neighbours had also asked why we had chosen Vis. Vis might be very beautiful, they said, but it was so primitive compared to other places we could have gone to. Not wanting to offend, we couldn't say that was precisely why we had chosen it, and we'd mumble something about the sunshine and the beauty.

The female members of the community also wanted to know how we lived in England. All they knew about it was what they saw on the old BBC series and sitcoms that were still doing the Balkan rounds, and they had a rather confused picture of what went on. However, an opportunity to find out more about us was provided when Ivana caught the flu that was going round and Karmela brought some neighbours to administer to her (I being deemed too untrustworthy to carry out such a task). I was working on the terrace while they were in our bedroom and Ivana was in

96

the kitchen, and I heard them opening drawers and cupboards and making a careful examination of the contents. Ivana's bras, particularly the more insubstantial ones, seemed to attract the most interest and were being handed round for structural analysis…

'And you can see right through it. Look!'

'How embarrassing! We couldn't wear anything like that. Our husbands wouldn't allow it!'

'Well, I suppose it doesn't look so shocking if you're small. The English aren't as big as we are.'

'Their shops must have all those small sizes.'

'What ever would *we* do if we lived in England?'

They also went through my drawers making disparaging remarks about my flowery boxer shorts, but they were most impressed by my M&S sweaters. (These were actually the only items of my wardrobe that didn't produce derogatory comments from Ivana). Good old M&S – an unsung icon of our indomitable and fearless country. M&S should be kitting out Her Majesty, the Cabinet, the SWAT Task Force and anyone else up at the sharp end of our once proud and ancient land. But M&S has to make do with late middle-aged codgers such as me trying to cut a dash on the Med in their 'Blue Harbour' range. Mind you, even the 'Blue Harbour' choices didn't always escape Ivana's censure. Some of what I put on still elicited cries of: 'My God! What *are* you doing in those?'

I did point out that God was probably even less well versed in the niceties of fashion sense than I was, but it didn't cut any ice.

I was enjoying my time at the bars. The only downside was the unreasonable demands made on my knowledge of English football – some of them got quite stroppy when I didn't know things like how many goals George Best had scored or what position Manchester United held in the current league table. Similar demands on my knowledge of technology also verged on the unreasonable at times. When I offered to lend my computer to Domigoy so he could email his girlfriend, Mara, I was asked to explain the workings of Microsoft Office and Student Word and Excel.

'I'm really not up to speed on that kind of thing,' I answered.

'But you must understand the principle of it,' said Domigoy's brother.

'Well, I'm afraid I don't.'

'But you use it all the time,' said Filip. 'How can you use something you don't understand?'

'Well, I just don't. Sorry.'

'But you're working with it every day, and so does Ivana,' he insisted. 'How can you say you don't know how it works?'

'I told you,' I said testily. 'I just don't. For Christ's sake, you guys, give me a break!'

'Maybe you could put Domigoy on this Facebook thing we're always hearing about,' said kind Bozo, trying to steer the conversation into less contentious waters.

'What's that?' asked Domigoy.

'You send pictures of your birthday parties to your friends or something like that,' said Bozo.

'I don't have any friends except my Mara,' said Domigoy gloomily.

'What about all your old school friends?' I said.

'Oh, they count, do they? Well, I've got some of those.'

'I heard on the radio that an American singer kid called Justin Bieber has three million Facebook friends,' said Zoran acerbically.

I ignored the comment. 'And, if you're on Facebook, Domigoy, you'll make lots more friends. My daughter has twelve hundred people who follow her page.'

'Twelve hundred followers!' said Sinisa, the geography teacher. 'And to think that Jesus only had twelve. He could have taken over the world if he'd been on this Facebook thing.'

One evening, Zoran took me aside to say that, because I frequented more than one bar, I was looked on as something of a 'floater'.

'The guys think it suspicious. "What's he up to?" they say. "He's shiftin' aroun' like a dog that can't find a corner to settle in. They're always cookin' somethin' up, those Northerners; especially those Germans."' He paused to scratch his stubble. 'Suppose they gotta point there. Look what happened the last time the Germans took an interest in what was goin' on down here.'

He suggested that it might stop the talk if I settled on a particular bar. His bar.

Karmela told us that my bar-going had gone down well. Apparently, people who didn't frequent bars were considered to have anti-social tendencies – or, worse, to be up to something they didn't want anyone to know about. This explained something that had been puzzling me. I had heard the bar-proppers saying things like: 'We never see much of Ivo ever since he started working at the post office. He must be having an affair with one of the post office girls and doesn't want us to find out.'

This was out of character, I thought, since most of them were a pretty uncurious bunch, but, when I mentioned this to Marko, he said that it was important to be seen. Even the promenade acted as a kind of roll call, and if someone was missing – and no doubt up to something they shouldn't be – their absence was noticed. This is one of the ways a small society kept its members on the straight and narrow.

From our experience so far, nothing escaped the eyes of the village. They peered out from doorways, shutters, car windows, shop fronts and church pews. One evening, I was at Marko's discussing my boat-chartering idea with three brothers from Komiza, and the next morning I found the whole cabal waiting for me at Zoran's.

'Don't do business with anyone who isn't from the island!' said Zvonko, a grizzled-faced wine grower who looked like he had been dug up from a potato field. 'You never know what'll happen once you get involved with outsiders like them.'

'But the Marovi brothers told me they were born on the island.'

'Yes, but sons of immigrants –from Montenegro. They're probably Albanians!'

'But they don't seem different.'

'Ah! They don't to you,' said Bozo, 'but they do to us. You be careful. Don't trust them. They probably speak their own language at home when no one's listening.'

'And heaven knows what they worship,' said Sinisa, the geography teacher.

'They probably face east when the sun goes down and no one's looking,'

99

said Zvonko's brother, a nice man apart from a tendency to dwell on his health problems and his heroic days with the Partisans.

'And they probably have boiled goldfish for breakfast,' said Sinisa.

'Well, at least no one's seen them riding a camel down the high street yet,' said Zoran.

'Well, they wouldn't do that sort of thing when anyone was looking, would they,' grunted Zvonko.

'Don't be ridiculous,' I said.

'You be careful,' said Filip sombrely. 'They may seem friendly enough and laugh and sing with you, but before you know it they'll be taking your money and you won't ever see it again.'

'What's more, they could get you into trouble,' said Bozo, wagging a chubby finger.

'But what kind of trouble could they possibly get me into?' I asked incredulously.

'Ah, you never know. But you take care! Before you know it, you'll find yourself involved in a drug deal or something like that. They're as bad as the Gypsies, those Albanians. If you went into their house, you'd probably find it's full of stolen goods.'

'How else would they have two cars?' said Domigoy, nodding solemnly.

'It's good to have people around who really have their finger on the pulse of things,' said Zoran looking despairingly at his cousin. The remark went over Domigoy's head.

'You all sound just like my grandmother talking about the Irish,' I said. 'Do Montenegrins keep pigs in their living rooms and coal in their baths, by any chance?'

Zvonko looked puzzled. 'Well, I've never seen a pig in their house, although I wouldn't put it past them.' He paused. 'But no one has any coal. We have wood for our fires.'

'Why do you want to know about their pigs and their coal anyway?' said Filip.

Luckily, I was saved from having to explain by the arrival of a one-armed man whom Zoran introduced as Mr Ilic, a cousin of his from the mainland. Talking with Mr Ilic, I learned that he had lost his arm in Sarajevo during the war. He was having a drink in a bar with a friend who was telling him about an affair he was having with an incredibly sexy married woman, when the husband of the incredibly sexy woman appeared at the door. He had just come back from the front line and had an assault rifle, and, before the other drinkers could subdue him, he had winged both Mr Ilic and his adulterous friend. The jealous husband was sent to prison for two years and the adulterous friend recovered, but Mr Ilic's arm had to be amputated, and, although the court awarded him damages, the gun-toting husband had no money.

I murmured sympathetically.

But the worst part of it all, he said, was that, when he got home, his wife took one look at his arm and screamed – and she'd gone on screaming ever since. 'That was five years ago,' said Mr Ilic dolefully.

I never used to have these kinds of conversations in the wine bars down the Fulham Road.

I was still thinking about Mr Ilic and the war the next day when I went on my early-morning walk. At that time of day, the line of houses along the shore looked like a row of staunch matriarchs, hardened by the wind and the sea who had raised countless generations beside the water. Solid and stark, their shapes were softened by the flowers on their balconies and the improvised alleyways that ran haphazardly down to the water – I presumed improvised, as I couldn't imagine an architect ever designing such a turmoil of steps.

Their shutters were closed when I started off, but as I progressed round the bay they began to open and I could hear the muffled strains of women's voices cajoling their families out of sleep. Never hearing the voice of a man, I always wondered if there were any men there for the children. Here you never knew. Maybe they had been carried away by the winds of war that have blown around here for so long. There were few families that hadn't lost someone, just as there were few that hadn't experienced actual physical fear – something that we who've lived in relative security since 1066 have been largely spared. It was easy for us with all the sunshine and bustle of the summer going on to forget about the recent terror, and it always came as a jolt when something happened to remind us.

At the end of May, Tomas the town librarian invited us up to his hamlet for Sunday lunch, so we drove up to the hills at midday and parked below the hamlet. It was a collection of a dozen stone houses, defensively stacked around a central yard and most with slits in their walls to keep out the sun and the enemy. On one side was a sloping meadow from where the sounds of bleating lambs were coming, and on the other was an orchard where Tomas and Mariana were laying out lunch on a ping-pong table, while children tumbled about on a grassy knoll beside them. The scent of the flowers and herbs crushed by their bodies wafted down to where we stood as Mariana came running down to us. Attractively petite with sparkling eyes and a frizz of springy dark hair that bounced as she ran, she hugged us as if we were long-lost cousins and took us into the meadow to pick some flowers for the table. Tomas went down to put the fish on the grill in the communal cookhouse as other family members brought up bowls of food. Once the children had been rounded up, Tomas brought up the fish and stood at the end to dissect them. On the island, serving fish is a ritual and has to be done correctly, and Tomas's bespectacled face was creased in concentration with his tongue sticking into his cheek as he sliced carefully away, while Mariana dished out the contents of the bowls – potatoes with garlic and parsley, French beans with bacon and olives, and three different types of salad gleaming with olive oil.

For the next two hours, we ate, talked, laughed and drank deliciously cool white wine as a light breeze stirred the apple trees above us and dappled us with golden speckles of sunlight. Sitting round the table with this extended family, surrounded by the flower-speckled meadows and stone houses, and with the sound of the animals in the background, I felt as if we were taking part in a biblical scene of an early Rossellini film.

Two hours later, when the children had long since left the table, the others stretched out under the trees for a snooze and Ivana and I walked up the hill to look at the other side of the island. It had rained lightly that morning and the rain had made the heather-covered ground give off that hot, mustily intoxicating Mediterranean post-shower smell – damp earth, wet grass, lavender, pine needles. Reaching the top, we had a 180-degree view of the middle Adriatic. We couldn't see Italy because of the heat haze, but on a clear day you could. The surrounding small islands hovered in the heat haze as if suspended above the water, and behind them the larger islands on the horizon extended their headlands into the silvery sea like sleeping crocodiles. We were turning to go back when we saw an old lady with a large bundle of faggots on her back coming up the hill and went to help her. Despite her protests, I took the bundle and carried it down to her croft at the edge of the hamlet, and, while I stacked it, she went to fetch a jug of lemonade.

Sitting with her on the porch sipping the cool drink and looking down over the valley, I said, 'How I envy you your view. It's the most beautiful setting in the whole valley.'

'Do your children come to see you often, or are they far away?' asked Ivana.

'Sadly, I have no children now. The war carried them all away.'

We started to apologise.

'No, no. Please do not apologise. We must all bear what our lives have to bring to us.'

She then told us that she had been forced to leave her home in Bosnia, but some distant cousins who owned this croft had offered it to her. She said she missed her homeland, but the people in the hamlet were kind and made her feel at home.

In World War II, her first husband and his brothers had been taken from their farm by the Germans and shot in reprisal for something the partisans had done. She had worked the small-holding on her own and tried to feed her son and daughter as best she could, but life had been hard. Her daughter had fallen ill and, because she didn't have enough money for a doctor, she died. A few years afterwards, she married a good man, a widower from the next village, and had another daughter, and things had looked up. They worked hard on their holdings, built a two-storey house for her son, and all seemed to be going well until the recent war with the Serbs started and once again the soldiers came. This time they killed her husband and her son along with all the other men in the village, and they put her and her teenaged daughter on to a truck and abused them all the way to the concentration camp. At the camp, being old, she was spared, but the young women, including her daughter, were abused by the guards for months, and, by the time the UN forces arrived, her daughter was pregnant. They were sent to a refugee camp near Split, but, shortly before the baby was due, the shame and the fear of the future drove her daughter to kill herself. Now alone and unable to return to her land, which was now in Serbian hands, her distant relations had given her a home in their hamlet.

'Oh, *Gospoda*,' said Ivana, almost in tears. 'How could life have treated you so unfairly?'

The old lady looked ahead and said, 'Some days, I sit here looking out over the valley wondering why it all came about, but I know I will never find the answer. Our lives are neither fair nor unfair. They are simply our lives.'

CHAPTER 15

MESSING ABOUT
IN BOATS

Owning a boat had been a fantasy of mine ever since I was a boy with a plastic battleship in my bath, and from the moment we arrived I had been looking out for something suitable. As with the car, I realised I needed something like my neighbours had – and I also thought that, once I had one, I would have something in common with my neighbours and be able to join in on the conversations about high seas, weather fronts, barnacles and splicing main-braces. With a boat I wouldn't be just another stringy, white-limbed foreigner; I'd be one of the island's sea captains!

As soon as I told the cabal that I was looking for one, I was swamped with offers, and by the end of the week Zoran had brokered a deal for a sturdy twenty-foot day-boat that belonged to Zvonko's brother. He had fished in it for twenty years, but had lost his hand in a hay-maker the previous year and had given up fishing. It needed a lot of work, but Zoran told me it was sound and could handle almost any kind of sea. So I now was spending a lot of my day down the hatch fixing things, and, as I had hoped, it gave me an instant bond with a lot of other islanders. The sea was still omnipresent for everyone, no matter what their occupation or stage in life, and with a boat, whoever you were, you spent a lot of time fiddling about with and cursing your engines.

* * *

I rather like doing things myself so I had brought out my state-of-the-art set of tools, and, ever since Karmela had broadcast their existence to the village, neighbours with car or boat engine problems had been asking me to help out. I liked helping out. I've always wanted to do things like heaving up my neighbour's roof like the Amish or giving my fellowmen a hand with their tyre changing, door hanging, weather proofing, piston grinding, tree felling and ditch digging. I'd never had much opportunity for this sort of thing in Fulham, but, whenever I had, it never failed to give me a kind of gritty masculine feeling, as if I was something in between a navvy and a carpenter – an attractively virile concept, I always thought.

Mechanical problems feature heavily in an islander's life, and scarcely a day went by at Zoran's without someone coming in swearing about something mechanical or asking for help. One afternoon, Zvonko came into Zoran's bar with his battered face a map of misery, and slumped on to a stool, his stubbly jowl drooping like a despondent hippo.

'What's that stuff on your shirt, Zvonko?' said Zoran. 'Has that wife of yours been throwing the frying pan at you again?'

'I've spent the whole day under that damned truck with my boy Icho,' said Zvonko, ignoring the loaded remark and taking off his cap. 'It's my Vesna's birthday this weekend and I was going to take her and the grandchildren out for a picnic. With no truck I can't get my boat into the water.' He rubbed his ears and scowled into his beer. 'F… all the gods of four-wheel vehicles!'

The bar-proppers made commiseratory noises.

'There isn't anyone who's got a van with a tow bar on, is there?' he asked, but didn't look anyone in the eye.

No one answered. Odd, I thought. Almost every vehicle on the island had a tow bar on it. But then, realising that this was an ideal opportunity to show what a neighbourly kind of fellow I was, I chirped up, 'I don't have a van, but my Renault's got a decent-looking tow bar on it. I could tow it if it isn't too heavy?'

'A Renault could do it. No problem.' Zvonko's grizzled features brightened and he called Zoran's assistant over. 'Another drink for both of us, Dragimir!'

Dragimir raised an eyebrow as if he knew something.

* * *

The next morning, I set out under a salvo of entreaties from Ivana – not to drive dangerously, not to put my back out by lifting heavy weights and not to get axle grease on my trousers again. Zvonko was waiting for me with his son Icho, a nice hefty-looking, open-faced thirty-year-old with arms like oak branches, a Cold Comfort Farm haircut and matching Cold Comfort Farm dungarees. I got out and saw the boat. Christ! Sitting on a rusty old trailer in the middle of the yard was four metres of heavy, waterlogged, worm-eaten timber. It looked like one of those Viking boats you see in magazines that have been lying in the mud at the bottom of some fjord since the twelfth century and have just been dredged up. Would it even float – and, more to the point, how was I going to get it up the slope from Zvonko's to the road with my poor little Renault? It must weigh over a ton.

Knowing better than to cast aspersions on another man's boat, I said, 'She does look a bit heavy, Zvonko. Are you sure a Renault can get her up to the road?'

'No problem! Renault pull her good,' he said in English, I think wanting to practise it without embarrassing himself in front of the other bar-proppers.

'Well, if you say so. As long as we can get her up this slope, we'll have her in the water in five minutes.'

Zvonko's flat nose did its best to wrinkle. 'We not put her in bay here. We put her in sea at Zaglav bay. That best bay. He waved his arm grandiloquently to the south.

'But that's on the other side of the island! We can't possibly get it over there. What about the hills! The engine's only 850 cc, you know. It'd have to be in first gear all the way. Anyway, I've never seen anything that looks like a launching jetty in Zaglav.'

'Zaglav have good place. Ten metre over sea, but we put rope on car and boat go down easy.'

'But, Jesus, Zvonko!' I said, looking at the haulage truck for the first time; a large battered green affair with a big winch on the front. 'The Renault's a dinky toy compared to that!' I protested. 'And how the hell can we lower the boat without a winch?'

'No problem! Rope on car. Car go back. Boat go down.' His face crinkled with pleasure at the thought.

I heard a voice telling me to get myself out of this, but then what about the other bar-proppers. It might make them think I was the sort of fellow you couldn't count on – and that wasn't a good label to have in an island community.

'Well… I suppose… Maybe if we had a few more people to help…'

'No, No. We no need more people. Three do job OK. Me, you, Icho. No problem!'

'But you can't lift at your age, for heaven's sake!'

(Zvonko couldn't have been a day under sixty-five.)

Zvonko bared his arm. 'I strong like bull!' he said indignantly. 'I pull like young man – Look!' He flexed a meaty but softening bicep.

'OK,' I sighed. 'We'll give it a try.'

Icho caught my eye over his father's shoulder. He had one of those endearingly wide faces that showed what it was thinking and it looked concerned. Moving to my side of the trailer, he whispered, 'The old man still thinks he's Superman, but he can't lift much anymore. I told him we needed more hands, but he just won't listen. I'm worried he'll have a heart attack.'

I made a mental note to stop off at the chemist for an emergency medical kit.

A young woman came into the courtyard and Zvonko introduced her. 'This is Vesna, the mother of my grandchildren,' he said.

I'd seen her before at the market; a mousey girl with the kind of straggly hair and vacant expression you see on followers of those oddball American religious sects – it must be the way you get to look after cold-water baptisms and serial polygamy with bearded, goaty-looking blokes. The girl smiled wanly at me and went over to her brother. As they talked, they were darting surreptitious looks at their father. No doubt the subject of heart attacks was under discussion. I mustn't forget to pick up the medical kit.

Once the trailer was coupled up, Zvonko went inside and reappeared in something looking like a variant of a 1920s flying helmet. With his grizzled square face and his greying box moustache, he looked like a cross between Alf Garnett and the Red Baron.

'What on earth have you got that on for?' I asked.

'I wear when put boat in water. Maybe I hit head.'

Hitting your head when launching a boat…? What had I got myself into? But I said nothing and we got into the car (getting into a car here didn't seem to entail buckling up or ceasing to smoke), and, with the smell of burning clutch plate added to the cigarette fumes, I managed to get up the slope to the road and we ground slowly up the hill, the engine groaning disconcertingly and the heat gauge flickering alarmingly upwards. Arriving at the top, I breathed a big sigh of relief, but things got even worse when we started on the first downhill slope. The heavy trailer pushed down on the tow bar lifting the weight off the front wheels and making the steering terrifyingly difficult to control. Zvonko, quite impervious to what was happening, was telling stories of how he and his brothers used to pull their boat along goat tracks, sail to the farthest islands, brave the storms and snaffle all the prettiest girls, but, being somewhat preoccupied with the steering, the heat gauge and the groaning noises coming from the radiator, I didn't take much of it in.

Finally, we crested the last hill and below us was a landscape that resembled my idea of paradise. Green vine-terraced slopes plunged down to a cobalt-blue sea dotted by an occasional white sail, and a lone steamer chugged its way across the straits. In the distance, the surrounding islands floated in the haze. It was a scene from a Disney movie. All it needed to win the Cutest Landscape of the Year Award was a tweety bird or two flitting around the edges.

'Isn't that the most beautiful view you've ever seen?' I said.

'Pah!' grunted Zvonko. 'Too much beauty view in our country. We like big development; not beauty view.'

What to say to that? But heaven help us if they ever discover something like oil down here.

Ten minutes later, Zvonko called out, 'Here! Here!' and I stopped. I looked down from the window at a twenty-foot drop to the sea.

We got out.

'Jesus, Zvonko! How the hell are we going to get the boat down that?'

'No problem! In war with Serb, we do like this every day!' He looked elated at the prospect.

For a second, I thought the Renault looked slightly nervous.

We unhitched the trailer and Zvonko tied the rope to the tow bar. He had to bend down to do it and was wheezing like a consumptive donkey when he got up. Damn. I'd forgotten to pick up the medical kit.

'All OK now!' he said, grinning widely with his gappy teeth. In a flying helmet, he now looked like Terry Thomas in *Those Magnificent Men in their Flying Machines*.

Zvonko and Icho slid halfway down the slope with the other end of the rope and I sat tensely in the car. The smell of the pines and burned clutch-plate was cloying and the cicadas rasped irritatingly. Perhaps they were trying to warn me of something – that the future held only two possible scenarios. One: that the car with me in it would be pulled backwards over the precipice squashing Zvonko and Icho, and that, after escaping from a submerging car, I'd have to support their widows for the rest of my life. Two: that, trapped inside the car, I'd sink like a stone and turn another scenic spot of the Med into a foreign field that would be forever England. Feeling like Lot's wife (who as you may well know got into all that unpleasant-ness with a pillar of salt when she turned round at the wrong moment), I looked in the mirror with dread. Be still, my pounding heart, I told myself and opened both windows to make for a quicker escape. Why had I got myself involved in this?

Hearing a shout from Zvonko, I gingerly engaged reverse and heel-and-toed the pedals to keep the engine revving (it was prone to dying at low revs). In the mirror, I saw the boat gradually disappearing over the edge, and I could hear Zvonko shouting hoarse instructions, but it's remarkable how difficult it is to understand someone shouting in a language you don't understand too well when you're revving a car engine. Hoping it was the right thing to do, I continued backing slowly, but the car suddenly began to slide. I stamped on the brake. It kept on sliding. I shoved it into gear but the wheels spun in the sand. Oh my God! Panic! I was nearing the edge! I was going to die!

Then there was a loud crack, a big splash and the car stopped.

Scenario One. They'd been squashed by the boat!

I jumped out and rushed to the edge. Relief! The boat was in the water but the boom had come off it. Zvonko, still in his flying helmet, was climbing astride the boom, hanging on with one arm and gesticulating to Icho with the other like a cowboy on a bronco. But booms in water are like fairground greasy poles and it rolled round, pitching him back into the water. He surfaced spouting waterlogged expletives – or were they gargled instructions? It was difficult to say which and Icho seemed to be having as much trouble understanding them as I was. I climbed down to help.

By the time I got there, Zvonko was hauling his barrel-like frame up on to the rocks like a prehistoric sea creature that had decided to evolve on land. With a great deal of grunting, he got upright, took off his helmet and shook himself like a wet Labrador. Rubbing a large lump on his head, he looked up angrily at me. 'Jesus and Maria! What you do? You go too quick! Boom it break! Why you go so fast? You want kill me? I lucky I not dead man!'

'I had the brakes full on, damn it!' I spluttered. 'The bloody car was skidding backwards. I told you your damned boat was too heavy. I nearly went over the edge after it. You nearly got us both killed!'

Zvonko rubbed the lump on his head sheepishly. 'Maybe you right. Maybe car too small.'

Icho looked up from where he was untying the rope. 'And maybe father too old.'

That evening, I found out why none of the bar-proppers had offered to help. Zvonko was famous for accidents. But, as he was also famous for his story-telling, the village got to hear about my selfless gesture and how I almost got to meet my Maker in a flying Renault 4, and according to Zoran it won me a few brownie points.

But, as near-death experiences weren't really my thing, I was going to steer well clear of that kind of venture in future, brownie points or not – besides, the operation had burned out most of my clutch plate.

With the boat came a change in our daily routine. Now we had a boat, as soon as the morning chores were over, I'd go off to tinker around on it like a man with a shed at the bottom of his garden, and Ivana would follow later with the towels and the picnic. There was always a sense of adventure in the air as we set out. I stood at the helm with the confidence of an experienced hunter-gather and steered her out of the harbour with what I thought was an impressive display of dexterity.

The first time we set out, the sky was brilliant blue as we scudded over the light sea and a wave of joy flooded over me. I felt like singing and dancing, but instead I put an arm round Ivana and, with a winning smile playing subtly about my thin but manly lips, I murmured into her ear: 'With thou beside me singing in the wilderness.'

Ivana looked up blankly.

'Omar Khayyam.'

'You just concentrate on what you're doing! You're going much too fast. Now mind that boat over there. You always behave like a boy at school whenever you get anything new. I should never have married you. You frighten me enough with the car, and now you've got a boat to frighten me with!'

'Hush now, my trusty crew. We're off for romance and adventure on the main! With thou beside me, we're bound for the Rio Grande!'

'You just keep your eyes ahead and don't run into anything.'

Undeterred, I took her up to warp speed (20mph). Sniffing the briny breeze, while my hair ruffled attractively in the breeze, I was Ragnar Hairybreeks, Captain Cook, Captain Ahab, Captain Kirk. Nothing compares with being out at sea on a bright, fine breezy day. Our bow cleaved through the clear water, splashing up spray that sparkled like jewels in the air and lightly sprinkled my face. The engine throbbed comfortingly underneath me as I took her past the headland and out into the open sea leaving a small but satisfying white trace in the cobalt blue behind us. Oh my beautiful boat!

Sometimes, we saw dolphins. Usually, they were in pairs, but one afternoon we came across a school of them. I slowed down and saw two of them break away and come plunging towards us like a pair of fighter planes. They first circled the boat, twirling up like ballet dancers on their tail-fins, and then swam alongside looking up sideways with their beady eyes before speeding back to report to the school. I thought they were going to disappear, but the report must have been favourable as they carried on playing. I turned off the engines and we watched as the smaller ones played about, making little jumps over each other, while the adults on the edge shot up out of the water in giant leaps. Solid compact grey muscle gleaming in the sunlight, they rocketed upwards, brushing against each other and sending thousands of sparking droplets into the air. Then in a manoeuvre I thought they only learned in dolphin circuses, two of them shot up towards each other and, suspended at the peak of the arch, they touched beaks as if kissing before spiralling back into the water.

And then they were gone. As if from a signal below, they suddenly vanished and the sea was once again a calm, smooth, undulating surface around us. We sat there stunned, feeling as if we had just witnessed a kind of marine epiphany. I started the engine, and we motored home dazed and in silence. If only the children had been with us. They'd never believe we'd seen the dolphins kissing. Why did I never have a camera with me when it was needed?

Bernard Shaw said that, when God had finished his creation, he looked down and the tears of joy he shed became the Dalmatian Archipelago. Created some zillion years ago by a gigantic volcanic eruption, the rocky shorelines of the islands plunged vertically into the sea like in a Norwegian fjord. So we could cruise right in to drop anchor, and then, after letting the chain rattle out until the boat was swinging free and the only sound the lap of water and crackling cicadas, it was clothes off and into the water.

The diving in Dalmatia is some of the best in the Mediterranean, and with the boat we discovered a whole new world. Because of the clearness of the water, the panorama of every cove gave you an undersea landscape of wonder, each one with its own sierras of rocks and jungles of ferns. The moment I was beneath the surface I would find myself in a miraculously coloured world of vivid fauna and surrounded by strange-shaped fish. Some darted about the rocks on their own and some swam around in the open, quite unconcerned at my presence. Some groups swam right in front of me in a stately formation like a family on a Sunday outing, completely ignoring me. Sometimes there were octopuses and squid scurrying furtively between the rocks, and, if I swam in front of the rock face, the silly old sausages would pulse with nervous luminescence and give themselves away. I'd then dangle a hand in front of the rock and, when they shot out a tentacle to grab it, all I'd have to do was close my fist and I'd have one.

Being the farthest island from the mainland, for centuries the island had been the nearest haven for ships caught in a storm, and lying on the seabed around the coast were the wrecks of those who'd just failed to make it into safety. Most of them had rotted away, but many of the Greek and Roman cargos of amphora were still visible. In some bays, I could see them twenty feet below encrusted together, and I'd dive down to try to work one loose.

The most exciting exploration grounds were the wrecks of the ironclads. There was also a World War II US bomber off the south coast, but I needed to take the next level of diving qualification before I could go down that far.

After our swim, we'd climb back on to the boat and lie in the sun before having our picnic, or, if there was a fisherman's shack serving food on the shore, we'd motor over to it. Sometimes we couldn't see one but could smell the grilled fish and baking garlic, and in that case we'd just follow our noses.

CHAPTER 16

ADVENTURE
AND ATTITUDE

Halfway through June, one of our cousins was coming to stay with her three small children and asked if we could find her an au pair. Marko's wife suggested a niece of hers in Split, so we rang her and, as Marin was going over there to renew the licence for his owner's boat, I went over with him to collect her. It was a sparkling, blue morning as we skittered out across the bay and, once out in the open sea, Marin gave me the wheel. I opened her up and, with a growling roar, 640 horsepower of engine thundered into life and rocketed us across the water. The surge of acceleration never loses its thrill. We lifted up on to the plane with a satisfying whoosh and sped across the water like a low-flying seagull. Nothing can be more thrilling than speeding across the water with a glittering plume of spray flying up on either side. Skimming over the waves at breath-taking speed with the engines growling pleasingly under our feet, we hurtled through the straits, clutching the wheel and hanging on to the grab-rail. With the wind in my face and Marin beside me, I was no longer a late-middle-aged has-been. I was Butch Cassidy with the Sundance Kid at my side, charging across the open space at the helm of a raffish piece of Italian machinery – my rapidly greying hair streaming behind me in the wind.

Marin first arranged the boat registration and we then took a taxi to the address Marko's wife had given us. We arrived at a lurid purple door off the waterfront and we opened it to find ourselves in a bar whose designer had unsuccessfully tried to reference Hollywood B-movies. It might perhaps have worked in black and white, but the neon-lit crimson-flocked walls were hard on the eye and the colour of the bar would have dissuaded an alcoholic from drinking.

'By my troth, this is a terrible place, Sir Lancelot!' I said in a low voice to Marin. I don't think he could quite place the quotation, but he grimaced back in acknowledgement.

Lolling against the flock were two girls with spiky hairdos talking in low voices, and, on a hideous purple sofa, two others with similarly aggressive hair were playing cards. This was no Norland Nanny agency. Back home, girls who looked like that would be tagged and reporting daily to their probation officer.

A barrel-chested man with biceps bulging out of the sleeves of his jacket appeared from behind a curtain. He had one of those faces that in the North of England would belong to someone good at blocking punts and stepping on people's faces in scrums rather than someone working in Social Services or writing poetry. 'You want Galina, yeah?' he said in an American accent.

'Oh, yes. We've come to fetch her.'

'She's not leavin'.'

'Oh! But my wife was talking to her about it only yesterday.'

'Yeah, that was yesterday. That was before she remembered she'd signed a contract to work here for the summer. That kinda slipped her mind when she was talkin' to your woman.'

'My wife.'

'Whaddever.'

'Is Galina here?'

'Yeah, but she's busy.'

There was a pause while we weighed each other up. The Gonzo was about twice my size, so I continued with my nice-as-pie manner.

'I only need a quick word with her. Her auntie arranged it all and she'll think something's wrong if we don't even say hello to her. You know how aunties worry.'

He hesitated for a moment (even Gonzos have aunties), but he then thought better of it. 'Like I said, she's busy.'

116

We could hear the voices of girls behind the curtain and Marin and I looked at each other. Marin moved quickly. In three strides, he was at the curtain and yanked it aside. 'Galina!' he called out. The voices stopped.

'Hey! Get outta there!' The man grabbed Marin's arm.

'Galina!' Marin called out again.

Marin and the man arm-wrestled each other as a figure appeared from behind the curtain. A waif of a girl with doe-like eyes, short black hair and too much make-up stood looking uncertainly at us.

The bouncer let go of Marin's arm and stood in front of the girl.

'You're not talkin' to her and there'll be trouble if you don't get outta here right now!'

'And just how do you think you're going to get us out of here?' asked Marin in a steely voice.

'I'll throw you outta that window. That's how.'

Marin stepped up to him, his jaw clenched. Though not as bulky, he was taller.

'We're going to talk to Galina outside for a moment, whether you like it or not. And, if you want to get rough, I'd remind you that there are two of us, and by the time your mates turn up, my friend and I will have made your face look like a pizza.'

Poised to kick the man's shins or give him a Chinese burn until he screamed for mercy, I stood behind Marin like I used to stand behind my elder brother. In my pocket was a standard ninja-issue biro, and I clutched it menacingly, ready to poke him black and blue if he made a move.

Clearly reckoning he wasn't a match for me, he grunted and pushed the girl grudgingly forward.

Once outside, Galina told us breathlessly that she had signed something she thought was a wages agreement rather than something that tied her into working there the whole summer. The money was good, she said, but for most of the day she was just hanging about in the gloom waiting for the drinkers to come in, and it was getting her down.

As we were about to leave, she remembered that her handbag was still inside and wanted to get it, but not feeling like practising my biro-poking expertise that morning, I persuaded her that she didn't really need anything that was in it. We dashed off to pick up her suitcase from the flat she was sharing and then high-tailed it back to the harbour in case the Gonzo had rung his mates and they were after us. We jumped aboard, the huge motors coughed into life and Marin wheeled the boat out of the harbour in a curl of spray. I felt as if we were trafficking illegal immigrants as we roared out to sea, and couldn't resist looking behind every few seconds in case a speedboat with machine guns was coming after us. Marin noticed and caught my eye.

'*From Russia with Love!*' he shouted over the noise of the engines.

We grinned foolishly at each other.

'Someday we'll have to grow up!' I shouted back at him.

Galina started to shiver and opened her suitcase, but there was nothing in it except jeans, T-shirts and skimpy dresses. I took the wheel and Marin went below to bring up one of the storm jackets. It was twice her size, but he pulled it over her and she sat with her head poking out of it like a puppy in a rug while he solicitously fastened the zips around her. She gazed up adoringly at him.

We'd have to keep an eye on her.

I asked them both not to mention our brush with the bouncer to Ivana, as I was worried she might want to go over and punch him. She does that sort of thing, and I've had to spend a lot of time refereeing altercations with other drivers and members of the public or talking our way out of police stations over the last thirty years. However, I have to admit that her 'attitude', as the children call it, did sometimes come in useful. When I had to stay on a nearby island to help a friend who had bought a house there, Ivana took the boat back on her own and got caught by a sudden storm. Unable to keep the boat on course, she was driven to the south side of the island – where she should have stayed until the storm had blown itself out. But, determined to show everyone (and me in particular) that she could bring the boat home in heavy weather if she wanted to, she set out to sea again and tried to make her way up the coast. Pounded by the waves, drenched by salt water and frozen by a force six gale, many times she thought of turning back, but she battled her way up and eventually

118

reached the safety of the bay. Marko saw her coming in and went to help, and he said that she was in a terrible state of bedragglement, but she had experienced what only true sailors can experience – that sense of achievement, when, after hours of struggling against all that the elements can throw at you, you finally make it into the harbour you've been trying to reach for so long.

For the next day, she was the talk of the town and her street-cred in the village rocketed. However, when I arrived back the following evening and she was helping me off the ferry with some boxes, I heard an old man on a bench say to the others: 'She did well in that Tramontana, you know.'

'True,' said the one beside him, 'but it had only just started to blow. If a full Tramontana had been blowing, she'd have never made it back without a man on board.'

The third nodded in agreement.

In Croatia, the sea is still a last bastion of the male.

We had, in fact, come across this attitude already. When we went to the harbourmaster's office to register the boat and pay the taxes, I had asked for the boat to be registered in Ivana's name and had been met with considerable surprise. The harbour-master knitted his heavy eyebrows together like a felted black sock and said, 'But we cannot have a woman's name down as the captain!'

'Don't be ridiculous!' said Ivana. 'Of course you can.'

The eyebrows did a quick *pas de deux* and he shifted uncomfortably in his seat.

'We have to put it in Ivana's name for tax reasons,' I offered as a palliative.

'But a woman's name is never on a boat register!' he said, the eyebrows continuing their dance routine.

Ivana fixed him with the oxyacetylene blow-torch look usually reserved for me and he fidgeted uncomfortably. 'I know what,' he said brightening up. 'We could put your husband's name down as the captain and then write your name underneath it. That way we'll have a man listed as the official captain, but your name will be there, too, if it's ever needed.'

119

Ivana stood there fizzling like a test tube in a chemistry lab. 'There are countries with a woman as their President these days, and you're telling me you can't put a woman's name on some silly boat register?'

The eyebrows clenched again. 'But it's just that… well… out here… you know…' He looked at me pleadingly. 'Wouldn't it be so much easier if we do what I suggest?'

I gave Ivana one of my 'please don't make such a fuss' looks, and with bad grace she submitted.

After leaving the office, we saw Marin sitting with some other skippers who had decided to devote their morning to beer and conversation, and Ivana peeled off to give them a broadside about the nonsense women still had to put up with from men – and seafaring ones in particular. Marko, always the diplomat, went over to sympathise with her, but came back to say we had done the right thing in going along with what the harbourmaster had suggested. At our stage, he said, the most important thing to do was to comply with local preconceptions, no matter how daft they might seem.

I went to prise her away from the table before she started accusing them of still wearing animal skins and clubbing their women into subservience, and as we left I whispered to Marko that he might warn the harbourmaster not to go down any dark alleys for the next few days if he saw Ivana in the vicinity.

Another boating issue also reared its ugly head around that time. Zoran and the cabal had actually warned me about it some time ago, but, although I had dismissed it as small-town misogyny at the time, I now realised they were right. Having one's wife as one's crew is definitely not a good idea. Whereas anyone else will do what they are told to by their captain, wives, being long accustomed to doubting the wisdom of their husbands, tend to answer back – and, by the time you've sorted that one out, you've missed your buoy, hit the sea wall, gone aground or run into a car ferry. An added problem with my crew was that, whenever it was told to do something, it would complain that its hair would get wet, its trousers dirty or its sunglasses would fall off.

Ragnar Hairybreeks wouldn't have put up with it.

One month had gone by since my cricket discovery, but there was still no sign of Luka, and, desperate for someone to talk to about my idea, I misguidedly mentioned it to Zoran.

'Cricket? You mean that dumb game where a lotta guys in white pants stand aroun' not doin' much. Right?'

'Er… yes, I suppose I do, but that's not exactly what…'

'I saw it in some of those old English movies on Channel 11. Why the heck d'you wanna start that up here? If you wanna play your Harry Potter games, play 'em at home.'

'Well, Marko thinks it's a good idea.'

A crafty look came over his face. 'Say, don't some cricket guys in India make a lotta money fixin' the odds an' bettin' on it?'

(The extent of Zoran's knowledge never ceased to amaze me.)

'Mebbe you an' I can start an island bettin' joint and I can make some decent money at last?'

'But do you think there will be enough men interested in learning how to play it?'

'I dunno. You know what our islanders think about anythin' new.'

'Oh.'

Being a P.G. Wodehouse reader, Filip knew something about it. 'But tell me. Do all those people really have to stand around doing nothing? With twenty-two people, surely more of them ought to be doing something?'

'Well, it's not really like that…' I began, but my words were drowned out by the hoot of the ferry and everyone moved outside.

It wasn't exactly the enthusiastic response I'd hoped for, but it was my fault. I should have waited for Luka to return as Marko had advised. I certainly shouldn't have opened my mouth about it to Zoran. Not that it was the kind of game that would appeal to him anyway – patience not being one of Zoran's more obvious virtues. In fact, whenever you were near him, you had a rather unsettling feeling. The sort of feeling you get when you're standing next to an overheating boiler that might be about to explode any minute.

CHAPTER 17

MUSICAL
EVENINGS

By the middle of June, we had begun to make some progress with our neighbours. Sometimes we were asked for supper or just to spend the evening with them, drinking and chatting (or rather putting on Oscar-winning sign-language performances when my Croatian failed me). The only drawback was the amount of drink involved. On arrival, I would be plied with something 200 per cent proof – usually *rakija*, their equivalent of vodka, or *Travarica*, another equally deadly gut-rot that they made from grasses, nuts or fruits. The first sip was always wonderful, as if an exquisite nectar had been put into my mouth; but a moment later a burning sensation would zap through my whole being, sending my nervous system into a St Vitus' dance – thrilling, but at the same time rather alarming. As my last interest in hallucinogenic experimentation had been many years earlier, I tried to side-step the hard stuff and get straight on to the wine, but this wasn't always easy. Men down here are expected to take an enthusiastic part in all the manly glass waving and toasting they go in for.

As women in Croatia hardly drink at all, Ivana was safe. She could refuse without offending. I first thought that this might make for a rather slow start to the evening, but I needn't have worried as the women seemed to devote the first part of their evening to making sure their men weren't exposed to any life-threatening draughts. Curiously, they didn't seem worried that the same lethal currents of air might strike down one of their own gender, but I dare say that was yet another of those things I'd get to the bottom of one day.

Most of the neighbours' houses were dark and Spartan. The main rooms were low and used as living-rooms-cum-kitchens and there was usually a stone cistern in a corner – which was needed. On the island there is little water, and, now that it was summer, it ran out in the late afternoon and we all had to get our water from our cisterns, usually with bucket, until the mains had filled up overnight.

Their interiors were minimal with stark furniture and old sepia family groups or religious pictures on the walls, but there was usually enough jumble of life's necessities – papers, books, tools, empty bottles, children's homework and homely collections of broken radios and kettles – that managed to humanise the rooms. The television took pride of place in most the houses; usually an ancient square set sitting Buddha-like on a strip of white lace on top of a heavy-looking chest of drawers. Most of the time this would be tuned into something like *Dynasty*, a Mexican soap opera or an ancient BBC sit-com like *Dad's Army* or *Are You Being Served?*. Island reception being somewhat sporadic, the colour veered towards an alarmingly purplish end of the spectrum, and I must say, the first time I saw Captain Mainwaring's bluey face looking at a spadeful of pigs' manure that Private Pyke had produced for his close inspection, I did find it rather off-putting. But, unlike at home where any variation in the spectrum sends every male in the room into a flurry of knob twiddling behind the set, no one seemed unduly bothered by it. After a while, actually, Clive Dunn's face tinged purple began to look rather endearing.

Most of what we were given to eat was delicious. The best cook was the postmaster's wife, an ebullient middle-aged lady, who for important occasions such as these applied her mascara in Dusty Springfield-like proportions. She made the most gob-smackingly delicious dish of cod, fennel and peppers and a triumph of an aubergine stuffed with soft cheese and figs. The next best was Dora, Grandma Klakic's daughter, who did a perfection of a steamed egg custard (*Rozata*) and a wonderful tomatoey fish stew (*Riblija Brodeta*) out of left-overs from the fish market (though I did find it rather disconcerting that she kept giving the flies buzzing over it hefty blasts from a highly toxic-looking can of insecticide).

The most common dish was grilled fish, and nothing else was ever served at Grandma Klakic's table, her son-in-law Igor being a fisherman. Igor had the universally bashed-up look of most fishermen and verged on the taciturn, but at least he had a full complement of fingers, and it was from him that I learned how each different fish should be scaled, cut and cleaned. Fish had to be filleted and cooked according to strict protocol, although Igor said he liked to add a small personal touch of his own – sticking a knife into its head to make quite sure it was dead. It might have been out of the water for some hours, he said, but he liked to be sure.

I usually paid decent enough tribute to the cooking, but, if the cook thought I hadn't eaten enough, a fierce hand would ladle more on to my plate despite my protests. Grandma Gokan was the fiercest, and she was also pretty fierce about the proper size of a man and the size of his family. Being on the skinny side and with only two children to boast of, I was wanting on both counts, but what shocked Grandma G the most was how few relations I had.

'Hah! I've seen what happens with those small families. When a child is the only thing its parents have to worry about, they think they've got a little miracle in their home, and those are the children who are always talking too much. Now it's all very well if you're going to be a politician or an actor, but, if you're going to be anything else, it's definitely not very well. Children should learn how to listen to others and not to the sound of their own voice. Our Town Hall is full of men like that, and look where that gets us! Pah!'

I raised my eyebrows enquiringly, hoping for more local low-down, but Grandma Gokan wasn't to be diverted.

'If you're born into a large family like I was, you learn to listen. With ten uncles and aunts and three times as many cousins, no one gave me much of a chance to talk. And that's how it should be!'

'It was the same when I was little,' added her daughter. 'I've got so many older cousins I could hardly get a word in. I've got so many I don't even know how many I have, but it's good to know they're all out there somewhere, should I ever need them.'

Coming from an average lukewarm Anglo-Saxon family, I found the attention they gave to children rather refreshing. Here, like in Italy, children are thrown into the air, tickled, hugged, kissed and smothered with affection (even though they don't let them talk too much). Mind you, from what I'd seen so far, it did seem to produce a lot of men with rather mother-inflated opinions of themselves. Being brought up in an English home, of course, my siblings and I were spared that fate – though I'm sure my mother loved us dearly in that 'don't spoil the children' English way. The attitude has changed over the last few decades, but many in England still look upon children in a different way to our Mediterranean counterparts. A male sturgeon, when he finds to his surprise that he has suddenly parented a million children, puts on as cheerful an expression as a sturgeon can summon and resolves to love them all, but the English have often had difficulty in doing this to the few that they have. Who can forget that newsreel clip of the Queen returning to Southampton after a long tour of the Empire and pushing away a little Prince Charles with an embarrassed hand when he rushed to hug her knees? No wonder the poor chap often looks like a spaniel that could do with some TLC.

I once volunteered to cook the supper. I thought it might be a good opportunity to drum up some advance publicity for English cuisine (and besides, if I was ever going to give *Slapdash Chef* demonstrations on TV along with Gordon, Jamie and Hugh, I needed a lot of people spreading the word about my wonderful slapdash cooking).

So I cooked up three courses, took it with us to Grandma Gokan's, and it was a terrific success. My cucumber and fennel soup was exquisite, the rosemary and garlic lamb was roasted to perfection and I was particularly pleased at how my dauphinoise potatoes turned out (I'd been worrying about them all day). At the end of the meal, everyone was wonderfully effusive in their praise and I accepted their compliments with suitable modesty, though, like all true artists, I do hanker after just a little bit of public appreciation.

I loved these evenings. What a delight it was to sit round a table with neighbours, eating, drinking and chatting the evening away. It must be one of life's greatest pleasures, and I can't think why I'd taken so long to find this out. Perhaps it says something about my retarded mind that I'd had to wait until I was over fifty and had come out here to realise this.

At the end of the evening, our hosts sometimes sang folk songs. Not knowing the words was a disadvantage, but we'd hum along to the chorus bits and I'm a dab hand at the spoons. Folk songs were very much part of people's lives, and, although we heard the same songs over and over again, they never seemed to tire of them. It's odd that one almost never hears folk songs in the West, but then pop music has almost taken over our entire musical heritage and the songs of Michael Jackson, Madonna and Abba are as well known in Beijing and Botswana as they are in Birmingham. Folk music, however, doesn't seem to travel and, besides which, few ever listen to their own. The only time you hear it in England is at folk festivals or when some clog-dancing beardies come clumping around your village pond in the Merrie Month of May. In Croatia, however, they play it on the radio, sing it while loading their vans, hum it while sorting their fish, whistle it while taking their pigs to market and, as any stroll down the back streets of Vis will confirm, they sing it in their baths. (Has anyone ever tried singing clog-dancing songs in their bath?)

The most usual form of Croatian folk music is 'Klapa' which means 'group of friends'. A Klapa can start up anywhere – in a bar, in a street, in a square, by someone's boat. The first time we heard it was outside the post office one night. A group of men were on the steps – a large bearded fellow in dungarees, an old man in a baseball hat and two stringy youths – and they were singing the same phrases over and over again and breaking off to huddle together like football players with a coach to discuss where they were going wrong.

'You're much too low!'

'You keep trailing behind me!'

'Your voice was better last week.'

The bearded one held up his hand. 'It'll never work with only the four of us. Let's get Davor. He'll make the difference.'

The thin one promptly disappeared into the nearby restaurant and came back pulling a waiter by the arm.

126

'For Christ's sake! I'll lose my job!' the young man was protesting.

'Come on, Davor – just a few minutes. You can't let us down. We all came and sang at your table-tennis final. Remember?'

Davor grudgingly joined the circle, the bearded one started with a phrase, and the others extemporised around it. The added voice worked immediately and the five voices melded into a close harmony. With no soloists, the voices conversed as equals. Occasionally, one of the voices dominated for a few bars, but then merged back into the general harmony.

Other passers-by stopped and gathered round, but no one dreamed of joining in. This was not a singsong. This was a *duende*; a moment of truth; a work of art, and the sound was deep, raw and ethnic. It swirled around the waterfront and out across the water, and we stood entranced as song followed song – about the sea, the girls they loved, their families, their lost youth, their love of their homeland. We wanted it to go on forever, but a harassed-looking restaurant owner appeared half an hour later and hauled the waiter away. The session now over, the four singers said goodnight to each other and went off in different directions.

Later that week, we heard another kind of music. We were passing one of the restaurants and the owner, Asija, a vivacious, sporty-looking woman called out, 'I am having party with my friends from Dubrovnik. They have brought musicians from the mountains. We have too much food. You come eat with us and then you sing. Yes?'

My innate Anglo-Saxon reserve twitched within. 'Well, it's awfully kind of you Asija… but we really shouldn't… and neither of us sings very well…'

'Oh, do stop being so English!' said Ivana crossly, before turning to Asija and saying in her most Sybil Fawltyish voice, 'Please excuse my husband, Asija. He's just being typically English, but we'd love to come and join you.'

Asija came out and took hold of my arm.

'But we really can't sing very well…'

'Nonsense! Everyone can sing!' Laughing, she pulled me inside. 'Come! First you eat and then we sing English football song!'

She sat us down at the end beside the musicians' table and plied us with a dish of small artichokes, fish soup, roasted lamb and flagons of wine. The musician next to us finished eating first, and, impatient to start playing, he took a bouzouki-style instrument from the case behind him and unwrapped it lovingly as if it was a ticking clock. This made the other players wolf down what was on their plates and take up their instruments, too. They formed up on a podium at the end of the room, and, with a flourish of fingers, the mandolin player sent out a fountain of notes that spiralled around the room like a plaintive coda until the others followed in and filled the room with wild, jagged, gypsy sounds. The music bounced off the walls and out through the windows. They played with their eyes shut as if transported by the music, and when they finished there were shouts of applause and calls for other songs. The next song was 'Volga, Volga', which in my wine-induced haze I mistook for 'She was Poor but She was Honest', and I stood up to lend my enthusiastic vocal support. I don't think anyone understood a word and I was singing slower and slower towards the end, but there was great applause when I finished, and, in tribute, the band played a creaky version of 'Tipperary' (often taken as our National Anthem in these parts). Mercifully they then reverted to their own music and played the old Croatian National Anthem, but once again I mistook it for one of ours ('The Dawn is Breaking' by the Seekers, that sixties, long-haired, Beatnik lot), and lurched to my feet, with Ivana hissing, 'Do sit down, darling! You're being embarrassing!' and pulling on my arm. But I had drunk enough to have a sense of invincibility and the bit was between my teeth.

Determined to better my last efforts, I trumpeted away, and I was just finishing off with what I thought to be some pretty impressive *basso profundo* when a group of four ruddy-faced yachtsmen in brightly coloured sailing gear appeared in the door. Seeing that they had blundered into a party, they started to back out, but Asija pulled them back in, saying they could eat and drink as long as they joined in the singing. Hearing the ear-bashing in English that Ivana was giving me, they introduced themselves as yachtsmen from Portsmouth and chatted with us until their food arrived – which they fell upon as if they hadn't eaten since they left Dogger and Forties. When they finished, the music started up again, and they kept their part of the

128

bargain by joining in. All of Asija's friends sang mellifluously, as most Dalmatians do, which rather showed up our English male voice contingent, which sounded like Lee Marvin singing 'I Was Born Under a Wandering Star', but by that point I don't think anyone noticed.

'Everyone's so friendly tonight. What's got into them?' I shouted across the table to Ivana.

'They're not islanders; they're from Dubrovnik. That's why!'

The music and the shouting was now deafening – like anywhere else on a Friday night, I suppose, just with more Xs and Zs in the words. One of the Dubrovnik men went over to Asija, lifted her up from her chair and whirled her around the room. Others followed suit and two of them whisked up Ivana, and she was tossed from one man to the other like a ragdoll, her feet off the ground, her hair flying and her dress swirling. The musicians were giving it their all and the screeching violins and throbbing balalaikas had worked themselves into a fever pitch. Those not dancing were singing and shouting as those on the floor spun faster and faster around the room, bouncing off the walls and cannoning into each other. I grabbed hold of a pretty, dark girl at the next table and whirled her dizzily around, my body feeling as if it could do anything it wanted to. Of course it couldn't, but it didn't matter as everyone else was tripping over each other and ricocheting off the walls as we careered around in circles.

Eventually, the band stopped and everyone collapsed back on to their chairs like marionettes with their strings cut.

The Portsmouth yachtsmen then thought they ought to contribute something to the evening's entertainment and sang a sea shanty. Standing on their chairs, they gave a spirited rendition of 'Bound for the Rio Grande', and the musicians struck up behind them. They acquitted themselves pretty well and ended with a rousing let's-give-the-krauts-a-kicking crescendo amid tumultuous applause. Just then, Asija came out of the kitchen, dragging an old woman wearing a black headscarf – the cook. She was the size and shape of an elderly Susan Boyle and was protesting volubly, but the protest seemed to be a token one, as, once on the podium, she took off her shawl and launched into a heart-breakingly soulful rendition of a *Svedlinke* (a kind of love song that always seems to end with the death of both lovers).

Huge applause when it ended, and for her encore she sang a song of gob-smacking lewdness about a cook who bonked anyone who came into her kitchen. Roars of laughter throughout and wild cheering when she finished. She retired back into the kitchen grinning from ear to ear.

'Must be a lot of fun out here with parties like this!' shouted one of the Portsmouth sailors. 'Does this kind of thing happen all the time?'

'Well… kind of… sometimes…' I said, not wanting to admit that it was the first party we'd been to.

The Dubrovnikites were now doing a folk dance – one of those one-two-three-hop dances that go round in circles.

'Interesting that folk dances in this part of the world always seem to go round in circles,' said one of the yachtsmen to an elderly guest sitting next to us. 'I'd have thought that one of your immigrations would have brought some criss-crossing variation or something that goes in lines.'

'In Dubrovnik, the only immigrants have been the Jews, and they dance in circles, too,' the old man replied.

It was past midnight when we left with the men from Portsmouth, and the musicians were still playing. After wending our way along the waterfront in a not very straight line, we left them at their yacht and continued on home. What a pleasure it was to come to a courtyard bathed in moonlight and look up at the ink-blue bowl studded with stars above us. We went up the silvery steps and I took Ivana's hand and pointed. 'Look. Can you see the Corona Borealis twinkling up there? Dionysus loved Ariadne so much that he put her bridal crown of jewels in the night sky for everyone to see.'

'Well, I can't remember you giving me any jewels for our wedding. All I ever got was that Magimix!'

Once in the bedroom, while Ivana rustled around the bathroom, I dropped my clothes on the floor and tumbled on to the crisp, cool sheets, thinking how wonderful it would be if we could live here for ever. Surely, with more evenings like this, it would all turn out well. Surely the community would accept us one day. The moonlight flickered through the shutters and on to the wall as I lay listening to the murmur of the sea mingling with the sound of the fishing boats creaking gently at rest, and drifted off to sleep.

CHAPTER 18

ISLAND
ROMANCE

In June, our friends Richard and Sophia came to stay. They had bought a house on the neighbouring island, and I had been over to help them buy it, but they were now having problems getting their title to it registered. As was often the case on the islands, their house had been abandoned around 1900 after *Peranospera*, the dreaded vine disease, had wiped out the vineyards of the Adriatic. It had created such a famine that nearly three quarters of the island population had been forced to leave the lands they had tilled for centuries and emigrate, mainly to the west coast of America where vineyards and fishing fleets needed men. Within ten years, the Vis population had reduced from 10,000 to 2,500, and a hundred years later the descendants of the owners of the abandoned houses often couldn't be traced. This, of course, threw up no end of problems when it came to conveyancing. Richard had paid for the house, but he couldn't register his ownership and the sellers couldn't pocket all the money until the missing branch of the family was found. Richard and Sophia had come over to Vis to meet the member of the family who was trying to track down the missing relatives.

As I sat on the terrace the next morning, munching my cornflakes and waiting for Richard, I felt an almost childish glee at not having to grab my breakfast and rush off to work. For the past thirty years, I'd never had time

131

for a proper breakfast or to chat with Ivana or the children. It was my own fault. I'd always been in such a rush. Looking back on it now, I realised I'd neglected to do an awful lot of things I should have done. I now feared that perhaps this lifetime of neglect was going to haunt me. I was already missing the children terribly, even though we rang them regularly (and they rang us often, too, to check that I hadn't lost their mother at sea). Ivana would talk to them first, to make sure they were OK for underwear, and when she'd finished I'd have long chats with them, but it just wasn't the same as seeing them.

My thoughts were interrupted by Richard coming out with his bowl of cereal. He sat down next to me and looked thoughtfully out to sea. 'Are you sure I won't get bored out here?' he said, almost to himself.

'I used to worry about that, too, but so far I haven't been bored for a moment.'

'Hmm. It's just that I do find it quite difficult to take things easy.'

'So did I when I arrived, old chap, but taking things easy seems to be my strong point these days. Maybe it always was, and I've spent my last thirty years in denial!'

Richard laughed, but he didn't look too convinced.

After breakfast, we went over to Marko's to meet the member of the family who was in a great state of excitement. The missing cousin had died some years ago, having had no children, he announced. Of course, Richard and I summoned up our suitably serious faces and began to express our condolences, but he threw up his hands, laughing. 'Now I am such happy man! Now I have all of money!'

Richard, being both a worrier and a lawyer, was hugely relieved, and, after downing a celebratory coffee with the man, we went off home. Passing the square by the Town Hall, we saw a crew of men pulling up flagstones and putting up a wooden construction and stopped to look. As usual, a collection of villagers were standing around telling the men how they should be doing their jobs, and Marko was among them. 'They say it will be an open-air café,' he told us, 'but how can a café pay for all this work? It would take ten years for my café to pay it off.'

'Look at that bar top,' said the local carpenter. 'That's polished Slovenian oak, a fortune's worth of wood!'

'And it's so wide you could dance on it!' said someone else.

'Maybe we'll have dancing girls on our island at last?' said the carpenter. 'I've been telling you for years, Marko. What you need to jazz up your old café is girls with no…'

Marko frowned and indicated the presence of Karmela and two other grannies, but Karmela hadn't heard the carpenter and was pointing to a sign that read 'Men at Work'.

'*Men* at work! Pah! There ought to be a sign outside every house in the village saying "Women at Work". That's all we ever do, while our men sit around and talk!'

'Be fair, Karmela,' said Bozo, who had joined the gathering. 'Look how I put up with my mother-in-law and help Nora with her whenever she's with us.'

Not accustomed to being challenged in public, Karmela shot him one of her eagle looks. 'Putting up with a mother-in-law once in a while, are we? Hah! Well, putting up with an awful lot all year round is all we women ever do!'

Bozo knew better than to argue back, and Marko, always the diplomat, quickly moved the discussion back to the construction work.

Richard and I left the discussion and continued on our way. At Dinko's, the town's newsagent and stationer, we went inside to buy a paper. Coming in from the bright sunshine, we couldn't see too well at first and didn't notice her, but, as our eyes got accustomed to the gloom, we realised that an exquisitely beautiful girl was behind the counter, the kind of dark-eyed, raven-haired beauty you see in perfume adverts standing in front of tropical waterfalls with a flower behind her ear. For some reason, she smiled at us, and the effect was instantaneous. It was as if the sun had burst from behind a cloud; it was the kind of smile that could make a traffic warden tear up a ticket or put a grin on the face of Gordon Brown – or even Boyana. It certainly stopped two late-middle-aged Englishmen dead in their tracks. Flustered, I took a sudden great interest in a magazine rack consisting entirely of car, truck and muscle-building magazines (men do tend to be rather uber-blokey down here), and from that vantage point I observed her surreptitiously. She had that pouty-lipped and slightly sulky expression common in those under twenty, but when she smiled her face was transformed into the face of a mischievous Botticelli angel. (Sexy, I suppose, is what I'm really trying to say.)

Richard stood there with his mouth open, and the girl, thinking something was amiss, asked if he needed any help. He stuttered something incomprehensible in English and I quickly mumbled something about forgetting my wallet and we left. We were back within the hour with a lot of urgent photocopying that needed to be done.

One of the benefits of being over fifty is that you can start up a conversation with a pretty girl without making them feel uncomfortable, and, over the swish and clunk of the photocopy machine, Tanya told us that she had finished university in Zagreb, but, as she hadn't been able to find a job, she was back with her parents again. The trouble with that, she confided, was that all the interesting young men on the island had gone to the mainland and the ones left behind were pretty limited. She also confided that she was worried she was taking it out on her father whom she adored. Richard and I made suitably avuncular noises and she gave a shrug of her delicate shoulders and pouted at us so delightfully that my knees almost gave way.

On the way home, we saw Ivana and Sophia talking with Marin on the quay.

'There's someone in the photocopy shop, who you've just got to meet,' I said to Marin.

'Oh, really?' he replied in an oddly off-hand way.

'She's the most beautiful girl I've ever seen,' added Richard.

'Maybe I've seen her already. I can't remember.'

'You'd remember if you saw this one!' said Richard. 'She looks like Penelope Cruz and she's got...'

Sophia shot him a look that stopped him in mid-sentence.

'I'll introduce you,' I said smugly. 'I'm on quite good terms with her, I think.'

'Thanks, but don't worry,' he said diffidently. 'I've probably seen her around already. You don't have any matt varnish, do you?'

'Er, I think I do somewhere. I'll have a look when I get home.'

He smiled politely, picked up his tool bag and left.

Our wives rounded on us.

134

'How could you both be so insensitive?' said Ivana.

'Couldn't you see the look on his face when you were going on about her figure, Richard?' said Sophia. 'How can you be so dense?'

'Um…!'

'Poor Marin. He looked so embarrassed. Wasn't it obvious he was already keen on her? Couldn't you see he was trying to change the conversation?'

'Er, no, not really.'

The wives went off, tutting to each other.

'Are we really that insensitive?' I asked Richard.

'Hmm, I always thought I wasn't entirely without emotional awareness.'

'Maybe the know-how fades when it's not your bag anymore?'

'Well, as no one's fancied me for so long, it probably has,' sighed Richard.

'Oh, I don't know. As late-middle-aged men go, we still cut quite a dash, don't you think? There must be some out there who still find the weathered Sanders of the River type something of a turn-on.'

'Well, you've certainly got the right baggy shorts, but I must say that I've always put you down as more of a Graham Greene colonial-seeking-solace-in-the-bottle type.'

'Thanks.'

'But we shouldn't delude ourselves. We might think we're wearing pretty well, but, as the saying goes, we're just about invisible to anyone we might fancy.'

'Suppose you're right,' I said. 'Here I am thinking I look like a slightly jaded version of Ralph Fiennes, but what I really look like is a silly, sad, old sod.'

'Sad, yes. Old, yes. Silly, certainly,' said Richard, laughing. 'Look at the two of us! Two sad old gits in our M&S "Blue Harbour" summer wear still thinking that someone might fancy us. What could be sadder than that?'

We went home to get a drink.

As usual in these matters, the wives were right, and during the week I noticed that Marin was spending most of his time at the café beside Dinko's stationery shop rather than at Marko's, his usual haunt. But Marin had competition. The word had quickly spread that Tanya was there, and a steady stream of young men were coming into the shop and they didn't look the sort who were too interested in stationery products.

A few days later, the four of us were sitting at Marko's when Marin came up to ask if I needed any odd jobs done during the winter.

'It seems such a long way to come for very little money,' I said. 'It wouldn't really be worth your while coming down from Sarajevo.'

Richard agreed.

As soon as he had gone, our wives rounded on us again.

'How can you always fail to see anything? Isn't it obvious he's got another reason for coming here in the winter? What's wrong with you men? Honestly! How did you two ever manage to make a living?'

'Well, we're both action men, not cognitive conceptualists,' I answered huffily. 'Names like John Wayne and Clint Eastwood rather than Graham Norton and Sigmund Freud come to people's minds when my friend Richard and I are mentioned.'

Richard and I went off to console ourselves with some of Zoran's beer. I do find beer such a help when it comes to understanding matters beyond my usual ken, and over two of Zoran's *Karlovacs* we came to two conclusions. One – that we were perhaps a bit slow on the uptake when it came to matters of the heart. Two – that our wives seldom missed an opportunity to point out our failings.

Despite the smoke-screen of insensitivity that he habitually deployed, Zoran didn't miss much, and he quickly spotted that something was up with Marin. I caught him in the street outside Dinko's pretending to adjust his bicycle seat but surreptitiously peering inside. I came up quietly behind him and said, 'I saw you!'

Zoran jumped, but quickly regained his composure. 'Just checkin' what Marin's gettin' himself into,' he drawled. 'She was a little stringy thing goin' off to college last time I saw her, but she sure looks OK today!'

Bozo was coming across the square and Zoran beckoned him over. 'Have you seen Dedo and Draga's girl?'

'The skinny one who went off to Zagreb, you mean?'

'Yes. That's the one. Take a look in the shop.'

He went inside and emerged a moment later to give a low whistle and say the equivalent in Croatian of 'Cor stripe me pink!'

136

Marin's rivals still trailed in and out of the shop, but he stepped up his presence as if staking out a territorial claim, and every few days he asked our advice. We found ourselves watching the progress of his suit with certain vicarious pleasure. Their youth, their affection and Marin's plans for their future together made us feel quite parental – a mixture of happiness and concern – and in a funny way it gave us our first feeling of belonging to our new community.

I had given a lot of thought to the matter of 'belonging' since arriving here. Strangely enough, the house never gave me a sense that it 'belonged' to me. I might have renovated it, given it a new roof and rebuilt the sea wall, but I never felt I possessed it. It felt more as if it was keeping an eye on me. The stones I had laid, the pillars I had erected, the balconies and porticos I had rebuilt were just watching me while I eked out my time here, and it gave me rather an eerily existential feeling. I know that London has been around for just as long, but somehow it never gave me the same sense of mortality and continuity of life – it certainly didn't in Fulham. But, standing here on the terrace, wherever I looked there were reminders of the passing centuries – outlines of settlements, Roman ruins, terraces of ancient vines, remains of fortifications – and, when the traces of life's continuity are so omnipresent, it's hard not to feel that you have a place in the continuum, whether your name is Stancomb or Stankovic.

Late in June, we were on the balcony watching the sun go down when we saw Marin and Tanya walking along the promontory. With the lowering red sun behind them, they resembled cut-out silhouettes; Marin so tall and broad-shouldered and Tanya so slim and lissom. It was as if they were taking part in a Biblical play about the love of Ruth and Boaz and the awesomely beautiful surroundings were just there to provide them with a backdrop.

'Now, there's a union that must have been destined,' said Ivana, as Marin bent to kiss Tanya's forehead. 'Do you think we looked as romantic walking hand in hand down the Kings Road in our flares?'

We went inside, took down the photo albums, and sat on the sofa to see. In fact, Ivana did look quite the part (very Ali McGraw in *Love Story*), but I had to admit, I did rather let the side down – more like Worzel Gummidge than Ryan O'Neal.

Flipping through the pages, Ivana gave one of her wifely sighs. 'Why do you always have to look like you've just escaped from a prison camp? You're even worse since coming out here. Just look at you!'

'I'll dress like Rab C. Nesbitt if I want to,' I replied grumpily. 'One of my earliest ambitions was to be a POW in Colditz and escape with Douglas Bader and his pals disguised as a Bulgarian grandmother or a Dutch turnip salesman. My clothes might be slightly out of date, but I'm going to get a lot more mileage out of them. So there!'

'You really are impossible! None of my friends have husbands who carry on like this. Whatever did I see in you? I should have married that nice Rafa who played polo and was so good to his mother.'

There followed more cross words and threats to burn my favourite corduroys (in perfectly good condition apart from the knees), but I let it ride. Since coming out here, that kind of psychological coercion and threats of banishment from the bedchamber had been falling on increasingly deaf ears.

'Anyway,' I answered defiantly, 'the way I dress makes me feel at home with the guys at Zoran's who have a similar taste to mine in practical attire and manly footwear.'

With a snort she'd learned from Karmela, Ivana left the room.

CHAPTER 19

LOST IN TRANSLATION

The ability to learn languages seems to be as natural to Slavs as it is unnatural to the British, but inhabitants of Vis, being islanders, were the exception to the rule. Some of the young ones and those like Zoran and Marko who had travelled spoke English, but, to communicate with anyone else, I had to speak Croatian.

The bar-proppers were surprised when I told them that Ivana wasn't teaching me the language and repeated the oft-quoted adage that the best way to learn a language is in bed. What I didn't tell them was that Ivana had started to teach me, but it was soon apparent that she was not made to be an ideal teacher, nor I an ideal pupil. Our lessons had rapidly turned into the most frightful arguments, and, for the sake of harmony in the home, I thought it best to stick to my trusty Croatian primer.

I actually spoke four other languages and considered myself a fair linguist, but, when I started on Croatian, I realised I was not the linguist I thought I was.

But mistakes always gave me trouble. Trying to show how good I was to the crowd at Zoran's, I told them I was off to fix a mechanical problem on the boat using the future conditional. I was greeted by a gale of laughter and snorts and told that I had just said I was off to copulate with the boat mechanic.

Another problem was not being able to tell if someone was joking.

Deadpan humour is very much part of Croatian conversation, and unless someone laughed or smiled I never got it. I was getting better, detecting a slant of an eye, a movement of the chin, a deflection of the hand, but mostly I took what was said at face value and felt very silly when it turned out to be a joke. Then I suppose humour has always been the most subtle form of human communication – the dents in our kitchen wall from flying objects bear witness that, even after thirty years, Ivana is still able to misconstrue the tender affection hidden in my witty ripostes.

My improved Croatian also meant that I was now able to eavesdrop on conversations. One evening, when Grandma Klakic was sitting on the steps outside our door with some of her family, I heard her granddaughter, Mira, reading aloud from a magazine. It was about a mother who had caught her son wearing his sister's underwear. The aunties were tutting and the teenagers were giggling.

'I'd sort him out in no time,' said Grandma K. 'Send him down to me and after a week of working in my fields he wouldn't want to be a girl anymore! Boys are just spoiled these days. With no men's work to do around the house any more, all they do is look at fashion magazines and other rubbish! No wonder they don't know who they are. Sister's underwear! Pah!'

'And what do children have to worry about these days, anyway?' said one of the aunties. 'Their schooling's free and their parents do everything for them. All they have to worry about is buying the right clothes!'

'That's not fair, *Baka* [Grandma],' said Mira, a nice-looking girl with a smiley face. 'You don't know what pressures we have at school these days. Anyway, I'm sure when you were our age you were always dressing up for the promenade so the boys would notice you.'

Grandma Klakic allowed herself a chortle (a rare occurrence). 'You cheeky little Missy!'

'I bet you did!' Mira giggled. 'I bet you wore one of those silly big hats and walked up and down in front of *Nonno* [Grandpa] hoping he'd notice you! And I bet you were always saying to Baka Zora, "Please let me buy a new frock! Please!"'

Grandma Klakic's hatchet face splintered into a smile and she put an arm round her granddaughter to hug her. 'Mira, *dusa*, you are my sweetest little pudding and I know you work so hard at school. We are all so proud of you.'

The hug made Mira drop the magazine and her gangly fourteen-year-old brother picked it up and started to read it. She snatched it back and whacked him over the head with it.

'You're not old enough for things like that!'

The brother pulled a face, but, not wanting to tangle with his older sister, moved two steps down and sulked.

The letter now prompted a heated discussion among the aunties about contemporary morality. I didn't understand everything, but a summary of the findings of the select committee seemed to be:

1. The young have too soft a life and don't know the meaning of the word 'suffering'.
2. All they do is smoke cigarettes and dress up in provocative clothes.
3. They never help their mothers in the kitchen or their fathers in the field.
4. Life in the cities is so peculiar these days, it's no wonder that mothers are coming home to find their sons dressing up as Doris Day.

By the end of June, I thought my Croatian was good enough to talk to a technician without Ivana's help, and, when the rain started coming through the garden wall and turning my lawn into a pond, I went on my own to talk to Constantin, the engineer Marko recommended.

It was a glorious evening when I set off with my dictionary in my pocket. At this time of day, the winegrowers on their motorised wheelbarrows were wending their weary way home o'er the lea, and, the road being too narrow for overtaking, I had to follow behind at a stately ten miles an hour with ample time to admire my surroundings. The sun was lowering over the peaks and the heat haze rippled like gauze over the terraced hills. The view around me was a harmony of landscape and man. The greatest charm of the Dalmatian Coast is that, even though the hills and shores are wild, it gives you a sense that man has always been there. Everywhere you look there is something to remind you of our passing – crumbling farmsteads, abandoned settlements, ancient terraces. Quite moving really, if you're that way inclined.

The sun was well over the hills when I left the car in the hamlet below Constantin's farm and started the trek up. Looking out across the slopes to the sea as I walked, I realised that there was something else special about the Adriatic landscape; there were no grand towering mountains, sweeps of sandy beaches or unbroken expanses of ocean, and there was always something for the eye to hold on to to give you a sense of proportion – a harbour wall, a tiny hillside hamlet, a monastery on a shore, a cluster of fishing boats in a cove – and it was all so welcoming.

Reaching Constantin's yard, I saw a prize collection of rusty farm implements, metal pipes and bent sheets of corrugated iron, and at the far end, by a stack of old bedsprings overgrown with morning glory, was a dozing donkey, its head hanging down, and chickens pecking in the dust around it. The door of the farmhouse was open, so I knocked and went in. The single large room was dark and beamed, and every available surface was piled so high with books and papers that I didn't see Constantin until he appeared from behind one of them. A slight man in his early forties wearing braces and a faded denim shirt, he had short prematurely grey hair that stood up brush-like, and a sharp alert face framed by pebble glasses. He came across the room with the precise, measured step of someone whose every movement was forethought.

'Mr Anthony, I presume!' he said in perfect English, and when I hesitated he said, 'I believe you are supposed to reply, "Dr Constantin, I presume!"'

We laughed and shook hands.

'I didn't know you spoke English. I've been practising my drainage terms all the way up!'

His grey eyes twinkled behind the glasses. 'Yes, Marko has told me about your problem.'

'I can do some rough drawings of what I think is happening, and then you can draw in what you think we should do,' I said, jumping ahead as usual.

'No, no! Not so quickly. First we will talk, then we will go to measure, then we will draw. Come now. You must help me select the wine that we will drink while we talk.'

We went out into the yard and found the donkey now mooching disconsolately against the large barn door. Constantin pushed it aside and heaved the door open. The space was large and high-raftered with walls blackened by age and smoke. Against one wall was a stack of wine bottles and against the others were jars of pickled paprika stacked three deep. I'd never seen anything like it. Not even a Sainsbury's supermarket depot could have had so many. It could warrant a mention in the *Guinness Book of Records*.

'What do you do with all this paprika?'

He looked at me over his glasses as if I had asked a silly question. 'I eat it.'

'But this is a five-year supply for a family of ten!'

'Paprika is full of nutrition,' he said and shrugged.

Back in the house, he poured the wine, sliced the bread, cut slivers from a large smoked ham, and we sat on the terrace to talk about the problem. When we had got as far as we could, I asked about his background. He told me he had been brought up on the island by fervent communist parents, and had joined the party himself when he went to university in Zagreb.

'As you can imagine, it came as a surprise when it all suddenly ended. After all those years of being told what to do and what to think, it was something of a shock when we suddenly found ourselves free of everything. Just as children can't imagine life outside the schoolyard, it was difficult for us to think of our lives without it. We'd never thought of a world outside the system. It was like being without an umbrella. In that way, communism solved a lot of problems.'

He took a sip from his glass and looked across the hills. The green vines contouring the slopes had deepened in the evening mist, the swallows dipped in and out of the peach trees in the fields below us, and in the distance the sea stretched out a silvery-grey expanse with faint shapes of other islands on the horizon. We sat in companionable silence listening to the rustling of the fruit trees and the bees buzzing on their last evening foray in the lavender. A cracked bell in the hamlet church struck eight.

Constantin broke the silence. 'But we really did want to make it work, you know.'

'Make what work?'

'Communism, of course. Oh, how we all waved our little red flags. We loved the colour so much, we almost wore pink underpants!' He laughed. 'And now it's all gone. Pouf! Just like that!'

He took another sip and I made sympathetic noises.

'But the greatest blow was to realise that, all the time we'd been waving our little flags, our Glorious Comrade Leaders had been focused on their next Mercedes and the stripper they'd set up in a flat in Dubrovnik.' He let out a long sigh and got up to fetch another bottle. We had eaten all the bread and ham that he'd cut, but he was too lost in thought to think about cutting any more. I eyed the loaf, badly in need of something to underpin the amount of wine we were getting through.

'But, you know what?' said Constantin, sitting down again. 'It felt good to be part of a great ideal. I really miss that.'

I felt I ought to say something encouraging. (A few glasses of someone's wine never fails to give me a particularly warm feeling towards them.) 'I think the same feelings must have been going through the mind of Piers Ploughman when he looked out over the Lincolnshire vales… a yearning for the old days… a welling of emotion for how things had been… a feeling of confusion…' But I realised I had lost my audience. Constantin was gazing into the distance.

'Bastards! And all that time the party chiefs had just been working the system for themselves!'

I made more mumbling sounds.

'Did you have any political heroes when you were a young man?' he asked.

'Well, we don't really take our leaders too seriously in England, but I once saw Michael Foot speaking and that was pretty stirring. With his shock of white hair, he looked like an Old Testament prophet, and there was something about him that touched a chord. He gave you the feeling that he was bringing the tablets down from the mountains.'

'Did you ever see any of the Americans speaking?'

'Only on TV, but all that "I had a dream…" and "Ask not what your country can do for you…" stuff was quite impressive even on TV. All we've got in England these days are blokes like Cameron, Clegg and Miliband. Have you seen them?'

144

He shook his head.

'Nice boys, but who'd follow men like that into the trenches?'

We spent the rest of the time discussing the problems of the world and mourning our lost ideals – and got steadily more sloshed. But there on a terrace overlooking the Adriatic on a warm summer evening, all was well in the world for an ex-communist Croatian and a woolly English liberal.

By midnight, we had settled most of the world's problems and come up with a raft of projects that we'd do together. Constantin suggested that I spent the night on his sofa, and given the amount I'd drunk I considered it, but knowing that Ivana would be lying in bed imagining Bozo in a killer Skoda coming down the road towards me hunched like Mr Toad behind the wheel, I thought I'd better get myself back home.

I stumbled down the hill and, after blundering into various gorse bushes, managed to locate the car and, having eventually found the right place to insert the ignition key, I lurched off down the track. Luckily, at that time of night, there weren't any other cars on the road when I got to it, but I do remember feeling rather anxious about the width of the tarmac.

Why weren't there more people like Constantin on the island? I asked myself, as I weaved unsteadily down to the village with my befuddled mind trying to piece the evening together. The answer was obvious, even at that time of night. Constantin belonged to a new generation who knew something of the world and weren't frightened by outsiders. But they had all gone to work in the cities, and the island had been left with an aging population of grouchy old stick-in-the-muds (people like me, come to think about it).

The next day, I asked around about the special nutritional properties of pickled paprika, but no one seemed to know anything about it. I was going to have to do some further research. I rather liked the idea of the pickled paprika business with Constantin. I could see us strutting around international pickled paprika conventions posing as pickled paprika magnates and pontificating about the finer points of paprika pickling. It could be a definite goer.

Karmela said that, despite his political past, Constantin should be in the Town Hall. 'They wouldn't be doing all those stupid things they do if he was there. He's the cleverest man on the island, that young Constantin. But he was such a weak child when he was little. All skin and bones he was. But his mother fed him well, even though they were poor. She had to borrow the money to do it, but she made him egg custards and strained meat to make him beef juice. And he always studied so hard at school, he did; unlike that fat, lazy sister of his who never gets off her sofa except to go and buy herself cakes at the corner store. Pah! And he never wasted his time running around after silly girls in Split like those cousins of his – that fool Josip and that lying toad Simeon who went to prison last year for stealing his mother's car. No, Constantin was always studying or helping his mother. I can't think why he's still not married.'

'Hmm. Don't you think he might be a kind of a Switzerland where relationships are concerned?'

Karmela gave me a funny look and scuttled off into the garden.

CHAPTER 20

A PROJECT
AT LAST?

I was now spending a lot of time on my Internet cooking course, but I still hadn't found premises. I thought I'd found one some weeks earlier when an old fisherman agreed to let me have his place if I gave him a year's rent up front, but, after some covert investigation (I didn't want to lay myself open to global ribbing from Ranko quite yet), I found that no restaurants were allowed in that part of the village. The crafty old codger had known that all along and was just trying to get the year's rent out of me before I found out. I confronted him about it, but all I got was a gap-toothed grin and a shrug.

In need of some sympathy, I went home to tell Ivana, but as she wasn't there I told Karmela instead. But I should have known that Karmela wasn't in the business of dispensing pity, and what I got instead was the most frightful fustigation for ignoring her advice about doing business with fishermen. When she'd finished, she pointed a knobbly finger at me and said, 'And you make sure your children never marry anyone from a fisherman's family. Danilo Matusek let his girl marry a fisherman's boy last year and he's never seen a cent from all the money he gave them for a share in their laundrette. Not a cent!'

I promised to watch the children vigilantly, but she hadn't finished with me.

147

'And I just don't know what's going to happen when Marin and Tanya get engaged. That mother of hers is such a mean one. When the school went swimming, she never even let my grandchildren borrow her daughters' rubber rings. There'll be precious little she'll part with when it comes to the marriage settlement, I can tell you.' She gave one of her snorts.

'Don't worry, Karmela. I'll be Marin's coach when it comes to that.'

Karmela sniffed and went off to bang some pots around in the scullery.

Still trying to get Ivana enthused about my restaurant idea, I was talking about it in the car when she suddenly sat up in her seat. 'I know! We should start a vineyard, not a restaurant! Look at all the vineyards around us! That's what they've been doing here since time began – making wine; not cooking!'

'Steady the Buffs! We don't know anything about winegrowing.'

'I'm sure we can learn.'

'Did I hear you say *we*, my sweet pea? I don't see you with a jaunty red kerchief tied round your pretty head tossing around pitchforks of vine leaves or bouncing baskets of grapes about on your none too ample hips. Are you assuming that *I'll* be doing all the work?'

'I'm sure we could hire someone.'

'Well, as fishing seems to be the only other island occupation and I don't want to end up with a complexion like a fisherman, I suppose it's a vineyard then. There'll certainly be enough land for sale. Marko says no one wants to farm these days.'

I warmed to the idea as I drove towards the village, picturing myself leaning against farm gates with gnarled fellow winegrowers on warm summer evenings, complaining about leaf spot, grape droop and the weather.

'And having a vineyard will be a great way of fitting into the community,' said Ivana. 'Much better than running a restaurant!'

By the time we got home, I was picturing myself striding down my vineyard rows on dewy morns wearing Polo Ralph Lauren britches and one of those Harrison Ford hats, and by the evening I saw myself sitting on the harbour benches with the other seasoned winegrowers exchanging wise words about the future harvest and knowledgably discussing sugar content and acidity levels. And what about the movie with Joaquin Phoenix playing Zoran, the rough and ready *patron* with the heart of gold, Colin Firth playing the understanding priest, and a guest appearance by myself as the slightly jaded but still winsomely attractive winegrower who is secretly fancied by the Mayor's daughter?

Ivana was right again. It was so obvious. The islanders were winegrowers. How would they not accept us once we were fellow winegrowers? A new path had opened up, and it could be a lot of fun. Why hadn't we thought of it before?

The next day, I drove up to Constantin.

'That's just the kind of project I was thinking of,' he said, screwing the top on to yet another jar of pickled paprika.

'I was hoping you'd say that. I know absolutely nothing about winegrowing.'

His eyes glittered behind his specs. 'The conditions here are ideal for strong wine. The sun provides the heat to warm the rocky soil and the porous limestone absorbs the rain and stores it up for the roots to suck up later. Before the *Peranospera* blight killed our vines, the island was covered in their terraces. Half of them have been here since the time of Christ, and we were producing more wine here than in any other place on in the Mediterranean. But after the blight, with most of the population gone, we've only cultivated the low land. It's about 25 per cent of what we used to grow.'

He poured me some wine and we drank to our new venture. 'With the few acres I've got here and a few more on richer soil, together we'll make some really good wine! And we should make it organic. That'll make it something special and we'll get a better grant from the EU. You need a grant to start a vineyard these days, anyway. A new vineyard isn't commercially viable without one.' He gestured to the Renault. 'And, by the look of your car, you're going to need as big a grant as you can get!'

So the plan was laid and we had our partner. All we needed now was the land and the grant, so the next day Ivana rang the Ministry of Agriculture about the grant, while Constantin and I went off to scout out some suitable land.

Ivana had no luck with the Ministry, but discovered that they were shortly sending a fact-finding mission to Vis. I went round to the Town Hall to see if I could arrange to meet them, but the Mayor wasn't too keen. However, when I heard him telling one of his men that he didn't have enough transport to take them up to the farms, I quickly offered the services of the Renault, and got his agreement.

As soon as the delegation arrived, we set off for the hills in a cavalcade of two – the one municipal mini-van that was in working order and the Renault. Twenty minutes later, we arrived at the farm of Old Sime, a local veteran farmer and winegrower. His farmyard could have been mistaken for the stage set of a punk opera. Its walls were so covered in dung that it looked like someone had applied it with a trowel, and in the middle of the yard was a car, a washing machine and a muck-spreader that seemed to have collided together to form the kind of sculpture you see at the Tate Modern. Further along was a collection of rusty Ukrainian tractors leaning drunkenly against each other with vertical exhaust pipes sticking forlornly into the air as if trying to intercept messages from outer space. Behind them was the sheep pen where Old Sime, whose face bore evidence of a lifetime of toiling under the sun and behind a flock of farting sheep, seemed quite unconcerned with our arrival. He went on squelching about in his boots and left the delegation to range themselves gingerly around the pen trying to dodge the splashes and asking questions. He grunted his replies to them over his shoulder and continued shovelling.

Twenty minutes later, I was driving back to the village squashed into the Renault with four baffled functionaries and a disconsolate Mayor. The Mayor, who had been counting on Old Sime to toe the line and say what subsidies he and other farmers needed, was apologising profusely for his lack of cooperation. Old Sime's indifference puzzled me, too, but that evening, after the delegation had left on the ferry and the cabal gathered at the bar, Zoran put the matter into perspective.

'You can't expect a man knee deep in sheep shit, and knowing that's where he's going to stay for the rest of his life, to take much interest in men in suits talking about some new legislation that's only going to be changed again when the next lot get voted in.'

'Yes, he's seen it all before,' said Zvonko. 'He knows that, once they've done their bit of championing the Croatian farmer today, they'll be back in Zagreb tomorrow with the Croatian farmer forgotten and worrying about the down payment on their next Mercedes and their wife's Botox treatment.'

'But surely it would be better for Old Sime if they got the policy right, even if only for a year or two,' I interjected.

'What do you care? You don't belong here,' came a voice from the end of the bar. I'd seen the man before, a foxy-faced chap with one of those pudding-bowl haircuts you see in forties war movies.

Ivana turned on him, claws fully extended. 'My family have lived in this country for as long as...'

Zoran stepped swiftly between them and ushered Ivana outside. Coming back in again, he went over to the man. 'That was damned rude of you, Bruno. You should be ashamed of yourself. How can you talk to your neighbours like that? That's not *kulturni*!' (The word 'un-cultured' was a grave insult in Communist days.)

The man looked sheepish and mumbled something into his beer.

Ivana came back inside and smouldered on the other side of the room. I went over to the man, who was now as embarrassed as I was, and tried to explain that it was as natural to take an interest in your local politics as it was in your local football team. I think he got my point – at least I got a grunted half-apology – but he evaded any further discussion by retreating behind his beer and a screen of Walter Wolf smoke. Ivana was glaring at him as if he was an insect pinned to a board, so I thought it best to take her home and leave Zoran to pour oil on troubled waters.

'That man was incredibly rude. I felt like hitting him,' she said as soon as we were outside.

'That was fairly evident.'

'And he only lives in the next street; so it isn't as if he didn't know who we were.'

'Yes, that was the worrying part. But you needn't have gone at him like that. You must try to control yourself. We can't afford to antagonise anyone.'

'Well, he was rude to us first, and we shouldn't put up with that kind of thing. We should stand up for ourselves.'

'That's just what we shouldn't do, for heaven's sake! That's just the way to start a conflict. They're standoffish enough as it is, without you starting a war.'

'You shouldn't be so ingratiating. People take advantage of you.'

'Well, I'm only nice to people I need to be nice to,' I said crossly.

'I call that ingratiating.'

'Call it what you want, but, like it or not, that's what we'll have to do until we're accepted.'

'Well, if they're going to take that kind of attitude when all we're doing is taking an interest in what's going on, *I'm* not going to turn the other cheek, and you shouldn't either!'

By the time we arrived home, the argument had petered out. Our arguments seldom came to any particular resolution. Like most people who have co-habited for a long time, our arguments usually faded away and, by the time they recommenced, both of us would have slightly shifted our view-points.

Karmela, who had seen us talking with the delegation, arrived the next morning with her granite faced etched with concern.

'I'm sure it's not the same with your politicians in England, but, whatever our politicians promise, they never do. Don't you believe a word of anything they tell you.'

I refrained from saying that it wasn't really that different back home. I didn't want to spoil the image they have here of well-dressed, polite Englishmen sitting around in Westminster smoking pipes, drinking cups of tea and earnestly deliberating how to make the world a better place. I think we ought to keep that image going.

That afternoon, Ivana rang the Ministry on the number the delegation had given me, but the man she talked to was curt and unhelpful. Before they would even look at an application, he said, we had to belong to the Croatian Winegrowers Association, and, because we were foreigners, the British Government would have to vouch for us. 'This will involve several different departments,' he said with evident pleasure, 'and, as we are accustomed to applicants who already have vineyards and you don't, how can we process your application with no production figures to back it up?'

We rang off and looked at each other in despond. Without a vineyard, we couldn't get a grant and, without a grant, we couldn't get a vineyard. Another Catch 22 situation.

That afternoon, determined to start some kind of ball rolling, we went to the Town Hall to apply for membership of the Vis Winegrowers Association. But even that wasn't easy. We first had to belong to two other associations, we were told by a woman who looked like an unbaked loaf, before she slapped some forms on the counter. By the end of an hour's form-filling, I realised we were no match for the Croatian Civil Service. It looked like it would be some time before anyone would be suffering a hangover from Stancomb Pinot Noir.

Would any of our ideas ever see the light of day?

And yet another week had gone by and still no sign of Luka the cricketer.

It was hot that night as I lay in bed worrying about the lack of progress with any of my projects. I tried to focus on the good side of island life – the beauty, the food, the boating, the fun and the few friends we'd made, but I kept coming back to the surly faces of Boyana, the fishermen and the unbaked loaf. Hearing Ivana turning over, I said to the ceiling, 'If the bloody village is never going to accept us, maybe we should go back home and look for something with a few acres in the Home Counties?'

Ivana murmured something about things looking better in the morning and slipped back into sleep while I continued to fret.

I was still fretting next morning when we walked to the market. 'If I don't get started on something soon, it's going to get me down,' I said peevishly. 'And, if only I had something to get on with, I'd have someone to moan to. I used to have my cricket mates to moan to on weekends, but the only person I've got now is you! I'd have had a captive audience for another twenty years if I'd carried on playing cricket.'

'Rubbish! You won't be playing much longer. Look at the trouble you've got with your shoulder, and what about your knee?'

'Well, apart from that, I'm in pretty good shape compared to most of my contemporaries, and you can go on playing cricket for ever. W.G. Grace played until he was sixty-six and Charles Absolom of Fulham took 206 wickets in one season when he was seventy-six.'

'Go on. You can hardly bend any of your joints properly these days. You're almost fit for the scrap-heap. I should have married that polo player. He had a nice hairy chest and arms like tree trunks. I bet he still does press-ups.'

CHAPTER 21

MISPLACED ECOLOGY

We were in the middle of yet another of our circular telephone conversations
with the Ministry when I heard Mr Samka and his team of hefties arriving
in the courtyard. (Despite the advance payment, it had taken some time for
them to get round to us.) We quickly ended the conversation and hurried
down to where the men were lining up their entrenching tools along the
wall like surgeons lining up their instruments. Mr Samka introduced us to
his team and they started to inspect the terrain – a celebration of all things
masculine. Walls were tapped with wooden handles, flagstones were marked
with chalk, calculations were made on scraps of paper and the suitability of
various tools was debated. They then rolled up their sleeves, picked up their
pickaxes and were about to start when a diminutive figure in khaki fatigues
carrying a large sieve appeared in the entrance and announced herself as the
representative of the Ministry of Heritage. Neat and trim with cropped hair
and John Lennon glasses, she had a small sharp face that would have looked
quite pretty in a gamine sort of way if it weren't for her ferocious expression.

'Ha!' said Mr Samka out of the corner of his mouth. 'I know the type.
The bane of any sanitation man wanting to do an honest day's work!'

The burlies eyed her suspiciously, too, but unperturbed by the glower
factor, she proceeded to sweep every cubic inch of earth they dug into her
dustpan and sieve it. This made the digging painstakingly slow and for

much of the time the men had nothing to do except lean on their pickaxes and glower, so, trying to keep things off the boil, I chatted to her while she sieved and learned that there had been a fishing settlement here until our villa was built on top of it in the sixteenth century. However, when I asked her about our present drainage system, she wrinkled her nose contemptuously. 'Merely eighteenth century,' she sniffed.

On the second day, Mr Samka arrived with his florid face knotted in concern. 'Last night, I dreamed that she discovered some ruins.'

'Wouldn't that be rather interesting?' said Ivana.

Mr Samka looked at her in disbelief. 'Can't you imagine what will happen then?' he spluttered. 'Even if it's just a lot of old pots and pans that some housewife very sensibly threw away five hundred years ago, it'd mean a complete stop to everything while the entire Archaeological Department from Zagreb descend on us like a pack of seagulls on to a shoal of sardines. They'd probably suspend our project indefinitely.'

'Oh, they wouldn't go as far as that, would they?'

'Oh, yes they would! You don't know the Ministry. Their hearts are as black as my mother-in-law's soul.'

We were having lunch the next day when we heard a commotion in the courtyard and hurried downstairs. The woman from the Heritage was hopping about in the trench, excitedly taking photos. She looked up as we approached and, with a hitherto unseen air of command, held up a hand.

'Mind where you step! These are the walls of the medieval settlement.'

I looked down and saw a stubbly line of stones. It didn't look like much.

'It's a priceless find!' she enthused, scrambling up from the trench. 'And, if I could do some research and write it up, it could make my name in the world of archaeology!' She wiped her mud-spattered glasses and smiled conspiratorially up at me as if we were colleagues.

Surprised by this sudden familiarity, I tried to think of something encouraging. 'You could send the photos to museums and magazines. I've got a friend in the British Museum, if that's any help.'

She beamed up at me. Full of enthusiasm, she really did look rather attractive.

'And what about getting the *National Geographic* down?' I went on. 'If you make enough noise about it, your face might end up on the front of *Archaeology Today!*'

Enthusiasm is an infectious thing, and even the burlies were now taking an interest. She gave me her camera and I snapped away as she posed coquettishly beside them. It was then that I noticed Mr Samka glowering away at the end of the courtyard. I motioned to Ivana and we went over to him.

'Just what I feared. Bloody ruins! I can't knock the damned things down and I can't run a drain over them.'

'Why not?' asked Ivana.

His face took on a pained expression. 'Water doesn't run uphill; that's why,' he replied rather sharply. 'And that midget from the Ministry is clearly hell-bent on doing her second PhD on the wretched stones. God only knows what this is going to do to my work schedule!'

Just as he was about to voice his thoughts publicly, our next-door neighbour (under whose house the drain was going) came into the courtyard. A stocky seventy-year-old with a face nearly as fierce as Karmela's, Grandma Volov stopped in front of Mr Samka and put her hands on her hips.

'My cousin Josip tells me that I'll get damp in my konoba if you put your drain under it.'

'Whoever told you that doesn't know what he's talking about!' snapped Mr Samka. 'A drainpipe under a konoba creates no damp at all.'

'I don't care what you say. I can't risk getting a damp konoba. My mother-in-law has had one all her life and what a Calvary that's been for her. A lifetime of damp linen she's had to put up with, poor soul. She has to hang everything in the kitchen to get it dry. It's even there when we go for Christmas lunch. You won't find me living like that. You'll just have to put your drain somewhere else, and there's an end to it!'

She turned on her heel and stomped out without waiting for Mr Samka's reply.

Mr Samka's face turned from its customary red to the colour of a purple King Edward potato. 'My workforce and I,' he stuttered, 'have become subject to the whims of ill-informed women and government jack-in-offices. This is an insult to my department!'

We took him upstairs and I poured him a *rakija* while Ivana sat him on the sofa.

156

'I don't care what we have to do or what it costs, Mr Samka,' said Ivana, 'but you're going to get rid of that cesspit!'

'That is not the only issue!' he replied irately. 'It is a matter of principle. My department and I will not be pushed around!'

'Look,' I whispered to Ivana, 'if we're not careful, they'll be arguing about it forever. Unless we can find a solution that saves Mr Samka's face, we'll be sitting here with no drains at all until next Michaelmas.'

I poured Mr Samka another *rakija* and listened as he vented his spleen about government interference, inter-departmental duplicity and the state of modern democracy. But, two glasses later, his spleen somewhat mollified, he started to draw up a new plan and work out the cost. Twenty minutes later, I looked at the figure he'd come up with and I wished I'd had three *rakijas*, too. The existing plan had already eaten up our whole yearly budget and this was another 30 per cent on top. I took a deep breath and told him to go ahead.

Two days later, the new trench had breached the sea wall and the next morning Mr Samka came wheezing up the steps with a big smile on his face. 'At last a stroke of luck!' he panted as he sat down to catch his breath. 'The midget from the Ministry has to go back to head office for a few days!'

'Can we carry on unsupervised?'

'Ha! She had the nerve to ask me to stop the work until she returned, but I set her straight on that one all right. "This project is private, not municipal," I told her. "We're not a communist state any more, in case you hadn't noticed." That set her back on her heels. These days, you need a warrant to stop work on a private project, and she knows it.' He leaned forward conspiratorially. 'Once she's gone, I'll get the boys to do some overtime, and the whole trench will be dug by the time she's back. Ha!'

'But what about the sieving?'

He chuckled. 'I think she did ask me to sieve, and I think I might have said something about incorporating it into our schedule.' He chuckled again and slapped his knee. 'But our job is to dig, and dig we will! No time to stand around sieving!'

True to his word, Mr Samka had his team out from seven in the morning till seven at night, and the trench forged along the waterfront like in a Roadrunner cartoon with spades, earth and flagstones flying up on either side. Three days later, the woman returned from the Ministry and Mr Samka was there to greet her, looking very pleased with himself. 'And I can assure you,' he said with a straight face, 'that every piece of earth was carefully inspected.'

'Another instance of "subtle island diplomacy", don't you think?' said Zoran that evening.

(We called it 'lying' at school.)

The village had been watching the operation closely, so, on the day it was finished and the village children were splashing around in pollution-free water at last, I waited for the outburst of spontaneous gratitude from thankful neighbours. But by the evening no one had even so much as mentioned it.

I went round to Zoran's.

'Well, the operation was certainly a great success,' said Zoran. 'Another example of island ingenuity triumphing over mainland bureaucracy, I'd say.'

'And a very skilful handling by yourself and Mr Samka of a tricky situation,' said Bozo.

'But what about the health hazard? It was an ecological disgrace,' I protested. 'And we've gone to huge expense to rid the village of it. No one's even mentioned it. Doesn't that show how much we care about the local ecology?'

A volley of hostile glares came winging over the bar at me.

'Ecology!' exclaimed Zvonko. 'You mean all that Green stuff people in the cities go on about these days. Bah! No one's interested in that kind of nonsense here, and let's hope it stays that way.'

His brother joined in. 'Once those tree lovers get to hear we've got any of that ecology business going on here, they'll be swarming over the place setting up stray cat homes, donkey rescue havens and I don't know what else!'

My best Captain Mainwaring frown of disapproval passed unnoticed.

'Yes,' said another bar-propper. 'They'll be dancing by the light of the moon and playing their Afro-Croatian music to our goats. That's the kind you'll get once you start with that ecology stuff. Hippies!'

'They'll be bringing llamas from Peru,' said Zvonko. 'They like llamas, hippies do.'

'And they'll be dropping big brown ones all over the waterfront when they come to market,' said Bozo.

'Llama dung is full of marijuana,' said Domigoy.

What was it with these islanders? I protested to the night sky as I walked home. Was there anywhere else on earth you'd find such a curmudgeonly lot? What did they have against hippies anyway? I'd never given it much thought, but, now that I did, I liked hippies. Hippies smiled a lot and said nice things to you like 'peace and love, brother!' They'd certainly be a lot more fun as neighbours than those around us now. They can come and set up their donkey rescue havens and play Afro-Croatian music to my goats any time they like.

So the whole operation had been another misplaced effort. But we couldn't make a thing about it, as that would only highlight our outsider status. We couldn't even complain about the 6 a.m. jam-jar clattering or Grandma Klakic not letting us park the car in the shade of the palm trees. The cats liked to lie there, she said. Ridiculous, I know, but we got into a boiling-hot car every day without complaining. I did once think of just leaving it there and letting her complain, but, on second thoughts, I didn't see Grandma K waiting around for an ASBO to be served on me – more likely I'd be on the receiving end of a wielded frying pan and land up with a row of stitches down my nose.

I went back to Zoran's the next morning to see if he'd thought of a way we could get at least some sort of PR out of our drains initiative, and we were discussing it when we heard the unmistakable bullfrog voice of Boyana. Every head in the barroom turned apprehensively.

'Looks like she's after someone to water her garden again,' said Zoran, looking out of the window.

Everyone in the bar shifted uncomfortably or began to sidle out the back, but I jumped to my feet as if to a clarion call and shot outside. This was the opportunity we'd been waiting for. If we did her a favour, she couldn't keep cold-shouldering us. My offer was accepted, but she continued on inside to collar anyone who hadn't been quick enough to leave, and grabbed hold of Marin and Domigoy.

The next morning, the three of us presented ourselves at her door and after a cursory greeting she herded us into the garden.

'Now this is the tap for the green hose. Only water the tomatoes and lettuces with the green one and pay attention to how I adjust the nozzle. Like this. Keep it wide so the water won't damage the fruit. You can bruise the whole crop if you're not careful. Now you be careful, Domigoy. I don't want to see any damage!'

There were two other hoses: a black one and a stripy one, and both came with different instructions. Domigoy was sweating by the time she finished and, when she started to tell us about the way the leaves on the various different fruit should be turned, he voiced his thoughts.

'I'll never be able to remember all this, Boyana!'

'Well, you can write it down if you can't remember it. And, if I find any damaged fruit when I come back, there'll be trouble. Now you all can practise what I've told you.'

We stood with our hoses like convicts in a chain gang and Boyana marched up and down behind, barking at us like a gang boss. At least she didn't have a whip.

There were three watering times in the day, so we religiously did our stints, and, when she returned a week later, eager to consolidate our new channel of communication, I went round with Marin, expecting thanks and maybe a jar or two of jam.

Boyana opened the door looking more like a bilious bullfrog than ever. 'The lettuces are all limp!' she barked. 'Someone gave them too much water! Now who was it? It was Domigoy, wasn't it? I know it was. He was always the laziest in the school.'

'Well, I did notice the ground was a bit too wet when I did the afternoon session,' said Marin, catching my eye and winking.

'Yes, I did as well,' I added quickly. 'Much too wet.' I looked surreptitiously at Marin for the next lead.

Boyana sucked in her cheeks. 'That stupid Domigoy! He'd mix weed killer up with fertiliser if he got the chance. Wait 'till I see him!'

We continued to heap the blame on poor Domigoy as we edged towards the door.

'Yes, one really has to concentrate,' said Marin.

'It's so easy to get it wrong if you don't concentrate,' I added toadily.

I backed out into the street, consoling myself with the thought that sometime soon she would be dead.

Because of problems with my boat's engine, I was spending a lot of time with Marin. Marin went about everything he did with a purposefulness and discipline not often seen in this part of the world, and, as I'm the type who tries to fix things with string and Kirby grips, it was a learning experience. But the more I worked with Marin, the more I learned to appreciate his patient and methodical way of going about things.

We also saw a lot more of Tanya. Most evenings, they came and sat outside our wall to watch the sun go down on, and, although we'd pretend we didn't know they were there, we could hear their whispers and laughter trickling up over the wall. Afterwards, they'd often come up and sit in the garden to talk about their plans and ask for our advice. Dispensing my Victor Meldrew-style wisdom to members of the younger generation is something that comes easily to me, but, with Tanya beside me in a figure-hugging top and skin-tight jeans, I found it quite difficult to concentrate – and, whenever she laughed her tinkling laugh, I would lose complete track of what I was saying.

Towards the end of the month, I noticed that Marin wasn't his usual self. He had started fiddling around aimlessly and sitting on the harbour benches, staring listlessly out to sea. After three days of this, I took him off to Marko's for a beer.

'What's up?' I asked.

'I don't know what to do. I'm sure Tanya prefers me to the others. At least she says she does. But I can never get her alone. That's the problem with places like this; you can never get any privacy. It was the same in my family's village.'

'If I were you, I'd take her off on your boat for a day or two.'

'I can't do that! I'd lose my job if my boss found out!'

'Well, why don't you borrow our boat for the weekend? It'll get you to Hvar and you could find a room to stay in.'

'That's very kind of you, but her mother would never allow it. Have you met her mother?'

161

'Is that the one with the moustache who lives over the bakery?'

He laughed. 'No, that's the aunt. The mother's the one who looks like a prison guard.'

'Oh, yes, I'm with you now. The Rosa Klebb look-alike who lives above Filip.'

'Yes, that's her.'

'I'd just take her on the boat and go.'

'No, a boat is out of the question, but perhaps a car would do it. If I could take her to a beach with a car and get her back home by nighttime. That might work. All I need is to get her alone for a day.'

'Well, the car is yours whenever you want it, but you'd better take your tool kit with you. It breaks down quite a lot, and breakdowns are real passion killers. I know from bitter experience!'

That Saturday, Marin picked up the car and the picnic that Ivana had made for them. (Knowing that Marin's usual lunch was a cold pizza washed down with a beer, she had thought something more appetising might improve his chances.)

We stood on the balcony watching the charabanc of passion winding its way up the hill and blowing out smoke from the exhaust as if steamed up at the thought of what lay ahead.

Marin and Tanya's love affair had certainly caught the imagination of the village. Even at the house of cynicism (Zoran's), it had touched a nerve. The interest was probably triggered by Tanya's gazelle-like beauty, and, while the talk was less about the couple than the bar-proppers' own less than successful involvements with the fairer sex, the romance had certainly caught their attention.

We were talking about it one evening when a grim look came over Zvonko's knotty features. 'Just because Tanya looks so sweet and saintly, that doesn't mean she's any different from the rest,' he said. 'Once they've got the husband, out comes the cloven hoof. They're all the same.'

'That's not fair,' I said and Domigoy voiced a mumbled agreement.

'Zvonko's right,' growled Zoran. 'We hadn't been in Texas for three months before mine ran off with her chiropodist.'

Murmurs of condolence round the bar.

'The guy was on thirty thousand and I was on twenty,' he grunted. 'That's the way it is with women.'

'There's no over-estimating the shallowness of the human heart,' said Filip, shaking his long head sagely. 'I learned that from reading your P.G. Wodehouse.'

'I'd have thought that ten years of collecting taxes on this island might have taught you that, too,' said Zoran.

Filip ignored the dig. 'But perhaps you were lucky. I should have left mine long before she left me.'

'Yeah. Ditch 'em before they do you in is what I say,' said Zoran sarkily. 'Ever hear of Captain Bligh? They had the right idea there.' He cocked an eye at me. 'One of yours I think.'

'Captain who?' said Domigoy.

'Never mind. Long story,' said Zoran.

'The best ones always get away,' said Zvonko's brother.

'Yes, I should have gone with that Ana-Maria,' said Zoran reflectively. 'You remember the one? The daughter of that Split harbourmaster.'

The company nodded.

'I really went for her, but I was only twenty and, when she got that job in Dubrovnik, I didn't want to drop everything.' He scratched his stubble. 'But she was a fire-cracker she was. I should have gone with her. I wonder where she is now. Probably cooking three meals a day for some fat ex-party chief who's got a side line in imported perfumes.' He put his chin in his hands and turned to me again. 'Good things don't come along often in this goddamn life of ours,' he said in English. 'You gotta grab 'em when they do.'

'Gather ye rosebuds while ye may, old time is still a-flying,' I replied.

'Damn right!'

'Maybe I should have stayed with my mother like she told me to,' said Filip glumly. 'Now I don't even have a house of my own.'

'You should have stayed with your mother until you knew a bit more about women, that's what,' said Zvonko, putting a brotherly hand on Filip's shoulder. 'There's no shame in staying with your mother until you're a bit older. I lived with my mother until I was forty.' A slow grin came over his weather-beaten face. 'D'you remember how hot you used to get for that

Morena? You'd quiver with passion every time you saw her!' Zvonko's stocky frame started to shake with laughter, and the others snickered.

'Yes, I remember that,' gurgled Bozo, his stomach wobbling. 'You used to get so steamed up, I'd see you shaking with passion every time you saw her behind her dad's butcher counter in that apron!'

The bar rocked with laughter.

'When will man come up with a solution to marital strife?' sighed Zvonko wiping his eyes as the laughter subsided. 'We should learn from our animals, we should. None of them get married for life and they seem to get on all right. They even get all the sex they want!'

'And look at the ones that do marry for life,' said Filip. 'Those swans always look so bad tempered to me.'

'But Tanya's heart is pure,' said Domigoy with a dreamy look in his eyes. 'She's not like the others.'

'And what makes you think that?' said Zoran acerbically.

'Oh, I just have these thoughts. You know how it is.'

'You're a deep thinker, Domigoy,' said Zoran with undisguised sarcasm.

'Yes, I've always been a thinker, even when I was a boy.'

Zoran raised his eyes to the nicotine-stained ceiling and sighed.

Another evening, I was standing outside with Domigoy and Zoran at promenade time when Marin and Tanya passed by arm in arm. Domigoy gazed at them with the expression of a love-struck calf and the beer in his glass started to dribble down his shirt.

'Didn't your mother tell you not to stare at girls, Domigoy?' said Zoran. 'And, if you leave your mouth open like that, something'll fly into it.'

Debate not being one of Domigoy's strongest social skills, he mooched back inside. Filip had heard the exchange and came to put an arm round his shoulder. 'Cheer up, Domigoy. Starry-eyed young men have always been falling in love with girls they can't have. Some of our poets have spent their entire lives writing about it.'

'Er…' replied Domigoy, missing yet another opportunity for a deep and meaningful debate.

'Never mind, Domigoy,' said Zoran. 'In life, happiness isn't for everyone.'

CHAPTER 22

ANOTHER PROJECT AND YET MORE FRUSTRATION

In Croatia, men of temperament abound and there's no such thing as a stiff upper lip. By and large, we English are brought up to be private people, but, in Croatia, no one misses an opportunity to give a decent emotion its full due. One morning, I was passing Ranko's and saw him in the state that psychiatrists, for want of a better term, call 'Having a Wobbly'. He was in his forecourt ranting to the sky. I could only make out occasional words like 'beasts' and 'scum', but, as an angry Ranko wasn't someone you wanted to engage in conversation, I continued on to Zoran's.

'Oh, he's just voicing his discontent,' said Zvonko, when I told him what I had seen. 'He's had a letter from the Town Hall saying he can't get planning permission for his chicken coops.'

'Should we go and commiserate?'

'No, I wouldn't bother,' said Zoran. 'We all need to shout at authority sometimes. We've been so beaten down for so long that we don't know how to handle it rationally, and it makes us feel better if we can howl our grievances to the sky instead of writing a letter to *The Times* like you do.'

(The breadth of Zoran's knowledge never ceased to amaze me.)

'Here we've always treated our authorities as the enemy. Having a new lot of overlords every few decades doesn't exactly endear you to authority. What's the point in respecting them when next year Selim the Sot, Vlad the Impaler or Hannibal and his elephants are going to turn up from over the horizon with a new book of rules, and, instead of getting a year's supply of turnips or a free elephant for every Centurion's head you deliver to the Town Hall, you get the noose.'

Thinking about the authorities, judging by the language of those I saw coming out of the municipal offices, it looked as if it wouldn't be long before someone in the Town Hall was going to be throttled by an exasperated petitioner – that is if Grandma Klakic hadn't got there first.

Seeing me trying hard not to be over-emotional about the lack of progress with the vineyard grant and the horrendous overspend on the drains, Ivana tried to think of something else.

'What we need is a project that benefits the community. That might get the village behind us. Why don't you think of something the island needs and make that your project while we're waiting for the grant?'

The idea came to me as we sat at Marko's watching a gang of boys on the waterfront jumping boisterously in and out of the sea. 'Pity there aren't any dinghies around,' I said. 'Boys of that age should be messing about in boats, not making an infernal noise and annoying their elders.' I paused. 'Of course. What about a sailing school? Why didn't we think of that before? That's just what the island needs.'

The bay was a perfect place for a school. It was a well-protected anchorage and there was always some wind. It should be a Godsend for the island. The tourist season only lasts two months, but the young don't mind cold water like we do, and, with wet suits, a sailing school could function from May until November. It would bring employment and a steady stream of money into the island for half of the year. The perfect project.

'And, if the islanders don't bloody accept us when this gets off the ground, it's back to the Home Counties!'

That afternoon, I walked round the bay looking for suitable sites. The old naval dock by the headland was ideal. It had a concrete landing wide enough for about thirty dinghies and an old barracks behind it that looked like it could sleep about forty. The next day, I rang the British Sailing Association, and a man who sounded like a West Country version of Ragnar Hairybreeks advised me how to write the prospectus and told me that they themselves could help to fund the dinghies and lend us instructors to train local staff if the school was open to boys and girls from EU countries.

This was terrific news. That would look after half of the cost. But, to raise the other 50 per cent, I emailed my proposal to everyone I'd ever known who had as much as set foot on a boat. One of them was Carlo, an Italian gallery owner I worked with who was now on the board of the Italian Sailing Association, and he emailed me back that his association had funds for sailing schools, and, as long as I could send him a lease for a suitable spot, he could recommend the school for a grant at their next committee meeting.

I did a quick hornpipe round the kitchen table and rushed off to ask the island's architect to do some proper drawings from the sketches I'd made. Excitement! If the British Sailing Association gave us the dinghies and instructors and the Italians gave us the money, we'd have three-quarters of what we needed. A project that could see the light of day at last. All we required was the Town Hall to agree on the site and we were away.

I told Ivana the news when she arrived back and we danced a jig round the sofa.

The next morning, we made an appointment with the Mayor's office and, clutching copies of the proposal and the drawings, we set off in high spirits. In a dark, high-ceilinged room of the Town Hall, we found the planning committee already sitting round a long table and, with barely enough light seeping through the slats of the half-closed shutters, it looked like the scene in *The Godfather* when the heads of the families get together to plan the carve-up. The Mayor, with his thin helping of black hair slicked sideways over his forehead, rose to his feet as we entered and sidled over. Not my favourite hairstyle and not a man I trusted, but I'd always found him affable enough. We sat down, handed round the copies of the drawings, and I stood to make my proposal.

I spoke slowly and very ungrammatically, but with words that I thought were full of feeling and persuasion. My pitch focused mainly on the employment benefits, the financial benefits and the high profile it would bring to the island, and ten minutes later I sat down feeling fairly confident of an enthusiastic response.

A row of stony faces looked at me over the table.

'Where's the money?' asked one of them.

'I told you, it's being pledged by the Italian Sailing Association.'

'Ha! Italians!' said another.

'So you haven't actually got the money.'

'No, of course not. We can only get approval and the first payment once you have agreed on the plans and the site.'

'We should know the money is there before we give any promises about a site,' said the one with a square-shaped head and no neck.

I stood up again. 'These people have offered a large charitable donation and you are questioning whether they will send it?' I asked icily. 'Do you seriously expect me to ring them up and say, "Send us the money and we'll let you know if we've managed to get a decent site later"? Don't be ridiculous! They need to see a guarantee of a lease and the approved drawings before they send us a cent.'

'We've heard these kinds of promises before,' said a man in a purple shirt. 'Sometimes the money never appears. We're talking about Italians, you know.'

Laughter round the table.

'And they might have other motives,' said a man with a thin moustache. 'We've got to watch for people wanting to set up businesses these days; particularly those "Pan-European" organisations we're hearing about.'

A general nodding went on.

'But they don't want to start a business!' I spluttered. 'They're a charity. They just want to give you some ruddy money so kids can learn how to sail, for Christ's sake!'

Ivana kicked me under the table.

'Ah! That's what you say,' said the man with the moustache, 'but they

168

might just be trying to get their foot in the door. They still think our islands belong to them, those Italians.'

'And how do we know they're not trying to hide some commercial interest?' chimed in another.

'I beg your pardon! The British Sailing Association and the Italian Sailing Association are both state-registered charities of considerable standing. This discussion is getting ridiculous.' I could hear my voice rising and Ivana's grip on my leg was starting to drain the blood from it.

The Mayor muttered with the two men sitting beside him.

'If I'm going to get this reaction,' I interrupted, 'perhaps I should advise the Italian association to put their money to some better use. If you don't want it, I'm sure there are other Town Halls with forward-thinking members who are queuing up for donations like this…'

Ivana kicked me under the table again.

As we walked back along the front, I was seething with frustration and almost unable to utter a word.

'Don't be so upset,' said Ivana, taking my arm. 'It's hardly surprising they try to stop anything from happening. They're all ex-party members and they've spent their lives being suspicious of anything coming from the outside. In the old days, they'd lose their jobs if they backed a foreign venture and something went wrong.'

This reminded me that I'd forgotten to ask the Mayor about the progress of our Vis Winegrowers application. 'Damn!' I shouted. 'We forgot to ask the bloody Mayor about our bloody application!'

'Now why don't you go and fiddle about on the boat for a bit. That'll make you feel better,' said Ivana, showing a touchingly deep understanding of the complex emotional makeup of her husband.

One hour later, I was feeling a lot better. I never thought I'd associate the whiff of diesel with the feeling of happiness, but, oh, the smell of a familiar engine, the feel of a familiar tool, the satisfaction of a well-tightened nut. Poets never seem to write odes to this most masculine of seafaring occupations. They go on enough about all that *tall ship and a star to steer her by* kind of thing, but there's never anything about the bloke down the hatch with his spanner who's keeping the whole thing together. Mind you, from the pictures I've seen of Wordsworth, Keats, Shelley and the like, you could tell they weren't the DIY sort.

That night, as I lay in bed listening to the sea that never sleeps talking to itself on the other side of the courtyard, I thought that perhaps there was something I was doing or saying that brought out such a negative attitude from the Town Hall. Maybe if I found out what it was, I might have more success.

The very next morning, a lesson in Croatian psychology, given to me for free by Grandma Klakic, gave me the answer. I was watching the six-year-old daughter of one of Ivana's Croatian cousins trying to play with the kittens in the square, and saw that, even though they were only a few weeks old, they were already streetwise. They were hissing at her and edging back into the oleander bushes. Not receiving the usual cuddly-kitten response, little Julia started to cry, and I went down to console her, but, when I opened the courtyard door, I found Grandma Klakic already there. 'Our kittens have to grow up fierce and strong,' she was saying. 'They must learn how to kill rats and fight off dogs. If they were just sweet and cuddly, they would never survive, and you wouldn't want that, would you?' Seeing me arrive, she gave me one of her flinty looks. 'And that's the way it is with our people. We've been trodden down for so long that this is how we've become. Hard and difficult to deal with, some might say, but, if we weren't like this, we would never have survived.'

Suddenly, it all fitted into place. It was as if the whole panoply of Croatian psychological infrastructure had been unfurled in front of me. The problem I had with the Town Hall wasn't me. It was genetically ingrained. I felt as if a great weight had slid off my shoulders. Blessed be thou amongst women, Grandma K.

When I mentioned Grandma K's take on the Croatian psyche to Zoran, he was quick to turn it in another direction. 'I know the British only looked on Vis as another Gibraltar to keep your battleships in, but at least you were better than all the other invaders – those thievin' Italians, those Hungarian butchers and those goddamn Turks. And Turks weren't Turks if they weren't linin' our streets with our heads on spikes or makin' our skins into their war drums. They took a lot of us as slaves, too – those who weren't already part of someone's drum kit, that is.'

One could always rely on Zoran for an upbeat take on history.

I was on my way home from the bar when my mobile rang. It rang so seldom these days that it made me jump. I fished it out and was assaulted by a salvo of hacking coughs, the unmistakable sound of my nicotine-ridden Dutch ex-agent Kaes. Wheezing away like a retired Bulgarian asbestos miner who'd just won the pools, he told me that he'd found an artist in Africa whose work was what we'd been always been looking for. Would I come back into the business and help him launch a worldwide promotion?

I was all ears. Ever since working in Africa as a young man, I'd been hoping to spot a new expression of art and be the first to champion it, but for the last decade I'd been feeling like a fielder waiting in the slips for a ball that never comes. I told Kaes I'd ring him back and sat on a bench to think about it. If the promotion worked, it would be the greatest achievement of my life – and it would make me some serious money. We'd be able to fund the vineyard without a grant. But then did I really want to go back to all that again – the endless travelling, the legal fighting, the financial worrying, the ever-ringing mobile? I sat there watching the fishermen pottering about on the quay, the boats drifting slowly into the harbour and the villagers going unhurriedly about their daily business or stopping to chat with their neighbours. Wasn't this beyond any price? But, considering how badly we were being treated by the village as a whole, perhaps it might not be such a bad idea to take up Kaes' offer and come back here in five years' time and try again. The feeling towards outsiders might have mellowed by then. I rang Kaes back to tell him I needed more time to think about it.

But did I really need any new challenges in my life? I asked myself as I walked home, and I remembered the list I had made aged eighteen of all the things I wanted to achieve before I was fifty – scaling the Eiger, crossing chasms on rope bridges, sailing single-handed round the Horn, winning a Nobel Peace Prize, wrestling busty blondes on film sets like James Bond and having knickers thrown at me like Tom Jones. I certainly hadn't ticked off many, but there were still a few possibles left – skinny-dipping in a waterfall or dancing at moonlight beach parties painted in psychedelic colours? That sort of thing should be easy enough out here. But, on second thoughts, most of them needed the willing participation of at least one member of the opposite sex – and I could imagine what Ivana's response would be.

Still, there was always Saturday nights round the bar with Zoran and the boys.

CHAPTER 23

MORE BRITISH
LEGACY

Ivana had an important birthday at the beginning of July, and Marko and I organised a party at Fort George, the fort that the British built around 1811 and named after King George III, and which still commanded the entrance from the headland with a foreboding presence. We assembled the thirty guests by the portcullis at sundown and, after carrying the food and drink up to the parapet, Ivana laid out the food on the trestles Marko had brought, while and Zoran and I mixed up cocktails beside one of the deserted gun ports of the massive thirty-two pounders that could hurl their cannon balls three miles out to sea. The view from the ramparts gave an uninterrupted panorama of the bay and the surrounding islands. The gunners could have blown anything out of the water that came within range.

Fort George was a top-of-the-range fort of its day. Built to house five hundred men, it was an impressive piece of late-eighteenth-century fortification, and, perched on its rocky headland, it stood there starkly forbidding. I looked over the battlements as we mixed up the drinks. By now, the burning sun was darkening from orange to red and turning the bay into a pool of liquid gold. The roofs of the village were suffused with the glow and the stone of the ramparts around us were washed with fiery pink. We toasted Ivana, passed round the eats and laughed and joked, but I couldn't stop wondering what the Midshipman Hornblowers would have been thinking of as they stood here all those years ago, waiting for the French fleet to appear and feeling very far from home.

Horatio Nelson was a man who knew how to read a map. He saw that whoever held Vis would control the Adriatic, so, in 1806, Captain William Hoste, one of his protégés, was dispatched with a fleet of frigates to take the island and hold it for England and St George. Once they had secured the island, the engineers from England followed and began the construction of a massive fort. Hundreds of people were employed, thousands of tons of stone were cut, and within three years the fort was completed. It had been a huge bonanza for the island, said Filip, as we looked down at the village now in shadow. It had brought wealth to the island and the Battle of Vis was something they were very proud of.

When the French fleet had been sighted, he told me, Hoste had sailed out to meet them, and, from the reports he'd received, he was fairly confident that their fleet was about the same strength as his. But, as they neared, he saw that not only did they have more ships, but they were also bigger and more heavily armed – in all, 276 guns to his 174. It must have been an uncertain moment for a captain still in his twenties, but reckoning that with the superior seamanship of his officers and men he could still win the day, he signalled for his drummer to beat to quarters, and, hoisting the flags that spelled out 'Remember Nelson' to the rest of his ships, he went into the attack. Out-numbered and out-gunned, the fighting was murderous, but by midday the superior seamanship began to tell and by mid-afternoon the French fleet was routed. Hoste returned in triumph to the bay with prize ships in tow to set about repairing his battle-damaged ships and to build a cemetery for his dead.

The light began to weaken as we leaned over the battlements, looking across the water. No one spoke, but the past felt very close as we stood there with our drinks, watching the last flickering vestige of the flaming orb sinking into the stretch of water where Hoste and his men had fought so bravely that day.

Marko broke the silence. 'You gave us our golden years, you know. There are only two clothes shops in the village today, but in 1815 there were seventeen. We were rich in those days!'

'But most of the clothes shops must have been for the soldiers' and sailors' uniforms,' I said.

'But no. They were all women's clothes shops,' he laughed. 'When does it ever change, my friend? Whenever we make any money, what happens to it? Our women spend it on clothes.'

The talk then turned to the British occupations. The occupations had made us the 'least worst' of all outsiders, Filip volunteered, and World War II had been a particular PR success, he added. His grandmother had never eaten chocolate before, but, after the troops had spent two years giving her their chocolate rations in return for washing their smalls, not only did she become a chocoholic but she also rooted for England whenever we were in the World Cup.

The following week, Luka returned and told me about the plans he already had for starting a cricket team. His family had emigrated to Australia, and after returning to Vis, he read about the British playing cricket here in a book about the Napoleonic War.

So now there were two of us.

Luka was a delightfully laid-back young man in his thirties with an athletic, rangy build, a mop of curly hair and twinkly grey eyes that slanted mischievously upwards when he smiled. He had a quiet confidence and wasn't at all fazed by the prospect of getting together everything needed to start a new club. All that was needed, he said, were some stumps, somewhere to play and enough kit for three or four players. Everything else could be sorted out as we went along.

The question of where to have a pitch was a stumper, as the only flat piece of land without a vineyard on it was the Navy's original pitch beside the monastery, but Luka was even philosophical about that. 'It will all sort itself out. Wait and see. The only real problem we'll have is persuading enough men to play.'

'But I've spotted at least a dozen athletic-looking types.'

'Ah, you don't know our people. Suspicious of anything new, we are. It's going to be a struggle.'

Cricket was now all I could think about. All we needed now was eleven like-minded men.

A week later he had assembled half a dozen who I sensed all rather looked up to him – then he was the sort who others always did look up to.

He had explained the game to them, but they were still pretty sketchy on what it was all about. It had been the same with Ivana's friends when we first met, and I remembered that what had worked best were stories about the great players and the great matches – about the nimbleness of Don Bradman, the true eye of Jack Hobbs, the phlegm of Tom Graveney, the wrist mastery of Jim Laker, the ferocity of Freddie Flintoff and the devastating spin of Shane Warne. What got everyone really listening, though, were the stories of the teams that fought back when it looked like certain defeat and went on to win the day. They were also intrigued to hear that the game threw up unlikely heroes; the overweight number nine batsman who scores 50 and saves the day; the over-aged fielder who catches the crucial catch; the dull player who opens slowly but lasts the whole innings and ends up 100 not out. They got a bit lost on the psychology of team play – how a captain like Mike Brearley could instinctively create a team that was more than the sum of its members, how Len Hutton had such an understanding of his men that he knew just what they were capable of – but at the end of the evening they rolled out into the darkened streets, laughing and joking, their voices echoing down the empty alleys and up over the silhouettes of the rooftops into the night sky. I sat on a bench by the water listening to the clink of their footsteps on the stone fading into the distance and looking at the stars sparkling in the great wheel of the heavens. Orion's Belt was twinkling cheerfully away in the east and Cassiopeia was flashing her messages across the ink-black sky. A good omen. Maybe island cricket was going to succeed.

The greeny lights of the fireflies pulsed in the dark between the palms beside me, and, feathered by a soft breeze, the water lapped in a light staccato at my feet. Bliss.

CHAPTER 24

THE DOUBLE-EDGED
SWORD OF PROGRESS

At the end of June, we were getting into the car (nicely heated to oven temperature, courtesy of Grandma Klakic) when we saw Karmela scurrying across the square. Breathlessly, she told us that the expensive-looking café we had seen being constructed was going to be a disco.

We went over to find the villagers milling around some enormous speakers, a bewildering array of wires and a half-finished dance dais. One of the gathering filled us in on the background. Selling overpriced drinks to holidaymakers was a lucrative business, and some entrepreneurs in Split, hearing about the number of yachts now coming to Vis, thought there were rich pickings to be had. They had set about getting themselves a site with Byzantine diplomacy, he said, and, after weeks of clandestine coffees with the right people, they had persuaded a local to pretend he was setting up a café, and under this guise they had built themselves a disco bar.

The double-edged sword of progress had appeared in our midst.

The crowd hung around for a while then drifted off, and we did the same, telling ourselves that things might not be as bad as they looked.

They were worse. The next night, the boom of disco-rap vibrated every wall within a half-mile radius, and it didn't stop till 4 a.m.

In the morning, we went over to Marko's and found a crowd already inside. Marko was standing at the bar and people were calling out to him.

'How could the Mayor have allowed it? It's right in the middle of town!'

'Why didn't he make them put it on the outskirts? It wouldn't have bothered anyone there.'

'The authorities should have stopped it!'

'Something should be done!'

Not wanting to look pushy, we sat at the back assuming that, once the shouting stopped, they'd form a protest committee and we could offer to help then. But half an hour later it was quite apparent that the object of the meeting was to complain rather than decide on any action. No one had even mentioned a committee (and I'd always thought that communist countries were big on committees).

Eventually, I stood up. 'What about forming a protest committee?' I called out.

Silence fell like a brick, everyone twisted round, and the woman with a pudding bowl hair-do in front of us was glaring at me as if I was a carpet stain. Highly embarrassed, I quickly outlined the three or four target areas the committee could cover, but even as I talked I could hear the rumble of disapproval. I sat down as quickly as I could, and a very brief discussion took place before the talk reverted to the complaints again. I couldn't understand it. Why didn't anyone want to take any action?

We got up to slink out of the back and saw another couple following us – the only other foreigners in the village – Erik, an earnest Scandinavian doctor, and his pretty Bosnian wife Latia, who was expecting their first child. They had met in Sarajevo while working for the UN and had just bought the derelict house behind Zoran's.

I suggested that rather than conducting a foreigners-only meeting in public we went home, and on the way there Erik explained why no one had wanted to form a protest committee.

'We had the same problem in Kosovo. They were always afraid that the Secret Police were still somewhere in the background writing down their names. No one would come out and say anything in public, not even to support the self-help groups we were setting up. They were all frightened of being marked down as trouble-makers.'

'You could see why,' said Latia. 'In the old days, if we said anything in public, there'd be a knock on the door in the middle of the night. At best you'd lose your job, and at worst you wouldn't be seen again!'

Once home, we sat round the kitchen table with our chins in our hands.

'I know what,' said Ivana. 'You and Erik go round the bars and chat up the men. I'm sure you can charm them into setting up some kind of a pressure group.'

Latia wrinkled her pretty forehead. 'Well, I'm not so sure about that,' she said, putting an affectionate hand on Erik's arm. 'My Erik is the nicest man in the world, but Swedish charm is something like a Presbyterian Minister married to a pine tree!' She giggled.

'I have to admit that this is true,' said Erik and grinned bashfully.

In the end, we decided that a visit to the local police station would be our first action, and with a great sense of civic responsibility we struck off down to the Bill.

'What I am asking myself,' said Erik in his slow Swedish voice as we walked, 'is what level of policing is needed on a small island like this? Surely there cannot be much crime?'

'And what would be the most common crime?' I asked flippantly. 'Grape scrumping? Chicken rustling? Lobster poaching? Wife stealing?'

'I think it is the lobster poaching,' said Erik, sounding serious.

Latia winked at me and raised an eyebrow, but said nothing.

We walked on in silence until Erik voiced his thoughts again. 'Do you think the police will have arrest quotas and crime-solving targets like we do in Sweden?'

'I think that maybe they will not,' answered his wife with a touch of exasperation in her voice.

The policeman on duty (one-quarter of the entire force) was Dalibor, a square-headed, sad-looking fellow in his forties who had only come to the island a few years earlier. Marko had told me that he had been a policeman in his home town, but he had been on duty at a checkpoint when a car had failed to stop, and, having drawn his gun to try to shoot a warning shot, he had shot his brother-in-law, who was standing beside him, in the leg. The family had not pressed charges, but the police department were so angry with him that he was posted to the farthest station in the land – Vis.

Dalibor was agitated. He was not accustomed to four people in the station at one time, and was flummoxed by our complaint. The complaints he usually had to deal with were garden boundary disputes, barking dogs, drunken seamen and complaints from Grandma Klakic.

'We can't do anything about the noise,' he said. 'After all, it's only music, and anyone can make as much music as they want until midnight.'

'But that's just what we're complaining about! The music went on to 4 a.m.!'

'Oh… Well, I suppose we could measure the sound. I think Health and Environment gave us a sound-measuring device some time ago. I don't know if it works. We've never used it.'

'Why not try it out tonight?'

He chewed his tongue and scratched his ear. 'Well, we can't just try it out like that. There has to be an official complaint.'

'What do you think we're doing now?'

'But the noise is not happening now. You must ring to report it when it happens. That will be an official complaint.'

'But you can hear it in this office!' said Erik.

'Yes. I know. But we have to follow the correct procedure.'

'So what do you do after you measure it?'

'If it's too loud, we will ask them to turn it down.'

'And what do you do if they don't?'

'We tell them again if there is another complaint.'

'And what then?'

'I think that after several incidences we're supposed to send a report to the Department of Environment.'

'And what do they do?'

He shrugged. 'I don't know.'

We sighed.

'OK. So, if we ring you up tomorrow night, you'll go on recording until you've got enough readings to send to the Department?'

'Oh, no! You must ring every time the incident happens. We can't go running around every night because of one complaint. We've got important work to do.'

180

'Yes, I know,' said Erik. 'Lobster stealing.'

Dalibor looked perplexed.

'Can't we ring you up in the morning and say there was noise in the night?'

'No, you can't,' he said firmly. 'As I said, if you want to make an official complaint, you must report it when the incident occurs.'

'You mean stay up until midnight just to phone you. I don't believe it!' exclaimed Erik, his temples pulsing.

'Don't lose your temper,' Ivana whispered. 'Go along with him or he'll be even less cooperative.'

Erik gave a great sigh like Peer Gynt in that gloomy Scandinavian opera when the poor chap gets told he's got to wander the seas for eternity.

We left the police station with the sinking feeling that the disco was not going to disappear as quickly as it had appeared.

For the next week, we took it in turns to stay up and ring the police. The village was complaining bitterly about the noise and were moving their children and their elderly to the edge of the village so they could sleep, but still no one would join us in protesting. Despite what Erik had told us about the fear of the Secret Police, I still didn't understand it. The Secret Police had disappeared nearly five or six years earlier.

The only person who offered to help was Marin, but, being an outsider, that didn't really count. Anyway, at least Marin was back on his old form. The Renault had done the trick and he and Tanya were now seldom apart. What's more, scarcely a day went by without an update from Karmela on their chances of a future together. Given her previous reservations about Marin and Bosnians, this was a surprise, but I think the combination of his good looks and his courteous manner had won her over. As for the rest of the village, Tanya was the darling of all the grannies, and for them the young lovers were the island's Romeo and Juliet.

CHAPTER 25

WINE AND THE ART OF CRICKET PRACTICE

By the next meeting the prospective players had watched some matches on Sky and were excited, but until the club was registered we couldn't bring any equipment in, and this presented the club with its first problem. In Croatian, Cs are pronounced like C for Cedar, and so 'cricket' would be pronounced 'sricket'. So, after considerable discussion, the members decided that the club should be called *The Sir William Hoste Kriket Klub* (SWHKK) and the motto: '*Remember Nelson*', Hoste's battle cry. (Their idea, not mine.)

'But will they allow us to set up a cricket club?' asked one of the group.

'Why on earth not, and who's "they"?' I asked.

'You can't start a club up just like that,' said Luka and went on to explain that under communism you couldn't just start up Scottish dancing clubs, Michael Jackson fan clubs, lesser-spotted warbler watching associations and Tommy Cooper appreciation societies whenever you felt like it. The authorities had looked on clubs as sources of counter-revolutionary activity, so starting one had been made as difficult as possible. Even once approved, club get-togethers would be closely monitored by the Secret Police. Of course, get-togethers featuring generals saluting ranks of proletarian mothers wearing five children medals and marching behind phalanxes of missile-bearing tanks were OK, but for anything else you had to apply to the relevant

Ministry. (Imagine having to ask permission to start a village cricket club in Yorkshire. That kind of thing could bring down a government.)

'We just had to put up with it,' said Luka. 'That's what happens when government theory gets bigger than the people.'

'I never minded the theory so much,' said Sinisa, the geography teacher. 'That was just one other annoying political irritant. What I minded were all those damned policemen on every corner.'

Once we had got ourselves registered, I rang everyone I could think of to ask for equipment. The response was terrific and when the parcels arrived, the club members opened them excitedly. I was whisked back in time. A Gunn and Moore, a Tom Graveney County Pro, even a Colin Cowdrey Truespot! And the smell of Blanco on the pads was like Proust getting a whiff of his *madeleines*.

'Do we really need things as big as this?' asked Sinisa, holding up some old pads. 'You cannot run in these!'

'Do the other players try to hit your legs with their bats?'.

'No they don't, but a ball on your leg can be just as painful.'

'Do we need such things? Did the men of Nelson also fear a small red ball?'

'You wait until you get the first one on your shin. You'll see!'

Luka thought it better to leave it a day or two before telling them about the boxes.

As more players were needed, Zvonko's son Icho was approached. Having seen him heaving their boat about like a plaything, I could picture his massive arms smashing drives and slinging down fizzing swingers, but it turned out that Icho wanted to try his hand at a new sport because his fiancée's old boyfriend was a policeman who belonged to a football-playing crowd, and as Icho was rubbish at football he thought that, if he could show some form in another sport, it might help to get her away from the football-playing policeman whom he suspected she was still seeing.

But what the heck. Brawn is useful in any sport, and with Icho we'd be up to nine. I think Luka had a soft spot for Icho, too, as Icho had a tough time at home. Zvonko's idea of raising sons was to treat them like fruit trees – prune them back hard and you'll get a sturdier specimen. I'd never once heard him praising Icho to his face, so if he was good at cricket, it might give him a bit of confidence.

Practice on the municipal tennis courts began and how rewarding to see them experiencing for the first time that terrific sensation of hitting the ball just right. I dare say many will go to their graves never having known the feeling, but take it from me, when you get the ball smack in the middle of your bat with a well-timed stroke and it rockets off the blade like a sprung projectile, it's one of the most exhilarating sensations in the world.

It has to be said that perfect strokes like this weren't happening that often on the municipal tennis courts. One would think that the skill of hitting a ball would come naturally to Homo Erectus, but it seems it doesn't. Domigoy made extraordinary windmill motions, Icho waved the bat about like a semaphore flag and Bozo would let it fly out of his hands. It would either whiz like an Assegai spear straight at someone's head or skim like a whirling boomerang across the court until it found someone's legs.

As for the bowling, there were four who showed distinct promise: two fast ones (Petar and Luka) and two spinners (Sinisa and Filip). The star performer was Petar, who, at six foot five and weighing in at two hundred pounds, was already throwing down some pretty dangerous stuff.

I thought that Marin with his agile build would be a pretty good all-rounder, but he seemed to think that the others might not want a Bosnian on an island team. However, three weeks later something made him change his mind, and he came along to a practice.

At first he hung around at the back of the court watching Petar, but when he took up a bat, my talent as a scout was vindicated. He moved like a panther and within half an hour he was able to size up almost any ball and get his bat to it.

As practice took place in the afternoon, the heat was fair bouncing up off the hard red earth, and by the time it finished everyone was pouring with sweat and desperate for a drink. Usually everyone repaired to Zoran's, where some used his toilet area as something approximating a changing room. (It's amazing how quickly a few sweaty men, clammy T-shirts, smelly socks, old shoes, soggy towels, half-eaten apples and packets of cigarettes can turn anywhere into a black hole of Calcutta, but for me the familiar smells took me straight back to the pavilions of West Sussex.)

It was at times like this when I was able to find out more about island lives. Those in their forties had resigned themselves to island life, but the younger ones all wanted to leave. Like most young men, they wanted to move to the city to seek fame and fortune. An islander's life, they complained, was pretty basic and everything still revolved around the land, which had to be tilled, planted, pruned and weeded. And then there were roofs to repair, wells to dig and old machinery to be kept in working order. Their fathers and grandfathers might have known how to do all this, but they didn't, and, anyway, they had an education and shouldn't have to be stuck with that kind of existence.

Drinking time was also an opportunity to learn the intangible side of the game – that it wasn't just a matter of the play; it was also about an attitude, a particular way of behaving, a sense of belonging to a group of fellow-minded blokes. That W.G. Grace and Jack Hobbs in their different ways epitomised the spirit of the game – W.G., the amateur, the robust rogue, the British Bulldog, the heavy drinker who would turn up at the last minute in his tweeds and brogues and smash his way through the opposition bowling – and that Jack Hobbs, on the other hand, was an entirely different player. Modest, respectable, sober, he was an example of the ordinary man who could do exceptional things when he had to – and as *Wisden* showed, Hobbs still held the record for the number of centuries scored in first-class cricket – 197. (For film buffs, this was a jackpot question in the quiz of *Slumdog Millionaire*.)

Some of the players were inveterate Walter Wolf smokers and wondered if it would affect their play, but as Hobbs, Hammond and Hutton were all great smokers, there was no clear answer.

They also asked about food, but as Mike Gatting managed to keep to a sensible diet through his long career, and his stomach was there as proof of it, the jury was also out on that one.

The attitude of both the young and the old to their home life and the kitchen not exactly PC. Most would all go home and sit in an armchair with the paper or in front of the television, and from that vantage point watch the activities of their wives or mothers. That their wives and mothers had probably spent the day working just as hard as them never seemed to cross their minds.

But in defence of the male population, I did sometimes hear them discussing the best way to cook certain dishes, so perhaps the idea of men in the kitchen was catching on – although it certainly hadn't got to the stage where I'd be able to interrupt the talk of fishing or politics in a bar with a new recipe for *Isles Flottantes*.

Strangely, food seemed to be usually discussed by the women in terms of being for the men of the house. We were coming out of the local store one morning when a neighbour leaned confidentially towards Ivana and said, 'And what are you giving *him* for his lunch today?'

Ivana hadn't even thought about it, and mumbled something about warming up a stew she'd made yesterday as her nose grew an inch longer.

'Seeing the way that they feed their men,' I said as we left, 'the villagers might think you're depriving me.'

'Don't be ridiculous.'

'Might I remind you that, just because you don't like the smell of bacon in your hair, a bacon ban has been in force in our household ever since the day we came back from honeymoon. In some parts of the world it would be considered a *prima facie* case of deprivation. If I spread the word, I think I'd get a lot of sympathy.'

In the middle of July, one of the club members had a word with someone in the Town Hall and, hey presto, our application for membership of the Vis Winegrowers Association was suddenly accepted. I thought this a pretty significant step forwards, but Zoran was typically disparaging.

'Nah! That's just a sop. They'll string you out forever, you'll see. That always happens like this when you're dealin' with ignorant bastards. Bastards, the lot of them! Like I told you, it'll get you down in the end. I tell you; a place like this can bend iron.'

As usual, an up-beat take on the matter.

But how much longer would it be before I was also referring to the authorities as 'bastards'?

On the bright side, my involvement with wine had already produced one good side effect. After two thousand years of winegrowing, the discussion of drink was an indispensable part of island life, and now that I was seen to be involved with wine, even some of our less friendly neighbours would talk to me (about wine matters only, of course).

'No wonder we're always talkin' about wine,' said Zoran when I told him this. 'We've been the greatest winegrowing island in the Mediterranean since before Christ was born. Don't give up on it. One day you'll get a vineyard goin' and you'll be part of a great tradition. The Romans reckoned Vis had the best wine in the Adriatic. When we were the capital of Illyria in 200 BC, the Head of the Alexandria Library came here on a state visit and wrote: "The wine from the island of Vis surpasses all others." Of course, once our Comrade Brothers started telling us what to do, that was the end of our great wine tradition. Oh, yes! Once The People's Wine Cooperative was up an' runnin', we had to give 'em all our wine an' they'd send it off to Poland or somewhere in return for pig iron and sump oil. So, after a year or two, no one cared any more, an' our wines began to taste like the stuff you get from Bulgaria. But we're makin' some decent wine again these days, an' that's good news for you, my friend. We'll be gettin' known again as a top-class wine region just when you'll be bottlin' your first vintage!'

'If I'm not pushing up the daisies by then.'

He gave me a questioning look.

'That means if I'm not dead.'

'Bravo! Spoken like a true islander! You're learnin' to be as miserable as the rest of us. I've trained you well!' He then wagged a finger. 'But if you keep on drinking like you do, you'll be pushin' your daisies up all right.'

That was a bit rich, coming from him, but I let it go.

'How come all you English drink so much, anyway? Look at what your friends drink. Their wives, too. Those women you brought round the other week sure gave my white *Vugava* a beatin'. They got through a bottle each.'

'We don't let our women drink like that,' grunted Zvonko.

'You don't let Daska drink because she's at you with the frying pan if she does,' said Zoran with his usual tact.

187

Zvonko's oaken features turned red and he started to his feet, but restraining hands landed on his shoulders and Zoran quickly went over to put an arm round him and apologise. It looked like this had happened before.

When Zvonko went home, I remarked on how quick his friends had been to intercede.

'It's to stop the blood feudin',' said Zoran. 'Used to be quite a popular sport aroun' here.'

I didn't say so, but I did agree with what Zoran said about English drinking habits. When it comes to drinking, Britannia rules the waves. I've often wondered what it is about us northerners that we have to sink a large quantity of alcohol before we can enjoy ourselves when our southern brethren seem to do this on no alcohol at all. I once asked a friend in the medical profession about it and he said that, after thousands of years in a cold climate, perhaps our blood circulated slightly slower, and, as alcohol speeds up the circulation, this might be why we feel somewhat cheerier after a couple of drinks. (But then an aspirin will do the same... I still don't understand.)

I walked home that night warmed by Zoran's wine and the thought of Vis becoming an important centre of viniculture. Once again, I saw myself striding down rows of vines on dewy morns in my britches and sitting on the benches with other seasoned winegrowers, imparting wise but cautiously prudent prognostications to international wine journalists about future vintages. Acceptance by the community? There wouldn't be a scowling face among them!

But then how long was it going to be before we could start the damn vineyard? One year? Two years? Three years?

CHAPTER 26

IMPROVING
RELATIONS

By now, most of the children and the elderly were sleeping at houses on the outskirts and the rest of us were sleeping in the heat of the summer nights with our windows shut. Wanting to make sure that the police had sent the noise report to the Department of Environment, we went along to the station and found Dalibor at the kiosk again. Seeing us come in, he quickly said that they were about to send the report and shut the kiosk window as fast as he could. Our persistent phoning must have got to them.

To give them their due, they did pay a visit to the bar each time we rang and told the manager to turn the sound down. But it didn't make much difference. Even with the sound turned down a few notches, the bass notes still vibrated the village walls like a mole with a mini pile driver.

After another week, Ivana rang the Department of Environment and I listened in on the extension.

'Have you received a report about disco noise from the Vis police station yet?'

A woman's voice that sounded like its owner was wearing a white calico blouse and sensible shoes confirmed that they had.

'It's been keeping the whole town awake for weeks and neither the Town Hall nor the police are taking any action. Can you do something about it?'

'It is not the role of this department to issue specific instructional directives to local administrative governmental bodies about matters of local conduct.'

'What *can* you do then?'

'We will inform the relevant Town Hall authorities that we have received a notification from the Department of Police.'

'But the police could have done that themselves!'

'This is in accordance with legislative government guidelines for complaint procedures relating to breaches of environmental guidelines or contraventions and infringements of regional norms,' she said as if she was reading from an instruction manual. 'It is for your local authority to take the requisite measures that are deemed necessary.'

'You mean the Town Hall will have to do something?'

'That is the customary procedure.' (She probably had calico knickers too.)

I daresay a good cross-examining counsel would have harried her further for some more concrete information, but, not feeling up to it, we rang off and looked despairingly out to sea.

In the meantime, our complaining seemed to have produced the opposite effect to that desired. The nightclub management had put out the word that lowering the volume was losing them money, and they brought in Go-Go girls from Split to up the interest. It was now even noisier.

As soon as we heard about the girls, Erik and I went along to investigate. Lurking furtively behind a palm tree, we watched as three stunning girls with impossibly pert bottoms in spangly thongs were doing their thing to Euro-rap. They did look rather fetching, and for a moment we toyed with the idea of taking to the floor and getting on down to some mean moves beside them, but, thinking it might be taken as fraternising with the enemy, we took ourselves off home.

The view from the bridge didn't look good. In one corner were the four quadrophonic blasters, three exquisitely beautiful Go-Go girls and the Split Mafia, and in the other corner were Ivana, me and a Scandinavian doctor. Our chances of getting the place closed down now looked even slimmer than before. But the most depressing thing of all was that, even though our neighbours kept asking us to continue the protest, still no one would help.

Bugger, bugger, bugger!

I said goodnight to Erik and trudged home in the depths of despond.

Ivana was still at her desk, so I went to put the kettle on to make some Bovril. When I get really depressed, I make myself a cup of Bovril, put on the aviator cap I wore playing Captain Courageous in a school panto and listen to some Fleetwood Mac. Rather sad really. (And, as Ivana was around, I had to make do with just the Bovril and the Fleetwood Mac.)

At my age, it is rather sad.

It was during this week that Luka made a breakthrough discovery. There was a European Cricket Development Programme (ECDP), which had EU sports grants for start-up clubs in new regions. Grants were available for equipment, pitches and even coaches. The club members could hardly believe our luck.

'Imagine! With a proper pitch and a coach, English clubs might even come and play us!' enthused vice-captain Petar.

'Don't worry, they'll come anyway,' said Luka. 'Cricket doesn't stand on ceremony and it's certainly not the sort of game you need the right shoes or the right watch for. It's a truly democratic game. A game of the people.'

'Maybe some touring Australian teams might even come?'

'And what about a Caribbean tour?' said Sinisa, who was the geography teacher at the local school. 'Vis versus Jamaica! Maybe there's a grant for that sort of thing, too? Maybe the government might help? After all, we'd be sporting ambassadors for our country, wouldn't we'

'Did you see that film about the Jamaican Olympic bobsleigh team?' said Bozo. 'They got sponsorship.'

'I think you call it "public relations" in the West,' said Sinisa.

'Yes, we should definitely look into the possibility of a sponsored tour, but it might be a bit far-fetched for the moment. We'll need to get a lot of matches under our belt before we get into tours.'

But the bit was between their teeth.

'Perhaps there's a Jamaico-Croatian Chamber of Commerce or something like that? We might be a big boost for Jamaico-Croatian trade,' said Petar.

Sinisa raised an eyebrow. 'I think trade with Jamaica these days might be a rather one-way thing.'

'And what's that?' asked Luka.

'Ganga!'

'Jamaica...' murmured Domigoy with a faraway look in his eyes. 'Playing under the palm trees... waves breaking on the sands... girls bringing drinks in coconut shells... It says on the Internet that there are girl cricket teams. Maybe Jamaica has some girl teams? Isn't that the country where girls just wear those flower strings on top?'

'No, that's Hawaii,' snapped our geography teacher. 'Disgraceful ignorance of geography,' he muttered. 'Not uncommon in teenagers, but for men in their thirties. Pah!'

I didn't think it was the right time to say that the sort of girls who play cricket are usually large and white and have thighs that can crush watermelons, and that they were called names like Rachael Heyhoe-Flint.

Domigoy looked confused.

'Will there be pretty girls in Manchester when we play at the Old Trafford?'

'Steady on. The Old Trafford's for county and international matches,' said Luka.

'Well, that's not very democratic!' said Petar. 'I thought cricket was a game of the people...'

Mercifully, the conversation then moved on to the hard-fought matches and the glorious deeds to come.

Things seemed to be going in the right direction. We nearly had eleven men and it looked like we might get the grant. The future was looking good.

That Friday, the ECDP office rang to say that our grant had been approved. Jubilation at the SWHKK. All the equipment they needed, a pitch and even a proper coach. The latter was particularly good news as the players had reached the stage where they really needed some professional instruction. So two weeks later a stocky, balding Mancunian stumped off the morning ferry with an enormous sports bag, a lopsided smile and the dry humour that has made Manchester famous – which made it difficult to translate what he said without giving offence.

Once in the gym, he produced a plastic wicket, a bat and a tennis ball from the capacious bag and, during the next two hours, the players realised that it wasn't just a matter of getting out there and playing with enthusiasm. There was a lot more to learn.

That night, I lay in bed worrying the players had got into something that wasn't really for them. Could it ever be an intrinsic part of their lives in the way it was for Anglo-Saxons? For me, as for many other Englishmen, the summer was cricket and cricket was the summer – sleepy days lying | on the grass swards of West Sussex hillsides, soft light, lengthening shadows, and, in the evening, a pub with twinkling lights and warm beer. How were a bunch of blokes on a rocky island drenched in sunshine going to empathise with all that? They'd never been to West Sussex. Would they ever get the sense of it without the beech trees, the green swards, the low light and the slumbering countryside – and, above all, would they ever learn to appreciate such irredeemably English attributes as a stoic manner when things go badly and a sense of fair play?

The next day, the coach had the players out on the tennis courts, and for the rest of the week cricket balls rained down on the village like an Old Testament plague – on roofs, cars, fishing boats, terraces, patios and Grandma Gokan's cats, but I noticed that the players quickly learned to shout *Pasi!* (Watch out!) every time a ball was hit with any force.

'That's instinctive,' said the coach. 'The first golfers probably shouted "Fore!" and loggers "Timber!" the day they started. Seems we've got an instinct to preserve the lives of our fellow men. Lucky really, the way your lot go at it!'

The sun beat down all day, but unflinching, he stood there encouraging and cajoling.

'Much better! Keep your head down.'

'Swing through!'

'Watch the ball!'

'Front foot closer.'

'That's more like it.'

'Get to it quicker.'

'Watch the bloody ball!'

The greatest danger was Domigoy who still hadn't mastered his swing. Sometimes his windmill follow-through clobbered the wicket keeper and sometimes he clobbered himself. Bozo, who had decided to be the team wicket keeper, soon learned to stand well back whenever Domigoy was in, but the coach stood his ground, and, each time the bat came too near, he tilted his head just an inch or two out of range and called out, 'Just a touch lighter next time, lad!'

With the bowlers, he had to try to reduce the excesses I'd been letting them get away with.

'You don't have to do something different every time.'

'Be patient. Wear the batsman down!'

'Arm straighter! Use your wrist!'

'Pitch it up, lad. You'll never get anyone out like that!'

'Now don't lose your temper, or you'll bowl worse.'

'There, that's more like it, lad! That was a good ball and batsmen don't like good balls, do they? Give your batsmen what they don't like.'

It was music to my ears. I was back in my Aertex shirt and Clark's shoes with a brown paper bag containing a doorstep sandwich and a bottle of Tizer.

By the end of the week, the coach had galvanised a motley bunch of players into a moderately competent team and left them with a wealth of cricket jokes. Best of all, the whole village had felt involved, and when he left on the ferry there was a large gathering on the quay to see him off. Luka said a few words and they all cheered and clapped as he stumped off into the hold, chuckling and shaking his head.

CHAPTER 27

THE PITCH AND
THE MATCH

An approach was made to the monastery to ask if we could use their field as the pitch again, but, as soon as the word 'cricket pitch' was mentioned, the hitherto jovial faces took on the appearance of Job.

The Brothers were clearly aware that the Navy had dug up most of their vegetable garden to make the cricket field wider and the Brothers there at the time nearly starved to death.

Abject apologies on behalf of Her Majesty's Navy were made, but they still wouldn't budge.

'So much for that idea,' said Luka to the club members.

'Damn! It's the only flat piece of land for miles.'

'I think the British Navy probably came to the same conclusion.'

So off went Luka to look for Astroturf pitches on the Internet. Astroturf pitches have been used on snow, ice, deserts and aircraft carriers, so a bit of Mediterranean sun wouldn't give them any problem. The colours they came in, unfortunately, were iridescent green and virulent blue and a virulent blue was settled on.

It wasn't long before we received our first challenge – from the 'Stragglers', a village touring team. But would the pitch arrive in time and where would we put it? Luka had started to clear one of his vineyard fields and prepare it, but it wouldn't be ready for a year or two, and, as the only other piece of flat land had the emergency helicopter landing pad in the middle of it, we had to make do with that.

Four days later, Luka arrived at Marko's in a state of great excitement. 'The pitch has arrived in Zagreb! We can try it out this weekend.'

'Sounds like you haven't had many dealings with our Democratic Republic's Customs Department,' Marko said grimly.

'Why should there be a problem?'

'If there isn't one, they'll make one up.'

Luka called the customs office on Marko's mobile, and, sure enough, they'd already thought up a problem.

'We've never had a cricket pitch imported before, so we don't know what category to classify it under,' said the officer.

'That shouldn't be a problem,' said Luka breezily. 'You can classify it any way you want. We don't care.'

'Well, I'm sure you don't,' said the officer sourly, 'but it's an important matter of precedent for us. What will happen if more cricket pitches are imported and the classification turns out to be wrong? We'll never hear the end of it! You'll just have to wait a few weeks until we can get the classification sanctioned and put into the system. You can't rush these things, you know.'

'But we've got our first match in three weeks' time! What are we going to do without a pitch?'

'Postpone your match.'

Luka's face contorted and he was about to throw Marko's phone across the room when Marko reached over and took it. Luka stood with his phone hand still in the air unable to articulate. Marko put an arm round his shoulders and guided him to the bar.

After several days of wrangling, the pitch was eventually released, and Luka and Domigoy jumped into Bozo's van, drove through the night to Zagreb and were back with it a day later.

That weekend the pitch was rolled out on the helipad, but there was another problem. The concrete square wasn't quite long enough and so it had to be put diagonally across. Not ideal, but at least we now had a pitch. The shocking colour of a celestial-blue Tintoretto sky, it looked somewhat incongruous among the soft greens and browns of the surrounding valley, and it certainly startled the passing farmers, but the club members thought it looked beautiful.

Once it was down, the village came to see it. They walked up and down it, poked it with their fingers, stubbed it with their toes and some even lay on it. We also had a visit from the Chief of Police, but that was to tell us we should warn the Air Rescue Office about the colour in case the vivid hue gave the helicopter pilot a fright when he next came in.

With only two weeks to go before the match, a growing excitement spread. Originally, I would be playing on the team, but, as the interest increased and many more young men came forward wanting to prove their virility at the lists, I realised I wasn't needed. Actually, I was much relieved as both my right shoulder and left knee had now ceased to perform any useful cricket movement.

There were the usual last-minute panics. Someone pointed out that smart clubs had their own T-shirts, so Luka went over to Split to run up a few with 'Remember Nelson' emblazoned on them. Next was the problem of 'whites'. Not a lot of club members owned white trousers (considered impractical by the islanders), but whatever could be found was washed, repaired and altered by the players' mothers, wives or girlfriends, and by the end of the week eleven pairs were ready. Your first pair of whites is one of those things that you never forget. I've never forgotten mine and I'm sure the members of the Kriket Klub will never forget theirs. Come to think about it one could probably plot the course of one's life with one's 'firsts': first bicycle, first team match, first kiss, first pay-cheque, first child (and, at my age, first grey hair, first dodgy knee, first aching shoulder).

However, despite the keenness, the play was still pretty scratchy and, now that all eyes of the island were on them, their greatest concern was how to acquit themselves with honour.

Quite a crowd was on the quay to welcome the visitors off the ferry, and no time was wasted in getting them up to Luka's vineyard to start the drinking. The visitors needed no encouragement, and a riotous lunch took place at which the SWHKK heard all the classic cricket stories – the rudeness of Freddie Truman, the meanness of Geoff Boycott, the stubbornness of Len Hutton and that Fred Lilywhite, founder of Lilywhite's, played for England in a top hat. Such a lot of wine was consumed that I retired for a longish kip. The dinner was an uproarious affair; songs were sung, speeches were made, and, most importantly, by midnight all of the opposition were exhibiting definite signs of wear.

The next morning, the visitors alighted from Nano's bus and staggered unsteadily on to the field, dazed by the heat and the brightness of the sun, and while they spread themselves around the field, we set up our makeshift pavilion of ten plastic chairs and two tables underneath the only tree. The smell of fennel and rosemary hung in the air, blue butterflies fluttered over tiny wild flowers, bees hummed in the heather and the fielders made decorous splashes of white against the green. It looked like a Victorian idyll. All it needed to win the prize for the perfect cricket picture was a cow, a village blacksmith and a vicar smoking a pipe.

There was an impressive turnout of spectators and a TV crew had arrived from Zagreb to cover the historic event. Clad in the whites so lovingly prepared, Domigoy and Filip strode out on to the pitch like Sylvester Stallone and his co-pilot swaggering out to their gunship. Domigoy in pads looked even more gorilla-like than usual – but he was going to show the crowd (and his cousin Zoran in particular) who could win honour for the island.

Cries of 'Ide, Remember!' ('Come on, Remember!') rang around the valley, and both spectators and team members alike waited with bated breath as our two openers twiddled their bats and looked apprehensively around. The field of rough grass was actually slightly lower than the concrete square, but, before things had got out of hand the previous evening, both captains had agreed that it was a shared handicap and the bowlers would have to negotiate the three-inch step as best they could.

Domigoy took guard and there was an audible inhalation of air from the crowd as the opening bowler pounded towards the stumps. With an extra skip, he was on the helipad and delivered a ball, which whizzed down towards the off stump. Domigoy took a swipe at it and it connected, sending the ball chest high towards mid-on. It was actually a cow shot (frowned on in the best cricket circles), but the crowd applauded madly as the hungover silly mid-on moved to catch it, but tripped over his feet and the ball continued unmolested. Domigoy stood there for a second looking at Filip running towards him as if he couldn't think what he was doing, and then, remembering where he was, he pounded down the pitch. The crowd clapped in approval and both batsmen beamed around them. One run for no wickets.

The next ball was a short one. It bounced up sharply off the Astroturf and would have taken Filip's left ear off if he hadn't had the presence of mind to dive for the ground. The spectators gasped. Filip got to his feet, dusted off his trousers and waved his bat to the crowd with a big grin on his usually solemn face. This drew more cheers. Their team could handle anything that was thrown at them!

It was two runs for no wickets at the end of the first over, and Zoran came to put things into historical perspective for anyone who cared to listen. 'In this part of the world, we've been slicing at things with swords or bashing them with axes for centuries. It's the cult of the axe, and it was certainly around here long before your Captain Hoste turned up with his cricket bat. I reckon you'll be finding some powerful hitters among our men.'

The other players thanked Zoran for his brief historical footnote, and we were spared further sociological revelations by the arrival of Zoran's arch enemies – the Mayor and his entourage. He glowered at them and moved away.

A spin bowler now took the ball, and, like the rest of the team, he was a bit unsteady on his feet, but he was a wily-looking fellow and was trying on the tactic of standing in front of the batsman, spitting on his hand and flicking the ball in the air. It seemed to be working on Domigoy, and I could see him fidgeting uneasily. Domigoy didn't have much self-confidence and the continual put-downs from cousin Zoran had helped to whittle away the little he possessed. A pep talk about how to face down bowlers would be useful sometime later, but for now he was on his own.

The second bowler loped up to the wicket and delivered a ball that spun so hard you could hear the buzz. Domigoy didn't stand a chance. Spinning up at an abrupt angle, the ball shot through the gap between the bat and his pad and took out his centre stump. Domigoy turned and gaped at it like a spaniel at a bone that had been taken away. It looked as if he was about to cry, but he shouldered his bat and plodded stoically across the field, a portrait of despair.

Luka was next in and, with a scarf wrapped round his waist to add a dash of colour, he looked handsomely athletic. He smiled confidently as a call of 'Captain in' went round the field. The crowd cheered, certain of their captain's prowess.

The first three balls he played cautiously, but, even though he simply blocked, there was applause each time. This was their captain at the crease.

For the last ball of the over, the bowler fired down another buzzing spinner, a short one that shot up at waist height. Feeling more confident, Luka stepped back to deflect it, but realised too late that it was still rising. It clipped the top of his bat and went straight into the hands of the wicket keeper. The crowd groaned in dismay. The first duck for two hundred years! Their captain!

Now, in my old club, this would have produced an immediate strangulated cry from the batsman of 'I just don't believe it' or something to that effect, but Luka stood there looking at the wicket in disbelief. Seeing his distress, the kindly wicket keeper said, 'Hard luck, mate!' in a fatherly voice. This snapped Luka out of his trance and he walked back to his teammates.

The fact that hard luck played such a large part in the game was something else the team was going to learn. Which schoolboy cricketer can ever forget that the great Don Bradman scored a duck for his last test innings at the Oval. (Of course, Geoff Boycott, true to his usual miserable form, insists that a batsman makes his own luck, but what fields of turnip-like grass or unforgiving Astroturf surfaces has Geoff Boycott had to deal with ever since he was out of short pants?)

The next man in was Petar. Six foot five and built like a bulldozer, he strode out on to the field like Lars Porsena of Clusium in that poem we all had to learn at school. Towering over the fielders, he stood at the wicket, glared around the field and then hunched menacingly over his oversized bat. The fielders, recognising they had a slogger at the crease, stepped back a few paces. A murmur of expectation ran through the crowd. Now they'd see some action.

The fast bowler launched himself on to the concrete again and the ball whistled down. It was wide of the wicket and Petar sprang at it like a tiger. Wielded by his massive forearms, the bat flashed in the air and a mighty *thwack* echoed across the valley as the ball skied upwards. It hovered at its peak as if trying to defy the central discovery of Sir Isaac Newton, and then plummeted earthwards to where the bonnet of Zvonko's tractor was waiting for it. A resounding clang rang out, making the spectators wince, and someone shouted, 'A six! A six!' An eruption of cheering broke out. This was more like it! Our first six! As good as the one Albert Trot hit over the roof of Lords in 1899.

Zoran came over. 'There, I told you so! The cult of the axe!'

Petar now hit out at every delivery. As with all games, even though cricket's a team sport, in the end, it's all about personal glory, and Petar wanted to shine. But, although his strokes were just as fierce, his early promise began to pall and, after two more overs and two missed catches by hungover fielders, he was bowled out for twenty-one.

As no one seemed to have explained the game to the spectators, the consensus after an hour of play was that the object of the game was to hit the fielders with the ball. I think they'd come to this conclusion because the hungover fielders were either being struck by the ball or were trying to dodge it when they realised they couldn't see it well enough to stop it. One of the team gave a brief explanation of what was supposed to be happening, and when he had finished, someone asked when it was going to end. Having assumed it would be over in time for their Sunday lunch, they were rather taken aback when told it could last all day and maybe most of the next day, too. Ten minutes later, the crowd had dwindled to Ivana and me, the girlfriends of the players, the national TV crew and a handful of others.

In the meantime, things were not going well for the SWHKK. Having sweated off most of the alcohol, the opposition were rapidly sobering up, and, as a consequence, wickets were beginning to fall. By midday, we were all out and in time for an embarrassingly early lunch.

'This is dreadful,' I said to Ivana. 'It's going to be a humiliating defeat and it'll put the island off the game for ever!'

'Don't worry. Look how everyone's having a great time and it's not raining.

If it was England, it would be pouring down, the pitch would already be a wet sponge and I'd be sitting in the car in a monumental grump.'

After lunch, Luka placed the team, and Bozo stood behind the wicket in his pads and gloves looking like one of those Russian moustachioed wooden dolls. Petar was to open the bowling, and he paced back from the wicket like he'd seen the professionals do. He then swivelled round, thrust out his chin and almost pawed the ground before leaping off towards the wicket like a Vulcan out of the clouds. The ball left his hand with frightening velocity, but, fizzing like a top, it shot past the batsman, the stumps and Bozo's gloves to find its mark in Bozo's stomach. It sank into it like a cannonball sinking into the oak of a French frigate, bringing a hideous groan from Bozo before he toppled to the ground. The team gathered round, and, after some deliberation, they picked him up and carried him to the boundary. Having divested him of his pads, they gave them to Dali the postman, and left him there, in the care of his wife, three sisters and two daughters.

Once Dali was at the wicket, Petar hurtled towards the pitch again like Jonah Lomu coming at an England scrum, and once again his massive right arm flung down a ball with appalling ferocity. This time it was so wide and going at such speed that in two bounces it was over the boundary. Four wides!

By the end of the over, Petar had got his eye in, but Dali behind the wicket was struggling to cope. The speed of the ball was one problem, but the other was Dali's misconception that, if he thrust out his gloves, spread his pads and yelled loudly enough, the flight of the ball would somehow be arrested.

Our next bowler was Marin, who also spent most of his first over delivering high-velocity wides (at one point I wondered if we might qualify for an entry in the *Guinness Book of Records* for the record number of wides bowled in one match), but by the third over Petar had got the right pace and was putting more spin on his balls. One of them came down with such a turn on it that it shot up off the Astroturf at the batsman's head. Now there's only one way to deal with a bouncer and that's to swivel on one foot and hit it when it's almost on your nose, and the batsman tried to do this, but his timing was out and the ball caught him on the ear. He fell as if pole-axed. The fielders helped him up and he came off holding his hand to his ear in evident pain.

The play recommenced and the next victim was one of our own – Filip at slip, who got a ball on the kneecap and hopped about on one foot in agony like a clumsy stork before being helped off the field.

Forty-five for one wicket; one batsman and two fielders retired hurt.

But, try as they might, our bowlers just couldn't get the measure of the batsmen who by now were carting balls off to the boundary. The high point of the afternoon was when one of the shots put up a pheasant in the next field. (A descendant of the pheasants that Captain Hoste had brought over to provide sport for his officers, which have survived ever since on a nourishing diet of island berries.)

Finally, at six o'clock, we drew stumps. A crushing defeat some might say (although no worse than England's 2012 performance against India). However, no one seemed at all upset by the result and a terrific celebration party took place that night at Marko's.

For me the highlight of the evening was watching excerpts of the match on the national TV news and hearing the newsreader calling it 'a historic event in Croatian sport'.

CHAPTER 28

RETURN TO
THE METROPOLIS

Two important lessons were learned from our first match by the Kriket Klub. First, that English cricket players had an extraordinary capacity to down a phenomenal amount of liquor and still be able to wield a bat quite effectively, and, second, that practising on a tennis court wasn't going to get us very far. We needed some nets.

So, for the next week, every yacht flying a red ensign that came into the harbour was badgered for a contribution. The response was terrific, and soon there was enough for a net. Now we could get down to some proper practice.

On the opening practice, though, an almighty thwack from Petar broke the only oversized bat we had. As no one had seen a broken bat before, the others crowded round to look at it, but Petar was distraught. At six foot five, he needed it. However, as I was going to London to talk with my Dutch friend Kaes about his job offer the next week, I told him I'd bring another one back.

I had thought that a meeting with Kaes at the opening of the artist's exhibition in a Cork Street gallery would serve as a good crossroads. I'd be able to compare my old life shoulder-to-shoulder with my new one and come to a decision. I'd been thinking a lot about the offer and the more I thought about it, the more attractive it seemed. I wouldn't have the financial worry of owning a company, and, if it went well, the money would be good.

How at home I felt the minute I arrived in a sunny, bustling, August London. How safe and anonymous I felt in my funny-old-buttoned-up Fulham, and how strange it felt not having anyone to greet as I walked down the high street – but at least there was no one scowling at me.

The opening was well under way when I arrived at the gallery. I wasn't sure how I rated the art – large abstract expressionist paintings in shades of black, violet, red and green with a hint of realism. I'd take a closer look at them later. Right now, I needed a drink and I made a well-practised dive for the hospitality table in case the champagne ran out. Spotting Kaes talking to one of the art critics, I made my way over to him. He was holding an unlit cigarette in one hand and was clearly dying to go outside and smoke it, but the critic kept asking him questions.

Pleased to see me, Kaes motioned to a waiter to bring me another glass (he knew me well) and called to the artist. A sharp-featured, serious-looking young man from Zambia wearing a black T-shirt under a dark-grey Armani-type jacket, he smiled confidently when introduced and asked me about the American galleries. We started to talk, but were interrupted by a journalist asking a fatuous question about the scars on his cheeks. I moved away. We could talk later.

'You're looking tanned,' said a voice in my ear. It was Ben, an old colleague who looked like a cross between Alfred Hitchcock and Johnny Vegas.

'It's the outdoor life,' I replied.

'Looks more like George Hamilton III after a session with a lamp. Your tan looks ominously even, dear boy. I bet if you dropped your drawers, we wouldn't see white cheeks! What's happening on this island of yours?'

'Darling,' interrupted the editor of *Arts Today*, giving my cheek a quick peck. 'Don't you look wonderful! Must go and see your island one day. Sounds too divine for words!' She sighted someone else and disappeared.

'In the opinion of the wise, sunshine isn't good for you at all,' said Ben, who had the pallor of a blancmange.

'Coming from you, that's a bit rich. You must be the unhealthiest person I know. But to tell the truth, I do feel rather alien among all you pale-faces.'

'I never really went for that tanned look myself,' said Ben. 'I've always thought it shows a rather unmanly narcissism. Methinks a pale and interesting look befits me better.'

'You mean you don't think my masculine weather-beaten look suggests an active and adventurous life and might serve me well as an allurement to the fair sex?'

'Despite the tan, you still look like a scarecrow, mate. Mind you, you could always get yourself a part in one of those films where they have ragged, weather-beaten slaves rowing Roman galleys.'

'Piss off, Ben. You're just jealous.'

I rejoined the artist, but a younger critic was now with him. I listened in. 'Is the abstract engagement in the question of temporality really relevant to the current debate on whether art can truly be part of a society based on hedonism?' I heard the man saying, and then without giving the artist time to reply he added, 'And, if it is, how does it contribute to the ongoing didactic of art?'

Er…? Was I just unaccustomed to this art-speak or had the months of hanging around with the crowd at Zoran's degenerated my brain?

The artist seemed equally befuddled by the question and discreetly steered the conversation to the beginnings of African art. Bright young man. He'd go far.

Looking around, I could see all the usual faces from the other galleries and the usual bunch of art critics. Those I knew came up to ask how I was getting on with my new life, but I had forgotten how noisy these occasions were and how difficult it was to have a conversation. After the token questions, most of my ex-colleagues gave up and went to see what business was to be done in the room. No one seemed particularly interested in the art.

Had it always been like this, or had I just never noticed?

As the evening wore on, the crowd thinned and I was able to have a word with Kaes. He was very buoyed up by the show and we talked about what I might be able to do for the American promotion. We then looked at the work together. It was totally original and rather beautiful in an abstract way, but didn't exactly gladden the heart and quicken the blood. We'd have to put together a pretty convincing story if we were going to succeed in America.

I told Kaes I'd get back to him about his offer and took a taxi to the tiny flat we'd bought when we sold the house. Sitting in the back of the taxi, I realised how unsettled I had felt at the exhibition. I'd only been away for six months and yet I'd felt like a duck out of water. Why did it all seem so contrived, and why had this never struck me before? Did I really want to go back to all that again?

I spent the night being woken up by police sirens and I got into the minicab for Gatwick with a certain sense of relief. On the way, I stopped off at the Oval shop to buy Petar the bat, but, as the only oversized bats they had weren't knocked in, I bought a bottle of linseed oil as well. I didn't need a hammer as my father's old wooden one was decorating our mantelpiece on Vis.

Once back on the island, I went to tell Ivana about my meeting and then took the bat round to Petar. He listened politely as I explained how to knock it in, but I could tell that he thought I was just being an old cricket bore and that it wasn't really necessary. And, sure enough, a week later, it was broken. Shamefaced, he asked if I could get him another, and, since he always gave me a case of his best wine whenever I got him anything, I was only too delighted. I rang Richard who was coming out again, and, when he brought it, Petar was so happy that I got two cases. I hoped he'd break this one, too.

It wasn't long before the news of our first match had spread throughout the world of cricket. From Yorkshire to Delhi to Cape Town to Jamaica to New South Wales, websites, newsletters, blogs and tweets carried the historic news to every cricket-playing community on earth and the reaction was overwhelming. Clubs from everywhere rang and emailed (some thought Vis was a country). The players hadn't really believed what they'd heard about the worldwide cricketing fraternity, and were gobsmacked by the response. It was as if they had scaled Everest, sailed the Atlantic or got a date with Keira Knightley. Perhaps one day they really would walk down the hallowed, high-ceilinged Long Room in Lords and look up in awe at the giant painting of W.G.

Our next challenge came from a Royal Navy destroyer on a UN patrol of the ex-war zone, and the team were worried that they might be out-classed again.. Last time, they'd been able to laugh off our defeat, but how long could we continue to do that? As Richard was still with us and as he had played for his university (and could have played for his county had he not wanted to spend his life wearing funny wigs and talking the hind leg off a donkey), I thought that he might strengthen our hand, and took him round to Petar, who, as the only club member with an email and a fax, had been given the job of fixtures organiser and team selector.

Petar looked embarrassed when I said that we might have a chance of winning with Richard playing. 'I am sure your skills would be a great help to us,' he said apologetically to Richard, 'but every young man on the island now wants their wife or girlfriend to see what sort of man they are, and they are all wanting a place on the team. You would never think that not so long ago, we couldn't even find eleven men. Now there are so many wanting to play that we cannot possibly give a place to an outsider, even if it might help us win.'

'Of course you can't,' said Richard quickly. 'We've got just the same "locals first" policy in my club, too.'

'But maybe you can give us some coaching. Yes?' said Petar, clamping a tree trunk of an arm round Richard's narrow shoulders and squeezing hard.

That settled, Petar uncorked a bottle and told us that an Australian club had just telephoned.

'The Australian captain was talking in English, but there were many words I did not understand. What is the meaning of "stick-it-up-them" and "slaughter"?'

'I'm afraid our Australian cousins are not known for their silken tongues,' I said. 'They're world-class swearers and they've got more names for vomit than any other language in Christendom.'

'But do they use these words when they are playing?'

'Oh, yes. You can count on that,' said Richard. 'I sometimes think they could win the Ashes just by swearing at us.'

Petar looked apprehensive. 'My mother will be coming to all our matches.'

* * *

Luka was still worried about the possibility of another crushing defeat, but after a conversation with the ship's games officer, he felt better. 'Our opening bowler has a slipped disc; our opening batsman hasn't scored double figures all season; our number two only plays because Ian Botham used to patronise his mother's pizzeria; our number three is frightened of getting injured in case he'll lose some of his shore-leave allowance... Shall I go on?'

It sounded like we were going to be in good company.

The sight of a black rubber assault craft roaring into the bay and a bunch of horribly fit-looking young men leaping on to the beach as if it was a D-Day landing was slightly daunting, but, when our players saw the state of their equipment, they relaxed.

As they had to be back on board by nightfall, we went straight up to the field and the captains tossed. We won and Marin went in to open. This time he got to the pitch of it and Domigoy, in at number two, had much improved, too, and was making some pretty impressive wristy drives, even though his footwork still needed working on. He was also making some of the top-edged clips he'd seen the Indian batters doing on the coach's videos.

Petar, in at number three, had also improved beyond all measure, and chalked up thirty in three overs. He could now deal with slow spinners and was handing out some pretty aggressive drives when he remembered to be patient and play them late. Like most village cricketers, however, patience was not Petar's strongest suit, and in his fifth over he forgot to wait for it, and a good length ball spun off his bat into the hands of the wicket keeper. Fifty-one in six overs. Not bad.

The rest of the club acquitted themselves fairly well, too, but, when Filip was out for a duck, he took it badly. He stormed off the field, his tombstone face contorted like a man in the early stages of rabies. Bubbles weren't quite coming out at the corners of his mouth, but he was having difficulty swallowing and the only sounds coming out were X-and Z-filled words involving God and unnatural sexual practices.

None of the club had ever experienced cricket rage before and didn't know what to do. Luka and Petar went over to try to calm him down, but he stomped off, cursing as he went. Don't worry, I told myself, this was quite normal behaviour in most cricket pavilions the length and breadth of England, and I hardly even registered it when any of my old teammates used to throw a wobbly – first the ritual throwing of the bat across the changing room followed by the pads and perhaps the box, then the stomp round the boundary uttering expletives, and the eventual return to the pavilion where the teammates would do that English thing of pretending they hadn't noticed anything untoward. Mind you, if the player has a wife or a girlfriend, things end differently – usually with the loved one proclaiming that, if he behaves like that one more time, she'll never go to his stupid matches again and will most probably leave him. (There are usually a few side threats thrown in too; like sticking his whites into a mixed wash before she leaves or putting a virus into all his cricket websites.) But the members of the Kriket Klub had no experience of cricket-rage and were baffled by the sight of the most sanguine of their members in such a state of apoplexy.

I wasn't unduly worried. After a season or two of hearing the Croatian version of '*would you fucking believe it!*' being shouted and seeing bats being hurled to the ground or pads skied into the air, they'd get used to it.

In the end, Filip calmed down and we drew stumps at six. Our first win!

Now that we had acquitted ourselves with honour, I wondered if the players would now become interested in other niceties of the game, such as moralities and codes of behaviour. I had just read *Cricket*, written in 1884 by A.G. Steel and The Right Honourable Alfred Lyttleton (A.G. Steel scored the first Test century against Australia at Lords and The Right Hon. Alfred took four for eight at an Oval Test, bowling in his wicket-keeping pads!), and in it I found a rather telling passage:

> *A cricketer should live a regular life and abstain at table from all things*
> *likely to interfere with his digestion and wind. A captain should never*
> *hesitate to speak to his team on these matters should he think a warning*
> *or a rebuke necessary. The necessity of moderation in drink, of course,*
> *is happily a thing few cricketers need to be reminded of.*

I considered putting a translation of it over the bar at Zoran's and encouraging Luka to issue a few rebukes.

CHAPTER 29

THE STRUGGLE
CONTINUES

It was interesting to see how quickly the cornerstone of communism (collective housing), was being eroded by the cornerstone of capitalism (home ownership). In the bars, the talk of politics was rapidly being superseded by talk of price per square metre. However, the bar-proppers were beginning to find that the problem with property matters was that they weren't things that you could argue about – and what was the fun of talking about something you couldn't argue about?

Ever since I'd had my head bitten off by the rude neighbour after the Ministry of Agriculture's visit, I had tried to avoid arguments, but I now saw that getting involved in arguments was a sign of belonging.

I think I missed a lot of the best arguments, which seemed to hit top gear around midnight. Bozo usually missed them, too, as he left even earlier than I did. As early as nine, I'd catch him looking furtively at his watch dreading the time when he had to return to Nora, or, even worse, when Nora might appear at the bar and order him home.

Bozo and Nora's 'matrimonials' were fast becoming an open-air entertainment for the village. Zoran and the bar-proppers found it very entertaining, but Marko and Ivana worried. We were on our way to the Town Hall for a meeting with the Mayor one morning, when we heard Bozo's voice shouting: 'If you go to that damn sister of yours, I will never speak to you again!'

Turning the corner, we saw Nora flouncing past him towards the car.

'Woman!' hollered Bozo. 'If you dare get into that car, I am leaving!'

Nora grabbed the handle and yanked open the door.

'I've had it with you! You dare get into that car and I'm off!'

Nora got in and slammed the door.

'If you don't get out this minute, I'm off to my mother's and I'm never seeing you again!'

Nora started the engine and jammed it into gear, but let the clutch out too quickly and the car lurched forward like a kicked dog before taking off down the street, its wheels spinning up the grit on either side.

'And I'm taking the children with me,' shouted Bozo to the back of the disappearing car.

Heads appeared in nearby windows as Bozo shrugged his shoulders and trudged dejectedly back into the konoba.

Continuing on our way, we passed Marin sitting on bench. He was looking about as downcast as a Copenhagen mermaid, so we stopped.

'Tanya went to Split for the football match two days ago and she won't answer my messages. I don't know what's going on.'

'Don't worry,' said Ivana brightly. 'She's probably having a grand time catching up with her old school friends and looking at the shops.'

Marin didn't seem too convinced, but, as our meeting was in five minutes' time, we left him sitting there, like a character in a Greek tragedy. It was a painful sight.

Erik was already outside the Mayor's office and we went in to find the Mayor and his cronies already round the table. He got up to greet us, smoothing his hair down nervously.

'How good of you to come.' He motioned for us to sit. 'How's your boat? Just the sort of boat you need for these waters. You must be so happy with it. And I'm glad to hear you're now in touch with the Dalmatian Sailing Association about the sailing school. Of course we'll do all we can to help. It's so important to attract visitors and have things for young people to do on the island. Suitable activities on our island is at the top of our priorities! I've always said that we must…'

Ivana cut him off. 'Are you by any chance suggesting that the nightclub outside your office is a "suitable activity"? As, if you are, I'm telling you that it not only makes life a misery for your ratepayers, but a lot of visiting yachts up anchor in the night and leave because they can't put up with the noise. I imagine none of them will be coming back in a hurry.'

'Perhaps they were just going to fill up with fuel and they came back later.'

'In the middle of the night! Are you joking?'

The Mayor started to say something but Ivana carried on. 'And we've found out that the place only has a licence to function as a café. How come you're allowing a nightclub to operate when you know very well they don't have a licence?'

'I don't know how it all happened,' he flustered. 'We had no idea the café was going to be a nightclub.'

'What? With all those speakers they were putting up right in front of your front door?'

A dark colleague with thick hair coming up out of his shirt whispered something into his ear.

'Maybe the Department of Environment could help you?' said the Mayor.

'You must have received their report by now, damn it!' exclaimed Erik, steam blowing out of his ears. 'What is going on in this office? Is everyone asleep or are they just looking in the other direction?'

'Well, it's hard for the police to do too much. Some of the staff are their friends.' He laughed uncomfortably and looked at his two sidekicks for help.

'We can't go around closing people down just because we don't like their music,' said the dark one.

'But they don't have a licence,' repeated Ivana. 'If you can't close them down, who can?'

'Give us a bit more time and we'll sort it all out, you'll see,' said the Mayor patronisingly. 'Now let's be a bit patient and see how things go.' He got up to terminate the meeting and thanked us profusely for coming.

We left with a definite fobbed-off feeling.

'Something funny is going on in that office,' said Erik, as we went to Marko's for a strategy meeting.

213

'And something to the benefit of the Mayor and his friends, no doubt,' I said. 'That dark one who kept whispering to him is obviously up to his hairy neck in whatever's going on.'

'Oh!' said Ivana. 'I thought he had a roll-neck sweater on.'

It was time to invoke the mainstay of British politics – the petition. If we got the whole village to sign one and presented it to the Town Hall and the national newspapers, that might get the place closed down. So we bought some clipboards, typed out a statement and, as one does in suburban England, we sallied forth to knock on doors.

To our amazement, no one wanted to sign.

'I'd like to,' said the petrol-pump attendant, 'but we don't want to upset anyone.'

'Once your name gets on to the files, it never comes off,' said the baker.

'Oh, I couldn't,' said Nora. 'Someone in Bozo's family is trying to get a job in the government and it'll be a black mark against him if they see our family name on a list of protestors.'

'We've lived here all our lives,' said the builder. 'I don't want to make enemies in Split.'

'You should be very careful yourself,' said the postmaster. 'Immigration might have your name when you next come back into the country. They can give you trouble.'

'The nightclub owners might recognise my name,' said Filip. 'And they're a mean lot, those people.'

Even Zoran wouldn't sign. 'I've got my own projects to think of.'

'For Christ's sake, Zoran! Don't be so damn selfish! Now's the time to stand up and be counted, not skulk behind your bloody bar. Get a grip on yourself, man!'

'You've just had too much to drink,' said Zoran derisively and laughed. 'Gets you quite offensive, doesn't it? I like you better like this. Have some more wine. You're not such a stiff-arsed Englishman when you drink.'

'The rigidity of my buttocks has nothing to do with it,' I said stuffily. 'You're just avoiding the subject.'

'You don't know what it's like here. If that lot who own the nightclub see my name there, they could have a quiet word with one of their friends in the Planning Office. They all know what I'm tryin' to do. You don't want that happenin'. Doin' business is difficult enough out here without problems like that.'

'But they're driving everyone to distraction with their ruddy music. You've got to stand up to them!'

Zoran grunted. 'When the mouse gnaws at the pot, the cheese inside gets frightened.'

'And what the hell does that mean, for heaven's sake?'

'Think about it,' said Zoran and with a mocking grin disappeared out the back.

From the moment the nightclub started, Ivana had wanted to go directly to the owners with a lawyer and sort it out, but, thinking that going over their heads would make the village think we were throwing our weight around, Erik and I had put her off the idea. She was now adamant.

'But we don't want to get involved with lawyers,' I told her. 'We'll land up dealing for months with benches of Balkan judges, and we're not up to that.'

'After dealing with you and a Croatian housekeeper, a bench of Balkan judges would be a walk in the park!'

'Why don't we wait and see how things go?'

'Why do you always do this?'

'Do what?' I said, knowing very well what she meant.

'You know what I mean! Soft pedal, that's what! You always do it and it never gets us anywhere. Look at the way you used to fall over backwards for your clients – and half of them never paid you. I've been living in fear of being turned out by the bailiffs ever since we met. I knew it was a mistake to marry you!'

She telephoned the nightclub office and the conversation didn't last long. 'That wasn't very nice,' she said, putting the phone down. 'Someone's coming over to see us, but, if he's anything like the one I just talked to, I don't think it's going to get us very far.'

I went to Zoran's to tell the cabal.

'Are you sure you're won't get a visit from the Mafia?' said Bozo.

'Maybe you oughta think about plastic surgery and a one-way ticket to South America,' said Zoran irritatingly.

'Thanks for the support.'

'Well, at least you won't have to worry about a surprise attack. You can always recognise Mafia guys. They wear suits too large in the shoulders; call themselves names like Tony "The Finger" Cannelloni or Giulio "The Screwdriver" Ravioli, and they carry on eating when the man at the next table falls into his soup. But don't you worry. If they do turn up, we'll be ready for them!' He gestured to the bar. 'Bozo "Big Belly" Sanda, Zvonko "Turnip Face" Karela and your good friend Zoran "Mr Wiseguy" Karusa will be here to protect you! You don't have to worry about a thing, my friend. In an ex-war zone, there's still a lot of heavy armament under everyone's beds.'

Zoran continued making unhelpful suggestions until he was interrupted by Dali and Domigoy coming in covered in sweat and carrying their cricket gear.

'Two bottles of your coldest Karlovac, Zoran,' said Dali. 'We're celebrating! Domigoy has finally got the hang of chipping the ball to the off.'

'To the what?' asked Zoran.

'That's the right to you.'

'Don't give me that sport-babble,' he grunted. 'We've had to put up with communist politico-babble for the last fifty years, and we don't want any more of any babble.'

'Well, excuse us!' said Dali testily. 'Some of us call it human communication.'

'Yes,' said Domigoy, oblivious to the barbed exchange. 'I've really got the hang of what that Indian player with the big hair does on the video. You just flick the bat at the ball. I've really got it now!'

'Well, I'll give you a towel and you can have a turban, too,' said Zoran sarkily. (He'd been in one of his spiky moods all day.)

'Oh, come on, Zoran,' I said.

He exhaled and pushed his lank hair back with his hands. 'I'm just so damn pissed off with everything today.' He looked up at Dali and grunted. 'Well, does this mean Croatia might have a team that actually wins something for once? If so, that'll be a change. In the last World Cup, we lost to East Timor or someplace I'd never heard of.'

216

'Well, we'll get beaten by both East and West Timor at cricket if everyone carries on like you do,' said Dali, before draining his glass and picking up his gear. 'Anyway, I'd better be getting back or I'll be in trouble with Aunt Sida. She's run out of cigarettes, and you know how crabby she gets when she's nicotine deprived.' He slung his bag over his shoulder and left.

No one said anything, but we all knew that the reason he was going home wasn't Aunt Sida. It was Anni, his wife. A familiar pattern had recently appeared in the marriages of club members. I'd seen it before. The first stage is when the wife or girlfriend watches her beloved clad in crisp, manly whites striding across the greensward and is in full support, but soon comes stage two, which is a decline into resigned acceptance. Go on, play the silly game, the wife tells herself. At least she knows where he is and he's not off having an affair with her best friend. Then comes stage three when the phrase 'You and your cricket' begins to be heard quite often around the house, and after that comes stage four when the phrase becomes 'You and your f…ing cricket!'

Maybe I should have warned them.

CHAPTER 30

THE STAR CROSS'D LOVERS AND MAN'S BEST FRIEND

Refreshments during matches had been served on a collection of plastic plates and cups, but, now the visiting teams had told the club members about the elaborate lunches and teas that some clubs provided in England, Ivana and I were sent over to Split's equivalent of B&Q to upgrade the tea service. Waiting on a bench for the ferry with our purchases, we were watching the world go by on the promenade when we spotted Tanya strolling along with a group of young things. We called out and the arm draped over the shoulder of a dark young man with heavily gelled hair was quickly whipped away and she came over to us.

'Please don't tell Marin you've seen me.'

'Who's your friend?' I asked, indicating the matinee idol who was checking his hair in a shop window. (I've always wondered about gel. Doesn't it get all over your girlfriend's face when you're snogging?)

'Oh, he's just a good friend, but please don't mention him to Marin. He won't understand.'

She rejoined her friends and I noticed she was careful not to get too close to the matinee idol as they walked away. There was something going on between her and Mr Gel. That was plain to see.

Back on the island, we went to confer with Marko the Wise.

'Go and talk to Tanya's parents. Her mother will know what's going on. She doesn't miss much. But I don't think her ten-year plan for Tanya includes marriage to a Bosnian. She was always an ambitious one, Draga Tomic. We were in the same form at school and she always had to be the best even then.'

'Rougher than a boar's rear end, that Draga Tomic,' said Dali the postman. 'She should have joined the army. Dedo her husband's a good man, mind you, but he doesn't wear the trousers in that household.'

'Go and tell her that a mother who casts her net too wide may end up catching no fish at all,' said Marko.

The Tomics' house was tucked away behind the post office. It must have been an attractive building in the eighteenth century, but it looked as if the owners had been ashamed of it and had smothered it with add-ons. This was actually the case with a lot of Vis houses, each generation having turned them into a dire cobbling together of mismatched elements. But then, who were we to criticise with our middle-class sense of aesthetics? Families had modified their homes to suit their needs as best they could, and it was only us latecomers who could afford to indulge in heritage-friendly renovations.

The outside stairway led us up over the ground floor where Filip and his mother lived, and on the first floor we found a hunched old lady sitting on a chair crocheting a blanket. She blinked at us and called, '*Gosti! Gosti!*' (Guests! Guests!) up the stairs before shuffling off to clatter some pots around in the kitchen. Draga Tomic came down to greet us. A tall woman, there was an air of Queen Elizabeth I disapproval about her. She greeted us politely and we were led up to the next floor with the grandmother teetering dangerously behind with a tray of rattling cups and saucers. Tanya's father was sitting on their terrace, and rose to welcome us with the contented expression of someone who didn't want any more from life than he had. I could see where Tanya got her dazzling smile from. Draga took the coffee tray from her mother, shooed her downstairs and began to pour. I suspected she knew why we were here. She talked in a nervous, staccato voice about their married daughter who lived in Zagreb as she poured.

'Her husband is in the technology business, you know.'

Ivana made appreciative noises.

'But I cannot understand them. They have a perfect space for a vegetable garden at the back of their house and he has paved it over with stone. What a thing to do!'

Her husband put his hand on her arm. 'Don't upset yourself again, my dear.'

She shook her head crossly. 'They are putting sculptures there. What a ridiculous idea! At their age they should be more practical and think about what they eat. But what can you expect? Her husband was brought up in a city and only thinks about other people's opinions. He wants his friends to see he has the kind of house people have in magazines, and he wants people to think he has a sophisticated wife, not one who grows vegetables and worries about her husband's health. How will they bring up their children?'

Her husband patted her arm again. 'They are two sensible, hardworking, young people. We need not worry about them.'

But she wasn't to be consoled. 'And as for Tanya,' she exclaimed, 'she should be going out with our own kind.' (There is a Croatian word for 'our own kind' – '*Nasi*', meaning 'ours' – with all the hidden connotations the word implies.)

Ivana pointed out that Marin was hardly a foreigner as he came from Bosnia.

'Blood is not water. Those Bosnians have been under the Turk for so long they're not the same as us. Most of them are Muslims. How can one of them ever understand the heart of one of ours?' She gave a Karmela-like tilt of her chin.

I put in that Marin seemed a nice hardworking young man and the father nodded. 'He looks a respectable young man, but with those Bosnians you never know. Their values are so different despite how similar they look. I think it's best if I find her a job in Split and she can meet some nice Croatian boys.'

The conversation seemed to be slipping a cog, but, not wanting to be too obvious, I couldn't commend Marin too much without it sounding fabricated. It all sounded rather lame.

We left them feeling that we'd failed and went to find Marin. We found him sitting at Marko's with a letter in his hands; he put it on the table and then picked it up to read it again as if he couldn't understand it. He gave us a lacklustre greeting when we came over, and, in the sort of tone that an ancient Greek might have used when asking for a cup of hemlock, he asked the waiter to bring some more coffee.

'Her parents want her to stay in Split and find a job,' he said, gesturing to the letter. 'She says she still loves me, but thinks we shouldn't see so much of each other for a while.'

That didn't sound good. The 'I-love-you-but-we-shouldn't-see-so-much-of-each-other' was the line I used to get given when I was being dumped.

We left him looking about as downhearted as a young man can.

But the next day he had put on a brave face and was helping me out with my new navigation equipment. He was the sort who would do this anyway, but I think he saw us as a conduit to Tanya and was hoping that somehow we might help to get her back. Ivana was actually already on the case. Despite thirty years of my telling her not to get herself involved in other people's emotional entanglements, she finds it difficult not to, and I had twice seen her in a huddle with Karmela and the other wise ones of the village (and Grandma Klakic was in the group, too – so perhaps the old bat did have human feelings after all).

For the village matriarchs, Marin and Tanya were still the island's Romeo and Juliet, and they wanted to get the star-cross'd lovers back on track.

September was when the annual regatta took place and Richard entered his boat. He had brought out a Cornish crabber in kit form with their furniture and, after he'd assembled it in a disused naval hangar, he had sailed her over here. She now rocked at anchor with a certain prim dignity among the large sleek racing yachts that had come to take part. With her turquoise-green hull and rust-coloured gaff rig sails, for me, she was the prettiest boat in the bay.

Richard had enlisted Bozo as his crew, but, nonetheless, his regatta application created something of a stir. Some of the committee had objected to a foreign-owned craft taking part – and one so much smaller than any other boat. But luckily Marko and Filip were on the committee, and when they pointed out that most of the money for the regatta came from foreign sponsors, and that if more foreign boats took part they might get even more sponsorship, the objectors were overruled.

We stood on the terrace to watch on race day; Nora and Ivana with binoculars and me with a telescope. With the rust-red sails fluffed out in the breeze, Richard and Bozo bobbed jauntily across the bay, looking blithe and bonny, but, just as they got to the start line, the gun went off for the category 'A' class yachts, and the four monster super yachts came sweeping down on to them. I could see Richard frantically trying to get out of their way, but Cornish crabbers can't move very fast, and the first of the ten-tonners swooshed past, creating a wave that sent the little boat bouncing about like a toy. Bozo fell over, and through my telescope I could see him trying to get upright (difficult when you are almost spherical and in a confined space), as Richard's lips were mouthing words that started with an F. Bozo had almost succeeded in getting up when he caught his foot in a coil of rope and fell over again and rolled around like an upturned turtle when the second super yacht thundered past, missing them by a whisker and drenching them with a tidal wave of water. The half-submerged little boat was now wallowing dangerously with Richard hanging on to the tiller trying to keep it steady and Bozo trying to untangle himself. Nora was gripping her binoculars with white knuckles as the third ten-tonner bore down on the little boat. 'It's going to hit them!' she shrieked as Bozo finally managed to get up and grabbed hold of the boom to keep himself from falling again. But Richard then shouted something that made him let go and he fell again. The yacht passed behind them and, the danger now over, Richard untangled Bozo and put him to work bailing the boat out while he repositioned her on the start line for the correct gun with as much dignity as he could muster.

That evening, all those in the regatta and most of the village career drinkers had gathered at the hotel for the prize-giving ceremony. As most of the races had been won by island boats, the place was filled with *rakija*-fuelled cheering and inane shouting as if inmates from a lunatic asylum were celebrating early release. Eventually, Marko shouted for some quiet so the prizes could be given, and Filip, the president, handed them out to the winners; the highlight being the presentation of the prize for the Cornish crabber category to Richard and Bozo – the only participants in the class – but these were the kinds of boats the islanders used to sail, and the loudest cheers were for them.

After the prize giving, we spilled out on to the waterfront and moved along to Marko's. By now, the singing had started and soon the gathering was singing along to good old Croatian favourites such as 'Memories Are Made of This' and 'Yellow Submarine'. In the crowd, we saw Marin, whom we hadn't seen since he'd gone on holiday to Bosnia two weeks before, and went to join him.

'So you're back,' I said. 'Find any new girlfriends in the mountains?'

He gave his slow grin. 'Well, yes, but she went off with another sheep.'

'No news from Tanya?' asked Ivana.

'Not really. Her father's got her a job working with some fashion chain in Split. It's a great opportunity. I hope it works out for her.'

'Oh no you don't,' said Ivana sharply. 'You want her back here with you!'

He hesitated for a moment. 'Yes, I suppose I do.' He looked at us earnestly. 'I still can't stop thinking about her.'

'You see. It's love! Now don't you give up! You go over to Split and stand on her doorstep until she says she'll marry you.'

'Er… I wasn't quite thinking of marriage just yet,' said Marin, rather taken aback.

'Oh, men!' sighed Ivana. 'You're all hopeless!'

'Well… it's a big step, you know…'

Ivana took hold of his face and put hers up to it (difficult with her being a good foot shorter). 'If you really loved her, stupid, you'd want to marry her. Heavens, if we had to wait for you men to make up your minds, we'd all be old, wrinkled and single!'

Marin scratched his head.

'Go on, get on with it!'

Later, I saw him sitting on a bollard by the water, no doubt giving the matter some thought.

The festivities ended around midnight and we were walking home along the front when Bozo's van came reversing erratically down the quay towards us. He shot backwards past us and waved in the confident style that comes from sampling too much grape-based product at a public gathering. Just as he had passed, the unmistakable figure of Grandma Klakic emerged from a side street into his path. We thought he was going straight into her, but, silhouetted against the night sky, she loomed like a shipping hazard, and he saw her and somehow managed a reverse slalom around her. Then he swerved into his turning and a loud crashing and clanging told us that his dustbins had got themselves involved in his parking arrangements. We rounded the corner to see him opening the door, catching his foot on the sill and sprawling on to the ground.

The dustbins had woken up the neighbouring dogs and heads were appearing in windows. Just as we arrived, the front door flew open revealing Nora, silhouetted by the light like Judy in a Punch and Judy show. She shouted at Bozo who was still on the ground with his short legs waving in the air like an upturned beetle. With an effort, he rolled himself upright and lumbered into the house, trying to fend off Nora's cuffs.

According to Karmela, Bozo had never been able to stand up to Nora ever since he lost most of their savings. 'Bozo's business partner ran off with it all and Nora still blames him for not going and beating the man up. And she's right. What sort of man wouldn't beat up a thieving partner? Pah! And the man only lived over the hill. The problem is that Bozo was the only man in the house. His mother had five girls and his father was always away at sea. That's the problem there, I'm telling you. That's what you get when you have too many women in a household. They didn't even have a dog! Pah!'

She went off muttering to herself – no doubt about the psychosomatic factors at play in a post-Freudian society.

Despite Bozo's dog-deprived childhood, he seemed to be making up for it with two yappy West Highland Terriers (unless he kept them to drown out the sound of Nora's raucous voice). Pets were in fact something of a rarity, and the locals didn't seem too fond of them. Most island dogs had to sleep outside, and the sight of children having their faces licked by one would send mothers into a flurry of flannels and soap. This approach to dogs had already given us trouble, and on one occasion we'd had to physically restrain some of our guests from staging a midnight dog-rescue operation on the half-starved dogs of Komiza – our guests, of course, being English. We really are hopeless cases.

But there was one dog in the village that could do no wrong – Baldo, who belonged to Vinka, the widow who owned the corner store. He was a large, shaggy wolfhound who did nothing except lie snuffling gormlessly outside the shop all day, but at least he had served a useful purpose by giving Vinka someone to fuss over.

One morning in September, she appeared at our door to tell me her Baldo had died. I couldn't think why she wanted to tell me, but summoning up all my linguistic powers I started to commiserate (not easy – many subjunctives). I got so carried away with the linguistics that I didn't realise that she was trying to get me to bury Baldo.

No trouble at all, I told her, once I'd understood. I'd come round later with Marin.

But no. It had to be done immediately. Baldo had expired in the store and the government health inspector was arriving off the ferry that morning. She couldn't conceal Baldo by throwing a blanket over him and passing him off as a sack of potatoes as he took up half the floor, and, if the inspector saw him, he'd look round the rest of the premises and find out about all the cats she fed in the backyard. He would close her down!

How could I refuse to be a knight in shining armour? And, besides, I ought to encourage this image of me as the kind of neighbour who'll help out with day-to-day problems such as dealing with your dead animals.

I jumped into the Renault like Charlton Heston into his chariot, and a minute later I was reversing up to the shop ready for some dead-dog action. Stretched out as stiff as a board between the carousels, Baldo looked even bigger in death than he had in life, but I hauled him out and crammed him into the back of the car with as much of a show of gentleness as I could. He only just fitted in and, when I shut the hatch door, his face was squashed against the back window in a particularly goofy expression. Dewy eyed at the sight of her Baldo's face against the window, Vinka thanked me profusely and said she knew I'd find a suitable place for his grave. I hadn't yet given the matter of a grave any thought, but, now that I did, just the thought of digging made the small of my back twinge. Also, the entire island was rocky terrain except for the vineyards, and I didn't fancy being caught by an irate winegrower digging a hole in his vineyard and polluting his next year's crop with essence of wolfhound. And the hole would have to be huge. Baldo was the size of a doe.

A solution suddenly occurred to me. The corporation dustbins. Why not? Vinka would never know. I quickly reined in the Renault and headed for the refuse site. Once there, I parked in the shadows, and as soon as the coast was clear I hauled the old fellow out and pushed him up the side of a circular container. But, when I got him up to the edge, the damn dog wouldn't fit in. He lay rigidly across the top, looking at me with his stupid grin. The only way to get him into it was to break his legs (I quailed at the thought) or to get up there and jump on him (I felt a bit queasy about that one, too).

I was standing there wondering what to do, when to my horror I saw the lower class of the school, shepherded by two nuns, coming towards me. Panic! I could see the newspaper headlines: 'Englishman Mutilates Dead Dog!' or 'Is Nothing Safe from British Necrophiliacs?' and how would I ever face Vinka again once she knew I'd tried to stuff her beloved Baldo into a corporation dustbin? I shoved him off the top and crammed him back into the boot as quickly as I could, but, when I slammed the hatch door on him, his face ended up squashed against the side window with his teeth bared in a hideous grin. There was no time to rearrange him, and, seeing a magazine on the ground, I picked it up, put it over the window and pretended to be avidly reading it. Because in a place as small as this everyone knows everyone, the nuns said, 'Good morning, Mr Anthony!' as they passed and then each child repeated it in turn. Having to turn round and trying to keep my back against Baldo's face in the window, I stood there smiling foolishly and saying, 'Good morning, Good morning,' until the little blighters had all filed past – several of them craning their necks as they went down the street in case the funny Englishman wearing the panama and reading the Croatian version of *Hello!* might reveal what he was really up to.

226

Phew! That was a close one. I jumped back into the car and, hunched over the steering wheel like Mr Magoo, I gunned the engine and shot off, the wheels spinning up the dirt and the exhaust puffing out some quite aggressive-looking smoke rings, in the direction of the island landfill dump. Enclosed in a hot car, Baldo smelled even worse in death than he had in life, and when we got to the top of the tip, not wanting anyone to witness *this* foul deed, I quickly yanked the old chap out and swung him up into the air. Sailing majestically down over sofas, mattresses, fridges and broken TVs with his tongue hanging out and a goofy expression on his face, he looked like he was having the time of his life until, with an undignified bump, he came to his final resting place on top of a pile of beer crates, an old motorcycle and someone's collection of orange G-Plan furniture.

Thus, Baldo came to find his peace and the operation turned out to be our greatest PR success to date. Vinka became our greatest fan and spent the rest of the week telling everyone who came into the shop how lucky they were to have such wonderful neighbours.

I was just a bit nervous in case she asked me where to put the flowers.

CHAPTER 31

CHANGES

It was Harvest Festival so we went to the Sunday service, and, when it came to the communion, Ivana went up to the rail. I, as usual, stayed in the pew pondering on matters of importance, and had just about worked out where to put my new navigation system on the boat when I was jolted from my calculations by the sound of the gravelly voice of Don Romolo, the village priest. I looked up and saw Ivana kneeling in an unusually contrite position on the steps beneath him, her mouth still open for the holy biscuit like a supplicant halibut. Wagging his finger at her, Don Romolo rasped, 'Look at your naked shoulders! Don't come to Mass if you can't dress properly. We can't allow this sort of carrying on! It's indecent!' And, after sticking the wafer in her mouth, he passed on to the next supplicant. Ivana got to her feet blushing madly and came down the aisle as every head turned and whispered.

Afterwards, in the square, half the female congregation gathered around her like a cluster of pelicans, and, to my surprise, they took her side.

'How could Don Romolo humiliate Mrs Ivana like that?'

'He shouldn't speak to any of us in that kind of tone!'

'He certainly shouldn't.'

'And in front of the whole congregation!'

'He certainly shouldn't treat one of *us* like that!'

This was bold talk. The village priest was usually above reproach, but, even more significantly, this implied that Ivana should be accorded the same respect as them. This was a surprising turn. It might have had something to do with several of them being mothers of club members, but, whatever the reason, I felt it was some kind of a milestone.

In the course of the discussion, I learned the reason for Don Romolo's outburst. A month ago, the Bishop of Hvar had decided that the amount of indecently dressed women coming into his churches was reaching epidemic level, and this had to be stopped before women in fishnet stockings and garters were traipsing down his aisles. So he printed up a batch of dress-code posters at his local Prontaprint and sent them out to all his parishes, and, lo, Don Romolo went forth with tacks in his mouth and a hammer in his hand and nailed one up to the church door of Vis like Martin Luther nailing his articles to the church door of Wittenberg. We just hadn't noticed it.

Actually, Ivana usually dressed in rather more demure attire for church, but, because the temperature was 35 degrees, she had put on a rather wispy gypsy skirt and a shoulder-less top. As usual, however, it was my fault. As we walked back home, I was foolish enough to tell her that when she had come out of her bedroom to ask 'How do I look?' I had thought the outfit a touch on the provocative side, but, as another change of clothes would have made us late, I gave her the usual 'You-look-simply-lovely-my-sweet' reply. I now got the 'it's-all-your-fault-you-should-have-told-me' reply. (I'd like to know if men do really exist who actually tell their wives their bottom *does* look big in whatever they've put on.)

Luckily, I was saved from any further mauling by seeing Marin sitting outside Marko's and laughing with some friends. It was the first time we'd seen him looking so cheery for weeks. We went over and he got up, beaming, as soon as he saw us.

'On Friday, I went to Split like you told me to and I asked her.'

'And?'

'She said yes!'

Ivana wrapped her arms round his middle and gave him a big hug. From under his arms she smiled up at me. 'You see! True love always has its way!'

'Hmm. Maybe it was more a case of true persistence having its way.'

'Oh, you're such a killjoy! You and Oliver Cromwell!'

Marin couldn't have cared what anyone said. He was grinning like a Cheshire cat.

That evening, the lovers were at the promenade. In a short white chiffon dress, Tanya looked as adorable as one of the angels behind God's arm on the Sistine ceiling. She ran over when she saw us.

'I'm so happy to be back. We're having the engagement party soon and you must come.' Lowering her voice, she said, 'I don't know why I left when my parents told me to. It hurt Marin so much. No one is as good and kind as he is. I must have been out of my mind.' She hugged Ivana. 'Thank you for telling him to make up his mind.' She then turned to me and said hesitantly, 'Does Marin know about the boy you saw me with?'

I assured her he didn't and she flashed me such a heart-melting look of unutterable gratitude that my knees nearly collapsed.

We walked home with that wonderful feeling you get when you've been part of a winning team effort.

I was still thinking about the happy conclusion as I had my breakfast. The world was a rosy place once again, and, however many times I looked out over the bay, I realised, I never failed to feel massively blessed. What a delight it was to live with a new theatrical backdrop in front of me. Each day the bay presented me a different *mise en scene*; sometimes a bright-blue sky, green hills and sparkling azure water dotted with billowing white sails; sometimes the storm scene from *The Tempest* with white crested waves roaring in and black clouds scudding over the hills. Today, the bay was as calm as a millpond and the water so clear that I could see the stones on the seabed thirty feet below.

I suddenly looked at my watch. Why, I don't know, but, like a Pavlovian hound, some nerve had twitched and I had checked in case I might be late for something. It must have been a reflex left over from years of working. My heart rate had even accelerated. Ridiculous! I told myself and went back to the contemplation of the bay. The flagstones under my feet were warm, the scent of the herbs in the courtyard drifted up to where I stood and muffled sounds from the waterfront percolated up over the courtyard wall. Surely life couldn't get much better than this.

I ought to ring Kaes to let him know my decision, I thought as I went inside. I should have done it already, but I'd kept putting it off. So

I went down to get a coffee from Marko's and sat on a bollard to think about it one more time. Did I really want to go back to the old business? Look at what I had around me now. The day's work had begun on the waterfront, fishing craft were chuntering in and unloading their night's catches, the market was in full swing and the villagers were going about their business. Island life might be a bit spotted at times and some of our neighbours might not be exactly welcoming, but there were certainly a lot of compensations.

I took a deep breath and rang Kaes.

I shut the phone with a huge feeling of relief and went home to tell Ivana. She was in the kitchen putting away the breakfast plates.

'I have just taken an important decision,' I announced with suitable bathos, 'I have turned down the trappings of wealth, position and honour to devote myself to the life I have and the one I love' – a pretty impressive turn of phrase, I thought.

'Oh good,' she answered distractedly, as she put away the plates. 'Now, we're having tomato and mozzarella salad for lunch today. Should we have hardboiled eggs or anchovies with it?'

In need of some consolation, I went down to the courtyard to contemplate the mimosa tree – or rather sit there and sulk – and I was still sitting there when I heard the courtyard door creak shut as Ivana left for the market. I stayed there consoling myself with the contemplation of the mimosa's exquisitely sculpted, soft parasol shape, and slowly my furrowed brow was beginning to unfurrow when the phone rang. I ran upstairs to get it, but by the time I got to the drawing room it had stopped ringing. One of us had forgotten to put the answer machine on. Oddly, I didn't feel annoyed. A few months ago, I would have been highly irritated, but now things like that didn't bother me at all. So what if I missed a call? Whoever it was would call again if it mattered. I then remembered how angry I'd been when the air-conditioning part had stayed on the ferry for a week and I'd had to wait for it. How could I have made such a fuss about such a trivial thing? What an impossible sort of person I must have been for so many years. The island must have had a mellowing effect. I had even begun to get more philosophical about how long it was taking to become fully accepted as part of the village. Perhaps Ivana was right and it really didn't matter so much. I wasn't even that worried about the prospect of not having enough to do – and that really surprised me. I never thought I had it in me to become that laid-back.

Halfway through September, the villagers started rolling all their wine barrels out into the street to wash them out and get them ready for the coming harvest. A faintly sour but comforting smell pervaded the streets and there was a sense of expectancy in the air as the village waited for the oenologist to say when the grapes were at their fullest, the acidity level right and the sugar content high enough for the harvesting to start.

As the grapes had to be picked in the optimum week, many hands were needed, and by tradition every able-bodied person in the family was expected to join in, even those who lived on the mainland. It was in everyone's interest to lend a hand, as families relied on the harvest for income as well as for their wine during the year – and if the harvesting was not done speedily the quality would suffer.

We had offered our services as pickers to Zvonko, so, the day the oenologist told him his vines were ready, we donned sensible hats, put on stout footwear and piled into his van with the rest of the family. Once in the vineyard, panniers were issued, we fanned out along the rows and began to pick – and, I must say, stooping to lift the leaves, separating the clusters, cutting the stems, putting the bunches into the pannier and then lugging it over to the trailer was knackering work. Ivana still looked quite spry, but, after three hours of back-breaking work in the sun, I was drenched in sweat and suffering horribly. Let me count the ways: my back was hurting, my arms were aching, my neck was stiff, my fingers were sore and something very worrying was happening to my breathing.

Mercifully, at one o'clock, Zvonko's wife and sisters arrived at the bottom of the fields with our lunch, and, trying hard not to appear in an ill-mannered haste, I downed tools and was the first in line. What a delight it is to fall on to food and drink when you're dog tired, hungry and thirsty. Everything tastes simply wonderful, and half an hour later, having devoured a life-affirming amount of salami, ham, cheese, pickles and the local pizza-cum-pasty that they make, and washing it down with some cool lemonade, I felt on terrific form again.

We lay chatting and joking for a while in the shade of the trees, but eventually Zvonko got us back to the vines, and, by three o'clock, every muscle in my body was complaining again. By then, every ten minutes seemed like an hour, but the blessed hour of five eventually arrived and we bundled into the vans groaning vociferously and comparing our sore backs, necks, arms and thumbs. But those who had come over from the mainland were in holiday mood and it was infectious. By the time we were halfway to the village, the aches and pains were side-lined and the talk turned to the parties they were all going to that evening.

Zvonko dropped us off at home and we collapsed into a bath, vowing never to volunteer again (and at that point the last thing on our minds was singing and dancing), but the recuperative power of a gin and tonic never ceases to amaze. By nine o'clock, our aching limbs forgotten, we were out taking part in the festivities, and by midnight I was whirling Ivana around the floor at Asija's to screeching violins, frenzied mandolins and some feverish accordion playing by the diminutive man with a Hitler moustache who sells the ferry tickets. Reeling about in circles with one's fellow beings must be yet another of life's great pleasures, and, as we careered around the room in the galloping throng, I felt an intoxicating herd-like oneness with my fellow harvesters and wanted the night to go on forever.

CHAPTER 32

AUTUMN

The summer came to an end, but the autumn brought its own spell. The green rows of vines had turned orange and brown, and the hills were wrapped by the morning mist in a mystical veil. The days were still warm, but the air was clearer and the light sharper. The breeze off the bay swayed the cypresses along the shore, fanned the branches of the mimosa and ruffled the feathers of the swallows chittering away on our telephone wires about their imminent departure. The bay was now a deep dark blue, its surface speckled with white horses, and the wind blew in differently from the sea. It came in gusts, riffling the woods on the hills, bending the pines along the shore, skittering the russet-coloured leaves around the squares and humming up and down the narrow streets as if playing a game. Olive trees creaked and shutters banged.

A small amount of rain fell, which tinged the parched brown grass of the cricket field with green and gave a wet gleam to the Astroturf pitch. Luckily, the nets weren't affected, which was just as well, since we now needed more practice than ever. The MCC had telephoned! The MCC – the most important cricket club in the world! They had learned about us from the articles on the cricket sites and they wanted to send a team down. It came as something of a shock, but their fixtures secretary very decently said that they'd field a minor team. This did little to allay Luka's nerves, and even the club members, after an initial display of bravado, were somewhat cowed by the prospect. Never in our dreams had anyone imagined this would happen.

Of course, except for the players, no one else on the island knew who the MCC were, but the players soon made sure that everyone did, and by mid-October the tension was building.

On the day, everyone waited nervously as the fabled club came off the ferry, and were relieved that they seemed to be as easy-going a bunch as anyone could have hoped for. Most of them had come with wives or girlfriends.

The next morning, the sun was high in a clear blue sky as the captains shook hands on thirty overs a side and tossed. It was a hot day with no wind and a thin heat haze hung over the hills. The smoke from burning piles of vine leaves snaked upwards into the blue where the buzzards circled slowly on the thermals, and the monastery bell struck ten o'clock as the white-clad SWHKK figures fanned out across the field. Bees drifted lazily over the gorse, butterflies flitted about the flowers in the long grass, and beyond the boundary was an old man with a whetstone sticking out of his pocket leaning on his scythe to watch. All the scene needed, once again, was a church, a vicar and a village blacksmith.

Would Petar and Domigoy be decimated by their fast bowlers?

But with some defensive blocking and cautious chipping away at anything off the wicket, they both notched up a few runs.

We were up to their bowlers! We weren't going to be decimated!

Their second bowler was doing slow right arm stuff with a bit of turn, and although most of his balls were uncomfortably accurate, Petar and Domigoy had the measure of them. There were a few close shaves, and eventually in the fourth over Domigoy took an over-confident swing at a fast spinner and got caught in the slips. Luka was the next in, and with his signature scarf around his waist he strolled confidently onto the field waving his bat at the clapping crowd, but I knew how nervous he was. He didn't want to repeat his duck.

Blocking the first few deliveries, he worked at the bowling cautiously while Petar began to hit out. The spinner's balls now got the full force of the new oversized bat and he was peppering the boundary with anything off the wicket. By his third over, Luka had got the measure of the spinner, too, and was putting most of his balls through mid-wicket, but when trying to get an extra run he got himself stumped.

Filip was next and gamely faced the fast bowler. The first ball he drove forward, and silly mid-off, no doubt emboldened by his stumping of Luka, dived for it. I could see him trying to stop himself, but too late he remembered that the pitch was on a slab of concrete, and his thigh hit the edge of the helipad with a nasty sounding crunch. Players and spectators gathered round. The gash didn't look good.

The game recommenced and Filip continued to do well with the quicker stuff even though he still got confused by anything that was given a bit of air. The canny spin bowler saw this and came up with a something. What Filip did to it was one of the most extraordinary shots I have ever seen which had the effect of deflecting the ball straight onto the stumps. Filip turned to stare at the splayed sticks like a schoolboy at his broken bicycle, and for a moment I thought he was going to throw another 'cricket rage' scene, but this time he took it on the chin and walked off uncomplainingly.

Our next few batsmen acquitted themselves decently enough and Icho put on a particularly impressive display of dealing with some tricky spinners. This brought bellowed cheers from his new bride who he had by now successfully lured away from the football-playing policeman. I was pleased to see that island life had mellowed her taste for Travis and Perkins facial accessories. When Icho first brought her over, she was extravagantly studded about the face, but the display was now restricted to three, though I dare say she also harboured others in unseen places.

All this time Petar was wielding his oversized willow with great effect and was racking it up, but at the end of twenty overs we were 78 for 7.

Quite a crowd had come along for the lunch. I even saw Don Romolo (never one to miss out on a free meal), arriving and collecting a fair-sized gorse bush in the bumper of his Wartburg as he tried to park it. Noticing his arrival, one of the team took him a glass of wine.

'I know I'm the least frequent member of your congregation Don Romolo, but right now we could do with some prayers.'

Don Romolo looked up and raised the glass to heaven. 'Faith works wonders, my son!'

'Rubbish!' muttered Filip in the background. 'It's all to do with application to the job in hand.'

After lunch the visitors took to the field and we sat apprehensively. The two opening bats walked in wearing protective helmets. Was this was standard MCC equipment, or had they had advance intelligence of Petar's bumpers? I thought it best not to ask.

Petar thundered down onto the helipad and hurled down a fizzer. It was right on target and the batsman had to block it. He did the same with the second ball, too – and to our amazement, by the end of the over they hadn't managed a run. A maiden over against the MCC! A collective sigh of relief went round the team. Maybe we weren't going to be trashed after all. Their opening bats then scored three singles off Marin in the second over, but his balls were now truer on the wicket and had a nice swing to them. They certainly weren't carting him all over the place like the Australians had a few weeks before.

In the third over, a sharp catch bagged by Luka drew a warm round of applause, and in the fifth, a loping ball from Marin was driven straight into the hands of Sinisa at silly mid-on. But Marin had put so much extra spin on the ball that he sprained his wrist and had to be replaced by Icho. Icho had been glued to Marko's bar TV and it looked like he'd been paying particular attention to intimidation technique. He stood at the wicket staring at the batsman and then running up at a brisk pace with his new round arm technique (the forearm flexing perhaps a little bit more than the regulation 5 per cent), he delivered a humming off-break that shot up off the matting and caught the batsman's pad.

A bellow of 'How's that!' in Croatian accents erupted from every man on the field, and the umpire (ours) raised a finger.

The batsman clearly disagreed, but shrugged and walked back, the umpire's verdict unchallenged. Sometimes one can feel very proud of one's fellow countrymen.

In the next over, a ball with a hairy fizz on it from Petar glanced off an MCC bat and was caught in the slips, bringing tumultuous applause from the side-line and an enormous grin to Petar's usually impassive face. (The hours spent watchingShane Warne had paid off.) Then in the next over, a ball came off their captain's protective stroke and Bozo leapt backwards at the wicket to catch it one handed. Masterful play!

But even so, by the end of the twenty overs, the visitors had overtaken us with some wickets in hand. Nonetheless we had endured the onslaught of the MCC, and hats, gloves, and bats were thrown into the air as spectators converged onto the field. The MCC men looked slightly fazed by the onslaught of fierce embracing, but they submitted decently enough.

After an evening of jollity, I sat on the bench outside the hotel. The waterfront was almost deserted, and as I watched a courting couple wandering between the shadows of the palm trees, the fishing boats swaying gently in the inky water, and the moonlight gleaming off the rippled surface of the bay, a sense of utter contentment overcame me. Two hundred years after Captain Hoste drew stumps and sailed for England, we had a team up and running that was able to give the MCC a fairly decent game. No mean feat. Would we do even better next year, and would island cricket now carry on for ever? I didn't see why not. Perhaps one day we might even have a real pavilion just like at home and a real changing room, where players can complain about the ridiculous decisions of their captain, compare sprained ligaments and bruised shins, and tell awful jokes just like in west Sussex. And will there be honey still for tea?

I hoped so.

The engagement party for Marin and Tanya was announced the day after the MCC left. It was to be at Darko's, high above the central valley. Darko had turned his family's farmhouse into a restaurant and had decorated it with every object he had ever made, collected or loved. Empty demijohns, horseshoes, yokes, scythes, harnesses and pieces of RAF aircraft had been piled on top of each other like geographical strata, and it gave the tumbledown farmhouse a unique sense of place.

Tanya's aunts were out in force that evening – tall aunts, short aunts, fat aunts, thin aunts. I've never seen so many aunts together at one time. They were catching up on the gossip (having first completed the prerequisite check for life-threatening draughts), and were clapping at the good news and making signs of the cross at the bad. But the two families weren't talking to each other. They were standing in separate groups. Tanya's relations, led by Draga doing a passable impersonation of Cruella de Vil, were glaring at Marin's family, and the Bosnians were eyeing their hosts nervously. Luckily, Marin and Tanya were both so busy greeting everyone that I don't think they noticed, but, for us, the tension was palpable.

Once we were sitting down, Darko brought out a cauldron of steaming lamb and then bowls of roast potatoes and the special salad he made of caper leaves and tomatoes soused in vinegar. Once that was demolished, he brought out one of his lambs for the children to play with, and that was an instant success. They patted it, fed it with a bottle of milk and squealed with glee when the lamb butted them for more. Then, thinking that they'd like his donkey as well, Darko hauled the poor beast up on to the terrace. It was a lovely, old moth-eaten specimen with enormous ears, and stood uncomplainingly as the children swarmed all over it – while mothers hovered behind muttering about contagious diseases and washing hands afterwards.

By the time we'd finished the pudding and a lot of wine had been consumed, the cold war began to thaw, and the aunties of the opposing sides opened negotiations on the matter of the bridal linen – and, most importantly, how it was to be embroidered. One even dared make the audacious suggestion that the linen should not necessarily be white and that heavy embroidery wasn't what the young wanted nowadays, but this was treated as progressive heresy by the majority. As the older generation, they asserted, they had a duty to make sure the tradition of embroidery was handed down to the next generation. At one point, I thought the question of the bed linen was going to start another Balkan war, but, in the end, the wiser element prevailed and it was agreed that perhaps not everything needed to be embroidered, but the marital bed linen and tablecloths certainly did. That settled, they then itemised every sheet, pillowcase, tablecloth and napkin required, and a heated debate ensued about exactly who was going to supply what.

Tanya's father, taking the opportunity of speaking without Draga's interruption, launched into a eulogy about the heavens. 'The twinkling lights we see above are something that happened thousands of years ago, but it's only now that the light of it has reached us and is blessing our young couple. What wonders they are privileged to be part of! Standing here on Darko's terrace, they are simultaneously being whirled through the universe at a hundred thousand kilometres an hour by the forces of gravity at work…'

'Maybe,' came the laconic voice of Zoran from the back of the terrace. 'But what about all the other forces at work in the universe? The forces that attract women to clothes shops, men to televisions when the football's on and other people's mooring ropes to Anthony's propeller?'

Damn! He must have seen me docking yesterday. I thought no one had seen me.

By the end of the evening, aided by the wine, Tanya's family appeared to be adjusting to the idea of Bosnians as in-laws, and the bitterness of the war temporarily forgotten, wine-fuelled embraces and promises of eternal friendship were being bandied around. Emotions were running high. And, when Tanya's aunties started hugging Ivana and thanking her for her role in getting the couple back together, even I felt a bit teary.

Marin and Tanya made touching speeches and then stood at the end of the terrace, silhouetted against the star-lit sky, waving to us as we got into our cars and drove off into the night. We wove our way down the track in an unsteady convoy with the beams of our headlights playing like drunken searchlights over the hillside.

'Wasn't it good luck that brought us here and made all this possible,' said Ivana, as I tried to keep my eyes focused on the road ahead. 'Look what happiness!'

'And look at how much we've been able to do in spite of not being fully accepted. We've eaten more delicious food, drunk more wine and made more new friends than we ever would have at home.'

'And the children will love it. They might even marry someone Croatian – just like you did!'

I laughed. 'Well, there certainly isn't a shortage of dishy-looking young people in this part of the world.'

'It would be nice to have a Croatian daughter-in-law,' said Ivana, with that look on her face that meant a plot was already being formed.

'Don't plan ahead like that. It's tempting fate!'

We puttered down the hill road past the slumbering farmhouses and darkened terraces, and far below us I could see the lights of the village twinkling on the water like Christmas decorations. There it was – my village; sleeping in the moonlight beside the shimmering bay. How long had I been thinking of it as *my* village? Maybe it didn't reciprocate, but its streets, its squares, its bars, its routines were now a part of me.

Ivana had fallen asleep, and looking at her profile I thought how much it resembled Milena's, and my thoughts then turned to the minor triumphs and failures that had coloured our lives. Had there been some rationale behind all our ups and downs or had we just been bouncing from one thing to the next like in a pinball machine. Had it been purely chance that we ended up here, or was it all part of a pattern that I couldn't see, a hidden seam that had been running beneath the turmoil?

Ivana stirred. Looking down at the lights of the harbour, she sat up, rubbing her eyes and blinking. 'See what a good time we can have here, even with standoffish neighbours. And can you imagine the fun it'll be once we've got the vineyard and the sailing school going?'

'Hmm. Maybe you're right. And don't forget about the English restaurant!'

Ivana pulled a face.

CHAPTER 33

THE FINAL
STRAIGHT

The next morning, a staccato rap on the courtyard door announced the visit we had been waiting for. We looked down and saw the director of the nightclub at the bottom of the steps, an athletic-looking young man with close-cropped hair in an immaculate blue suit.

'Quick, put the coffee on,' I said.

'There's no time now, and, anyway, he doesn't look like the warm-drink-and-biscuit type to me.'

He came into the drawing room with the latent menace of a character in a Pinter play. Emanating the sleek self-assurance of the successful, he introduced himself in perfect English. With a dark, suave, intelligent-looking face and unblinking eyes, he looked at me coldly when I asked him to sit down, and started on what sounded like a well-prepared speech. Disco bars made their money between 11 p.m. and 4 a.m., he said. This was when young people would hang around listening to booming music and eyeing up the opposite sex – and this was when they spent money on drinks. But, if the music was not booming, they didn't come, he added with a smile that conveyed a minimum of humour.

'Loud music draws young people to it like moths to a light,' he continued. 'They are happy and they dance, but for most of the time they sit around and spend money on drinks. To start with, we did good business, but, after you and your Swedish friend started complaining, the police made us lower the sound and stop the music entirely at 2 a.m. This made our revenue drop by 25 per cent.' He looked at us coldly. 'And we don't like people who damage our business.'

'But half of the village can't sleep properly because of the music,' I responded.

'As the other half still can, that's not such a bad result,' he replied. 'Nightclubs mean progress, and some will always have to suffer because of progress.'

I could see Ivana bristling on the sofa, so trying to keep the meeting on an even keel, I pointed out that the charm of Vis was its peace and lack of progress. He didn't seem that interested and started off on a different tack. Intimidation is a common ploy in Croatia. Here, people shove their opponents or curse them and walk away, swearing to return later and punch them – and the tactic usually works. Turning up the menace knob to level eleven, he now looked pointedly at Ivana and said, 'My partners and I know how to deal with people like you.'

Ivana jumped to her feet. 'And what exactly do you mean by that? To have us murdered?'

'Now, now! Calm down, dear,' I said, sounding like Michael Winner. 'Why don't we ask the nice man what suggestions he has?'

Ivana continued to give him the oxyacetylene blowtorch look usually reserved for me, but I continued in my honeyed tone: 'Seeing that we seem to be at something of an impasse, what would be the most acceptable compromise? We do know that you are operating without a licence, you know.'

He had his answer ready. 'If you pay us, we will go. Pay us for our setting-up costs and buy our lease from us, and we will leave.'

There was an uncomfortable silence while I repeated the words in my head. The effect was no better the second time round. 'We'll certainly consider it,' I said, wanting to keep the offer open and give us time to plan.

'That is our offer, and, if you do not pay, we will continue.'

'Well, I'm sure we'll be able to come up with something,' I replied shakily.

'I believe we have understood each other. Let me know your decision,' he said icily, moving towards the door. He left without shaking hands, leaving a hint of expensive aftershave lingering in the air.

Somewhat shaken, we sat down on the sofa. What had we got ourselves into? I might be able to find some people to come in on the lease with us, but who wanted to cough up for their costs? And, if we didn't go along with his offer, would the Split Mafia turn up with violin cases to catch us on the church steps after a christening, or hang around Marko's spiking our coffees with Polonium 210? Apart from that, what would we do with a bar? We knew nothing about the business.

I got on the phone to see if I could drum up some investors. By lunchtime, I'd got the owner of the hotel to agree to run it, and by teatime I'd got Richard and a cousin of Marko's in Zagreb to come in on the lease, but, as I had feared, no one wanted to pay for whatever their costs would be.

'What are we going to do?' I said, looking gloomily out of the window. 'We can't possibly pay them on our own.'

'This is all wrong!' said Ivana. 'It's intimidation! They're telling us that, if we don't pay them off, they'll continue to make everyone's life a misery.'

We stood at the window looking out over the peaceful sunlit water and an idea occurred. Maybe the islanders' dislike of outsiders might work in our favour this time? As they seemed to dislike people from their own big cities almost as much as they did foreigners, perhaps, if we told them about the threats we'd just had, they might consider that the village itself was being threatened. Could it make them feel insulted enough to put some pressure on the Town Hall for the first time? It was worth a try.

So, for the next two days, we went around telling everyone about the man's threats, and I was right. It was taken as an insult to them.

'They think they can just come over with their money and do what they want.'

'How dare they try to intimidate us!'

'We'll show those Split boys that they can't bully us!'

'We're not the sort to be pushed around!'

Karmela blamed the Mayor. 'A fat buttock always looks for a comfy bench to sit on. That man goes along with anything that benefits him.'

Grandma Klakic marched into the Town Hall and told them they were a bunch of wimps, and for the rest of the week we saw several others coming out of the building flushed with the satisfaction of telling their elected representatives what they thought of them.

On Friday morning, the Mayor told the nightclub to close down.

We had finally done it!

During the promenade that evening, we were feted as if we were Captain Hoste coming back into the harbour with the French fleet in tow. We were patted on the back, offered drinks and thanked profusely – even by some of the usual scowlers.

I took the opportunity to point out tactfully that they might have lent their support to our protest in the first place, but the answer was always the same: 'You can protest but we just can't.'

At Sunday Mass, the theme of Don Romolo's sermon was David and Goliath – the victory of God's Little Village over the Disco of the Devil – and we sat in our pew glowing with self-righteousness. It was even better on our way home. By the convent, we were beckoned over by some nuns engaged in an argument with an old man. Their neighbour was complaining about their early-morning prayers, they said. Could we make him see reason?

Morning prayers used to be at eight, but now they started at six and he couldn't get back to sleep again, the old man protested to us in turn. Could we make the nuns see reason?

'What's all this got to do with us?' whispered Ivana.

'I think we're now seen as "fixers",' I whispered back.

So, with Ivana acting as referee, the discussion continued, and, after ten minutes of head shaking, hand waving and a lot of nun-tutting, the matter was settled. Morning prayers would start at seven.

Further along the Riva, we passed a house that a nephew of Karmela's was turning into a restaurant and he called out to us: 'You kick those Split guys in arse real good!'

'You make all Vis people so happy!' echoed his wife. 'You proper Vis people now. Yes?'

Ivana turned to me 'Proper Vis people! Good heavens! Have they accepted us at last?'

'Good God. Maybe they have!'

'Maybe we can stay here forever then?' said Ivana, hugging me and beaming.

'*Zdravi Bili!*' ('Feel well!') the man called out as we moved on.

Yes, we did feel well. How could we not feel well? We felt as if we'd just won the General Election.

We ambled on arm in arm past boats bobbing contentedly in the water, while the fishermen laid out their nets, and at the end of the Riva was our boat glinting in the water as it rocked beside our perfectly proportioned Venetian facade. The autumn sun warmed us through our light clothes and sparkles of light bounced off the water, dappling us with flecks of gold.

That evening, sitting on the terrace with my gin and tonic and watching the hills turning from green to purple, how far away I felt from my old life – the rollercoasters with the Japanese art market, the legal battles with New York lawyers, the artists with artistic temperaments, the uncomfortable meetings with bank managers. And how far away from the trials of raising a family in a metropolis – the bills, the orange hair, the hormonal strops, the anxiety that I wouldn't be able to keep it all going. It seemed light years away now. But the same questions I had asked myself before we left were still unanswered. What was it that drew us to places like this despite all the attractions of a city life? Were obscure backwaters such as Vis really the Holy Grail that had eluded us all our lives? Was this what we had worked for – to turn our backs on the very world we had spent our lives building? But, despite our human sophistication, maybe we are more primitive than we think, and once we hit fifty we instinctively seek out a more harmonious life, like an old dog trying to find a patch of sun to lie in?

Of course, it was all very well for me. I had sold my business and could sit here contentedly with my gin and tonic, watching the world go by, but for most islanders life was as full of financial worries, troubled marriages and obnoxious teenagers as it is in suburban London.

As I sat there musing, I suddenly realised that I couldn't remember being scowled at for some time. And not only that. For several days, I'd been vaguely conscious of a general congeniality. Small insignificant things – a wave from

246

a car, a smile from a schoolgirl, an acknowledging nod from a fisherman. It wouldn't have seemed much to an outside observer, but it did to me.

I was sitting outside Marko's the next day, when Boyana walked by and gave me a frightening grimace. I shivered. What had I done? Five minutes later, she came back from the market and did it again. And this time the penny dropped. The rictus on her face was her version of a smile. I sat there in disbelief. Did this mean that even Boyana had softened? It would certainly be a relief if she had, as being greeted by her scowl face every morning had been a pretty grim start to the day. I nearly ran over and kissed her.

That evening on the promenade, Boyana came to ask if I could give her a hand with her early-morning jam-jar loading. It came as such a shock that I missed my step – and I think she noticed, as she quickly added, 'The strain on my back is getting too much and I can't lift like I used to.' Recovering my composure, I answered that I'd love to, but it might be better to do it a bit later. And, to my amazement, she agreed. Then, never one for wasting time in social chit-chat, Boyana stumped off, and Ivana and I were left goggling at each other.

'I never thought I'd live to see the day,' said Ivana.

'I dare say it's old age rather than my charm that's worn her down, but who cares if it means there won't be a dark, brooding presence on the other side of the garden wall and we won't get woken up at six. That's real progress!'

I went to tell Zoran the news.

'God can come up with some funny tricks,' said Zoran, 'particularly after he's had a good bottle of wine.'

ACKNOWLEDGEMENTS

In admiration to Oliver Roki for his superhuman effort in managing to get cricket going again on the island, and with thanks to Steven Haslemere for all the information in his book *The Ascent of Mount Hum*. (And if anyone wants the definitive version of how the Vis cricket club started up, this is the book to read.)

CPSIA information can be obtained
at www.ICGtesting.com
Printed in the USA
LVHW100821270522
719901LV00006B/369

9 781839 012501